"A Dada Mind
is a terrible thing
to waste."

Old Chinese Saying of the Xia Dynasty
(ca. 2070 BC – ca. 1600 BC)

Rudy Ernst

ANATOMY
OF A DADA MIND

Drawings, Writings, Sculptures

Ernst, Rudy, 1937-
Anatomy of a Dada Mind-
Drawings, Writings, Sculptures
- 1st ed.
April 3, 2011

Published by QCC Art Gallery Press,
The City University of New York, Bayside, N.Y.
© 2011 by Rudy Ernst

264 p. - Format 8"x 10" (20.32 x 25.4 cm)

ISBN: 1460939301
EAN -13: 978-1460939307

Front Cover:
E.T. (Detail): 2005
Ink on Paper – 30"x 22"
Photo: Arpi Pap, 2009

Back Cover:
Dada Homecoming: 2009
Ink on Paper – 13½"x 9½"
Photo: Arpi Pap, 2011

Rudy Ernst

ANATOMY

OF A DADA MIND

Drawings, Tales and Dada-Poms

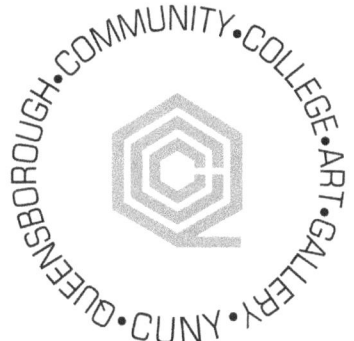

QCC ART GALLERY

THE CITY UNIVERSITY OF NEW YORK

About the Author

Rudy Ernst's life was marked by extremes. After his Ph.D. in economics, and following a horrific accident in 1965, he suffered a near-death experience with a 32-minute cardiac arrest, but went on to becoming independently wealthy.

In 1982 he pulled the plug from corporate life and immigrated to Manhattan with his wife and two sons to become a painter, sculptor and writer. Obsessed with the act of creation, he then lived years in isolation in his New York studio on the Upper West Side.

Ernst shares his time between the metropolis of Manhattan and the rural life of the Blue Ridge Mountains in southwest Virginia, where he built his large studio back in 1988.

Anatomy of a Dada-Mind opens a window into Ernst's artistic creations *from the guts* that bypass the rationality of his mind. His drawings and writings, as evidenced by the *Dada-Drawings*, the *Dada-Tales* and the *Dada-Poms*, are not the result of previously memorized -or planned- images or writings, but rather the spontaneous products of an *on-the-spot* creation.

Previously Published Books by Rudy Ernst:

The Story of Dada

Manhattan Flash Stories

Sculptomania

Magic (Computer Aided Art – CAA)

Ungeschminkt (German Childhood Stories)

Kurz belichtet und verdichtet (A Selection of German Poems)

Table of Contents

PART I

EXPLORING THE DADA MIND

PART I:

EXPLORING

THE DADA MIND

The Dada Mind

The word goes that when you meet a single person, you have just met all of humanity. By extension we can say that every person is born a Dadaist.

Whenever I walk around my neighborhood on the Upper West Side of New York City, I am reminded of that, and the myriad of different languages reaching my ears at every street corner are strangely reminiscent of the Tower of Babel and of how it all ended in chaos. I like that thought, it stimulates my Dada mind.

What an incredible contrast to the so-called realities in this day and age, where rationality and scientific breakthroughs are dominating almost every aspect of our daily life! Is it a sheer coincidence that the Dada movement is experiencing a renaissance throughout the international museum world? I don't think so.

As I explain in detail in my earlier book of *The Story of Dada*, the Dada movement was a short lived period that originated in 1916 as a reaction against the horrors of World War I. It came to an abrupt end in the early 1920s, when it was replaced by the surrealist movement. However, this basically nonsensical art form influenced the entire art history of the 20th Century in a major way.

The reasons for a *Dada Renaissance* today, however, appear to be different from those of the initial movement. Our world has become so specialized in every single aspect that, paradoxically, instead of becoming more structured, our planet seems to be more in chaos than ever before.

Take my case: I went to school for 21 years of my early life, but still have to learn on a daily basis the newest developments in computer technology, economic news, political events, health matters, etc, etc to remain what I would like to be: not only an artist, but also a global thinker (open minded and up-to-date).

And yet, while trying to achieve my goal, I find myself more and more in the position of Socrates who famously said two and a half thousand years ago "I know that I know nothing," and that of the Buddha who taught to "forget everything you ever learned."

At a late stage of my life I came to the same conclusion as Diogenes of Sinope (ca. 400 B.C.), that wealth, rank, honors and success are worldly aims that stand in the way of a complete independence of the mind.

I call it my Dada mind.

This is why, a few years ago, I became a self-declared Dadaist. In a world of chaos, where the most basic logical thought process has vanished from almost every aspect of our public and private domains, the only dictate of a basic survival instinct and defense mechanism may well be a return to the childlike nonsensical Dadaism where the questions and the answers are always **Dada**.

Let me illustrate this thought by bringing up a random example.

Semantic Externalism

Before writing this book, I engaged in a prolonged condition of self-education in the matter of the human mind. While sparing you the bulk of my findings, I would like to bring to your attention an aspect of modern philosophy that appears to justify my rational decision of becoming a Dadaist.

The following section represents an example of my serious academic research of the obscure world of modern philosophy, which borders on classical Dadaism and the pursuit of happiness thereof.

A Warning.
Dear Reader: Skip this section at any point when you think you are getting the idea. Life is too short to engage in *dadaistically misguided readings*, even when they sound fascinating like this one.

Ron Hubbard, the founder of *Scientology*, promised that once his *Basic Anatomy of Confusion* and *Embracive Concept of Life* were fully understood and used, there would be no confusion left that could not be reduced to an understandable simplicity, or even completely eliminated.

In his lectures, Whitehall Putnam, Cogan University Professor Emeritus at Harvard University, agrees. He has been one of the central figures in *analytic philosophy*, especially in *philosophy of the mind*, *philosophy of language*, and *philosophy of science*. Putnam is known for his willingness to apply an equal degree of scrutiny to his own philosophical positions as to those of others, subjecting each position to rigorous analysis. As a result, he has acquired a reputation for frequently changing his own position.

In his *philosophy of the mind*, Putnam argues against the *type-identity of mental and physical states* under the hypothesis of the *multiple realizability of the mental*, and for the concept of functionalism. In *philosophy of language*, he developed the *causal theory of reference* and formulated an original *theory of meaning* and of s*emantic externalism*, based on a fascinating thought-experiment called *Twin Earth*, where H2O would be replaced by an XYC substance:

Assume Fredrick and Frodrick are two physically indistinguishable citizens of each planet, both calling the abundant liquid here *Water* when they utter their respective words; but since that word has different meanings on each planet, it cannot be determined solely by what is in their heads. This led Putnam to adopt a version of *Semantic Externalism* with respect to meaning and mental content, rather than suggesting my own conclusion, which would be to call them both *Dada*!

Furthermore, in his *philosophy of mathematics*, Putnam and his colleague W. V. Quine developed the *Quine-Putnam indispensability thesis*, and in the field of *epistemology* he is known for his critique of the well known *brain in a vat*, which provides a powerful argument for *Epistemological Skepticism*. In metaphysics, finally, he originally espoused a position called M*etaphysical Realism*, but later became one of its most outspoken critics, first adopting a view of *Internal Realism*, which he later abandoned in favor of a pragmatist-inspired *Direct Realism*. In this theory, Putnam aims to return the study of metaphysics to an actual *experience the world* doctrine, rejecting the idea of *mental representations*, *sense data* and other *intermediaries* between mind and world.

Putnam is also interested in *metaphilosophy*, seeking to *renew philosophy* from narrow and inflated concerns. "Meaning just ain't in the head," says the famous professor. **…Do you get the Point??**

The World as Dada

A few years ago, when I finally became aware of the full extent of the almost infinite chaos that humans are attempting to hide all day long at every level of society by introducing manmade structured thoughts of dialectic proportions (the exact opposite of any truth is equally true), I decided for myself that Dadaism was the only way out.

Indeed, what I believed at some point to be common sense has become consistently upside-down at every level of our Government, the economy, the stock market, our value system, our health care system, and finally our approach towards our own personal body. Under the circumstances, my only refuge possible was to eventually see the whole world as Dada.

As I took up the study of world history and the history of philosophy once again, but with a different approach, I realized that indeed there is nothing really new out there that the world hasn't seen before, other than the fact that everything around us is moving so much faster in this day and age of instant communications. In other words: the world has always been Dada.

In the Beginning was the Child

No wonder that the first exclamation uttered by almost any child around the globe is the universal word "Dada!" Realizing the complexity of its developing brain and the impossibility to master the chaos all around, the child -in its infinite wisdom- cuts through the thick of it and simply calls the world and all the crazy things therein "Dada."

In that sense, not much change will occur between the child in its first stage of mental development and the grown-up person that has gone through life's many cycles of formal and empirical education stages, until finally reaching the conclusion that the best way to cope with all of the surrounding chaos is to become a Dadaist. It is the Buddha-like conclusion of *what is, is.*

Most adults ignore, or -worse- even deny the fact that every one of us has been born a Dadaist. But the child before its brain gets perverted by that mandatory higher education that everybody is bragging about -- that child knows exactly why it utters the first sounds of its young life all day long as: "Dada, Dada, Dada."

We adults, however, self centered as we are, interpret the word *Dada* rather to mean *Daddy* or another rudimentary expression that we want to hear and that fit our self-centered view of the world.

The unaltered influence of its natural *Dada-Gene* has not yet perverted the young brain of the child, when it begins to explore the Universe, of which Albert Einstein (a grown-up man) once said that the most incomprehensible thing about it was its incomprehensibility.

The child knows that, but doesn't get troubled by such deep thoughts when it sucks the milk out of its mother's breast. Soon enough its brain will be forced into the constraints of an education that channels its train of thoughts into a forced direction, until it becomes a *valued member of our Judeo-Christian Society*, where its main focus will be to make money as the yardstick of a successful life.

The problem is that -by the time the child grows up to become an adult- so much knowledge will be rammed into its young brain that the ability to activate its own Dada-Gene to become a creative human being has almost disappeared. In my book *The Story of Dada – and how to activate your Dada-Gene* I have extensively researched and written about that subject.

Chaos

The following images periodically come to mind when I draw from them in my creative hours by activating my "Dada-Gene."

a) When you hit the body of a grand piano with your flat hand, the result is a cacophony of an almost infinite number of sounds that evoke the impression of chaos. But the number of those sounds is not infinite, and in a weird way the resulting sound symphony appears to be somehow structured as those echo waves slowly fade away.

b) A similar thing may occur when we dream, and so many *memory cords* are being activated and reassembled into weird images that make no sense to the rational mind.

c) I grew up in the parish where Carl Jung's father was the pastor and where the famous psychoanalyst spent the first few years of his life. (Jung's father-in-law, Johannes Moser, was a business partner of my great-grandfather.) Jung and I were both marked for life by the thundering waters of the Rhine Falls - Europe's largest water falls- under a narrow wooden railroad bridge, no more than thirty feet above the deafening noise of the Rhine Falls.

Those were the same sounds of the river that so fascinated the young Buddha as being always different, yet always the same.

My Own Rorschach Test

For the past thirty years during which I have been concentrating on creating art, I have learned to express the vast experience of my life in ways that can best be described as my own *Rorschach Test* approach in the expression of my Dada mind:

- My lifelong small *weirdo* drawings
- The large Dada drawings
- My Dada-Tales, and
- The Dada-Poms

For the longest time in my life I felt disadvantaged by my lack of visual memory. That has changed; today I see my shortcoming of visual remembrance as an advantage that doesn't stand in the way of my artistic creativity. It has become a blessing in disguise, since my drawings and writings are not the product of some memory imprinted in my conscious mind, but rather the expression of my *gut feelings* at the time of their creation. As a result, there appears to be no obvious rational makeup in any of those spontaneous expressions.

However, looking at the bulk of my work, I believe there is some kind of a *personal handwriting* that characterizes each one of those products in a distinctive manner. Indeed, when I put my pen onto a piece of paper to either draw or write a *Dada-Tale* or a *Dada-Pom*, I never think ahead of what I am going to do next, but rather become my own spectator once the work is finished, after the fact.

PART II:

THE LARGE DADA-DRAWINGS

PART II:

THE LARGE

DADA-DRAWINGS

Genesis of the Large Dada-Drawings

Ever since I was a small boy I have been doing what people commonly call *doodling*. As a kid, my school buddies were looking over my shoulder, and later in life -when I was attending some of those boring business or political conferences- my neighbors looked onto my paper sheet and lauded the *artistic qualities* of my drawings. None of them survived, but after my move to Manhattan I started to keep, and even exhibit them in my gallery shows.

In 1986, Carmen Morin-Miller of the Morin-Miller Gallery on West 57th Street in Manhattan gave me a solo-show. After years of indifference, and often discouraged by what is called *the art community* (whatever that means) she was the first to detect uniqueness in my drawings and to encourage me to pursue my path of creating what I came to call my *Dream-Drawings*, or my *Dada-Drawings from the Guts*.

Indeed, those *Automatic Drawings* emanate from my most inner dream world, a world that lies deep below the level of consciousness, which explains their unforeseen originality.

The Large Dada-Drawings

One day in 2005, as I was looking for art materials in the *Pearl* superstore in Manhattan, I found a stack of fabulous hand-made 22x30-inch Japanese museum quality paper sheets. I decided right then and there to venture into a brand new series of drawings the size of which I had never done before. I also bought a box of .2 mm permanent ink pens and rushed home to embark on my new project.

Since I never know where my pen is going to lead me next, and since it follows that therefore I can never do an outline of what I am going to draw, I started right in the middle of the sheet with a minuscule image. Over the next several days I gradually continued my journey by extending outwards my Dada approach, until I had a large drawing in front of me that filled the entire sheet.

It was the beginning of my new series of large Dada-Drawings, which was going to be my next obsession.

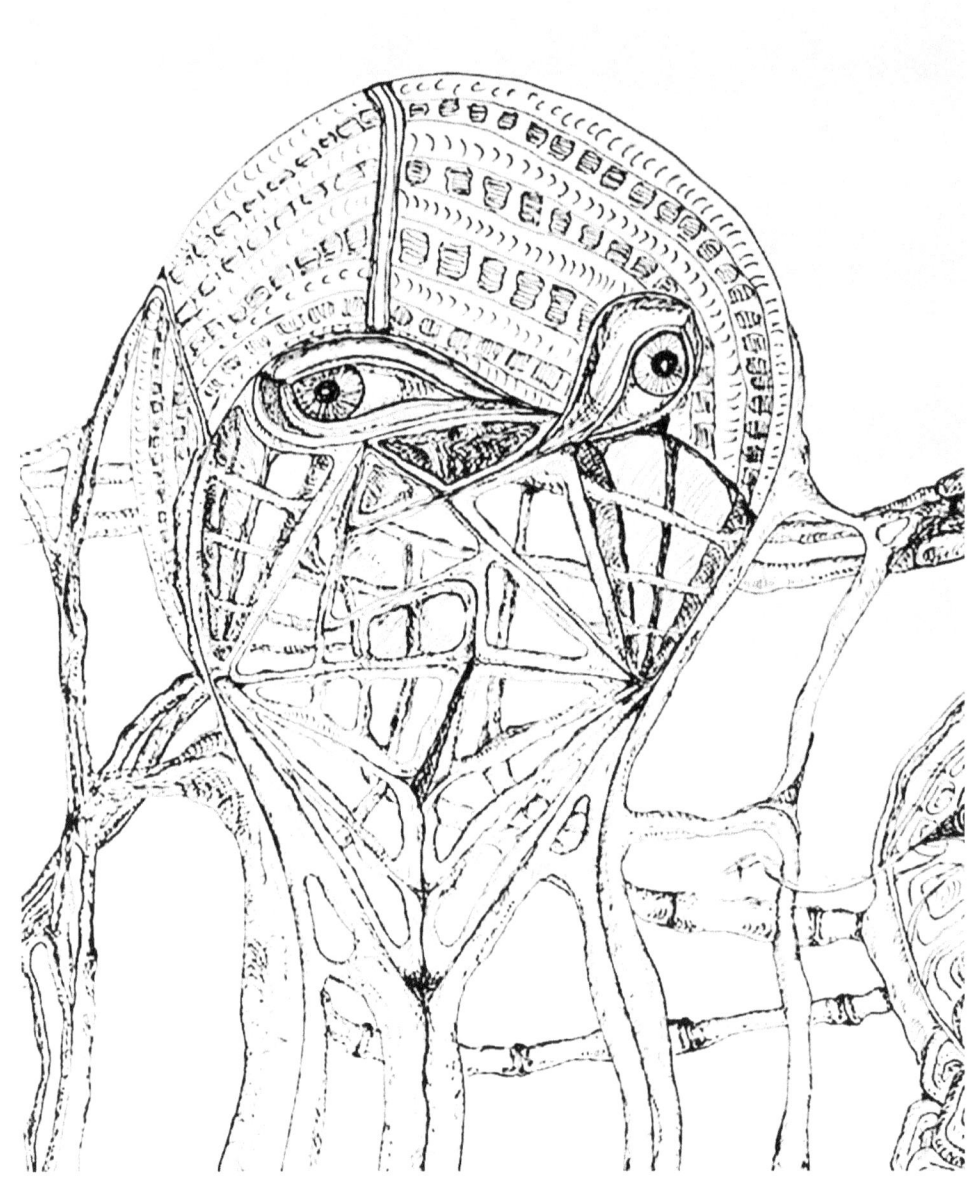

Above: Detail of *An Unusual Cell Colony*

Opposite: *An Unusual Cell Colony* (2005) Ink on paper - 35"x 25"

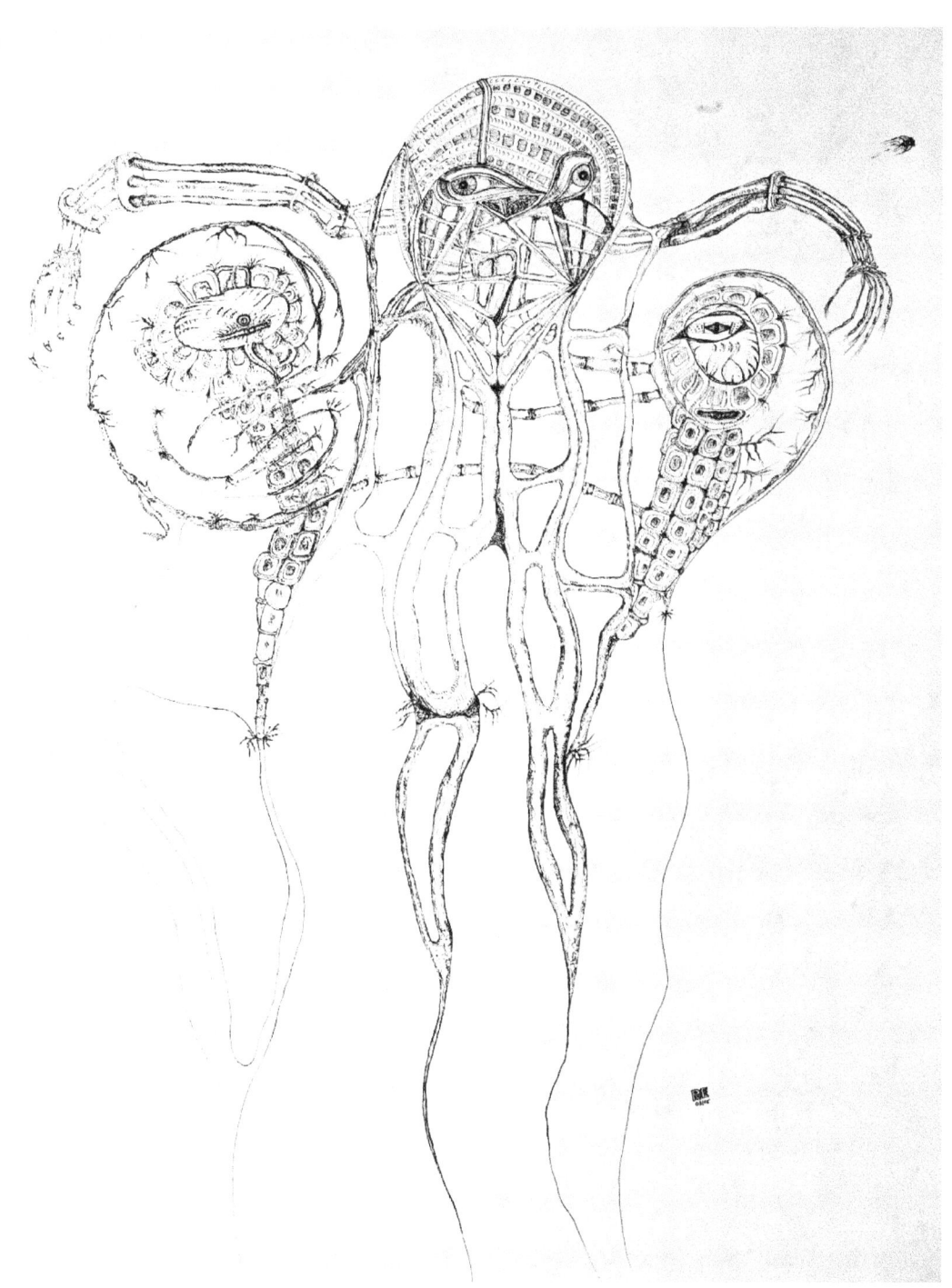

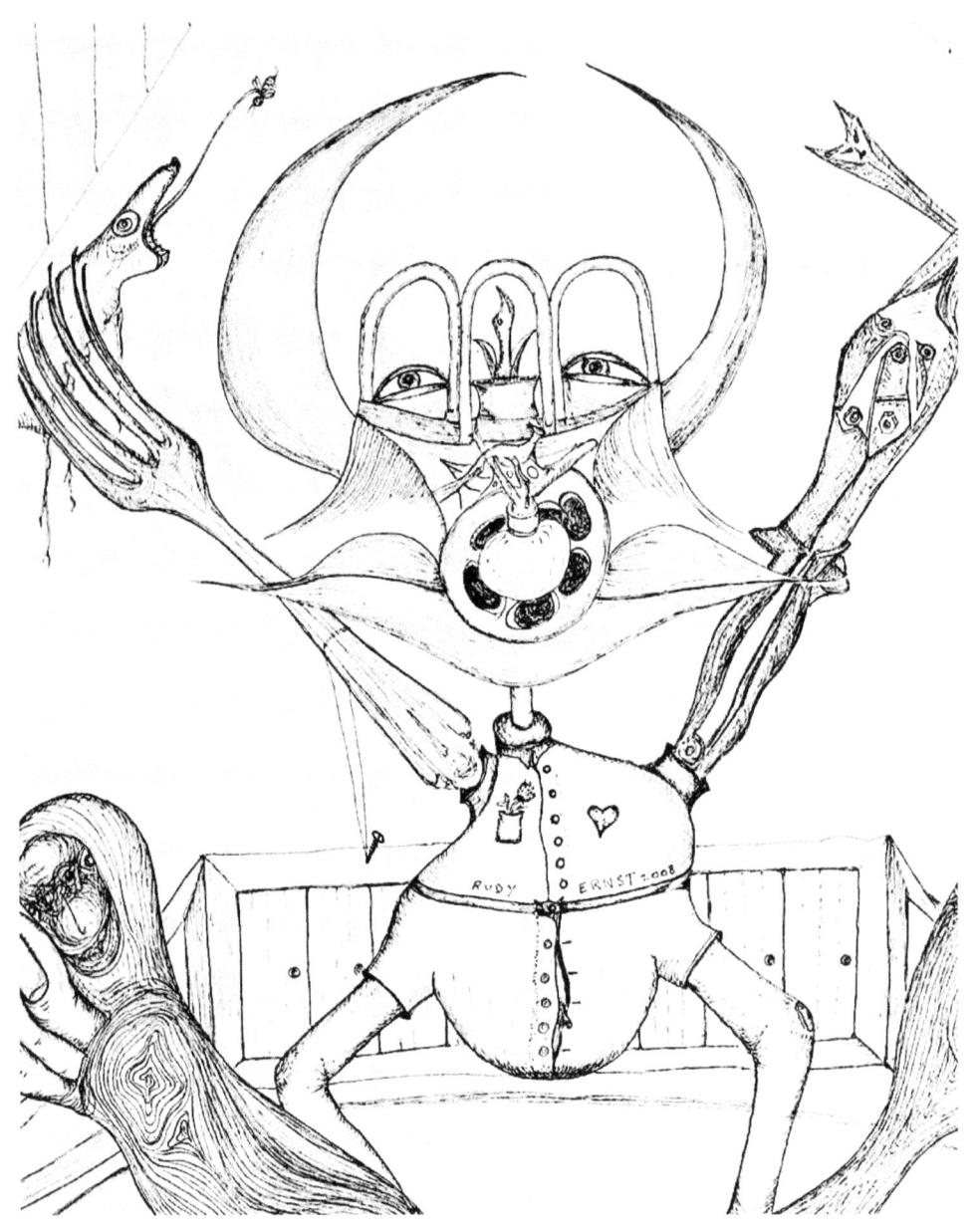

Above: Detail of *The Good Old Times*

Opposite: *The Good Old Times* (2008) -- Ink on paper - 30"x 22"

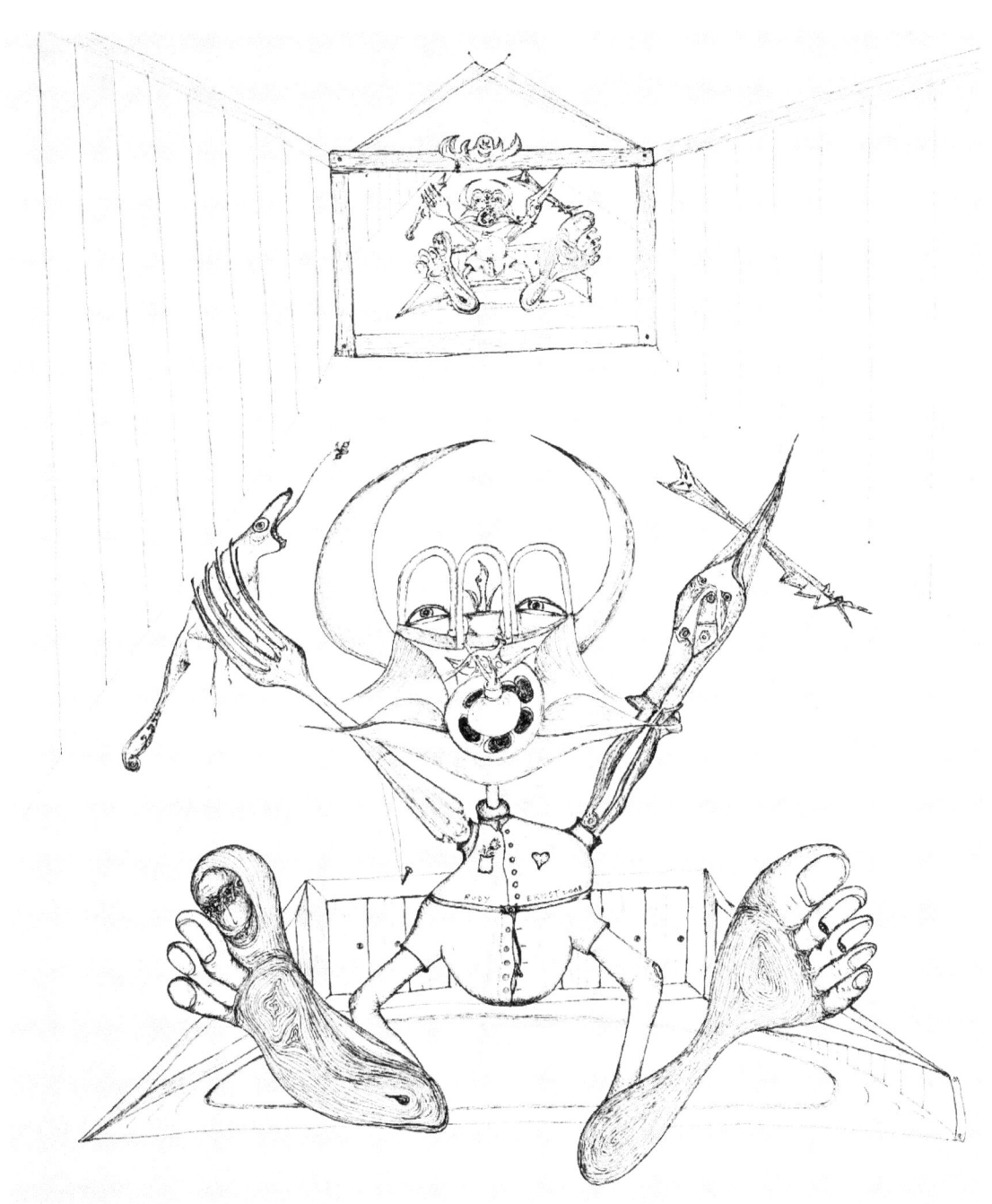

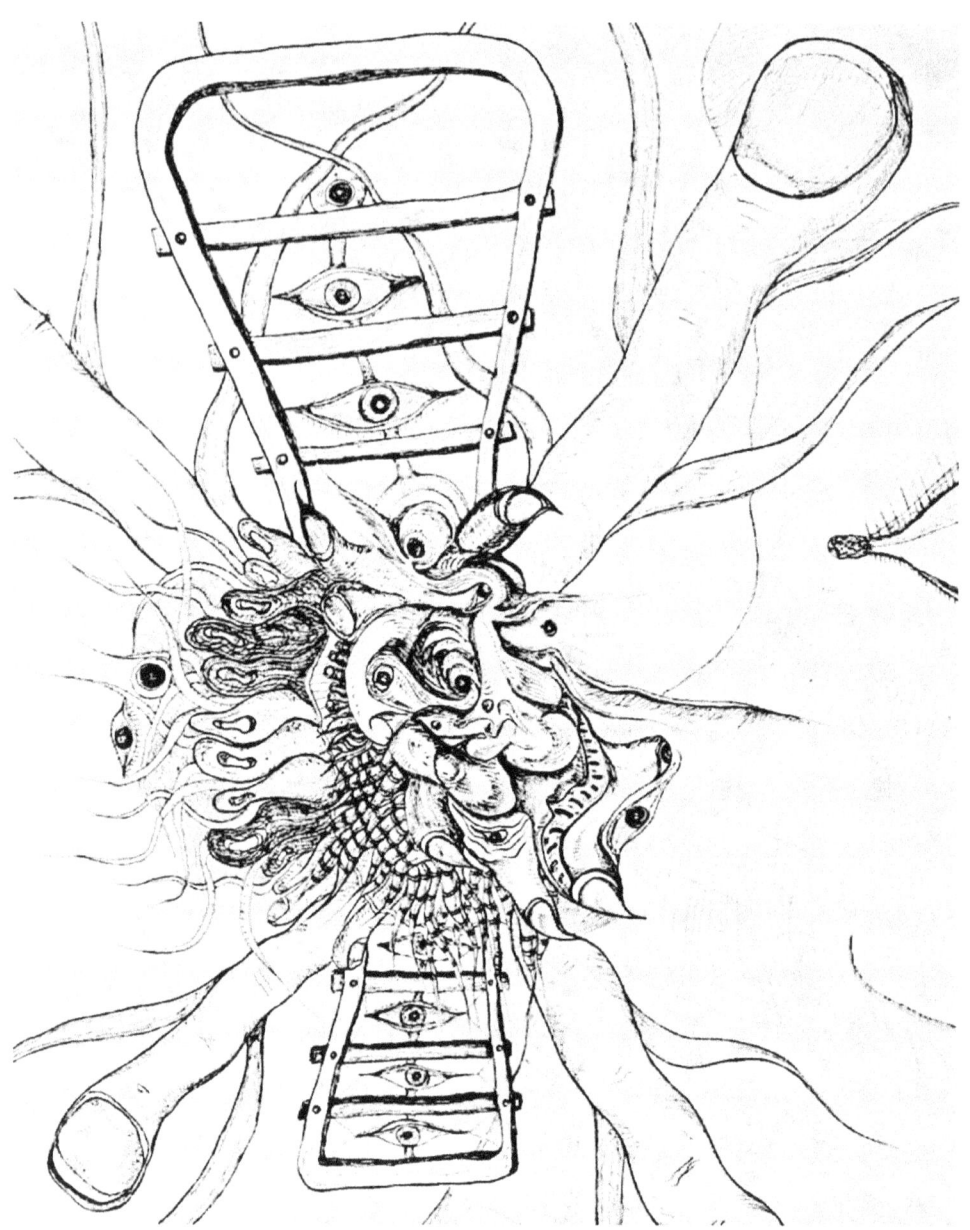

Above: Detail of *The New World Order*

Opposite: *The New World Order* (2005) -- Ink on paper - 30"x 22"

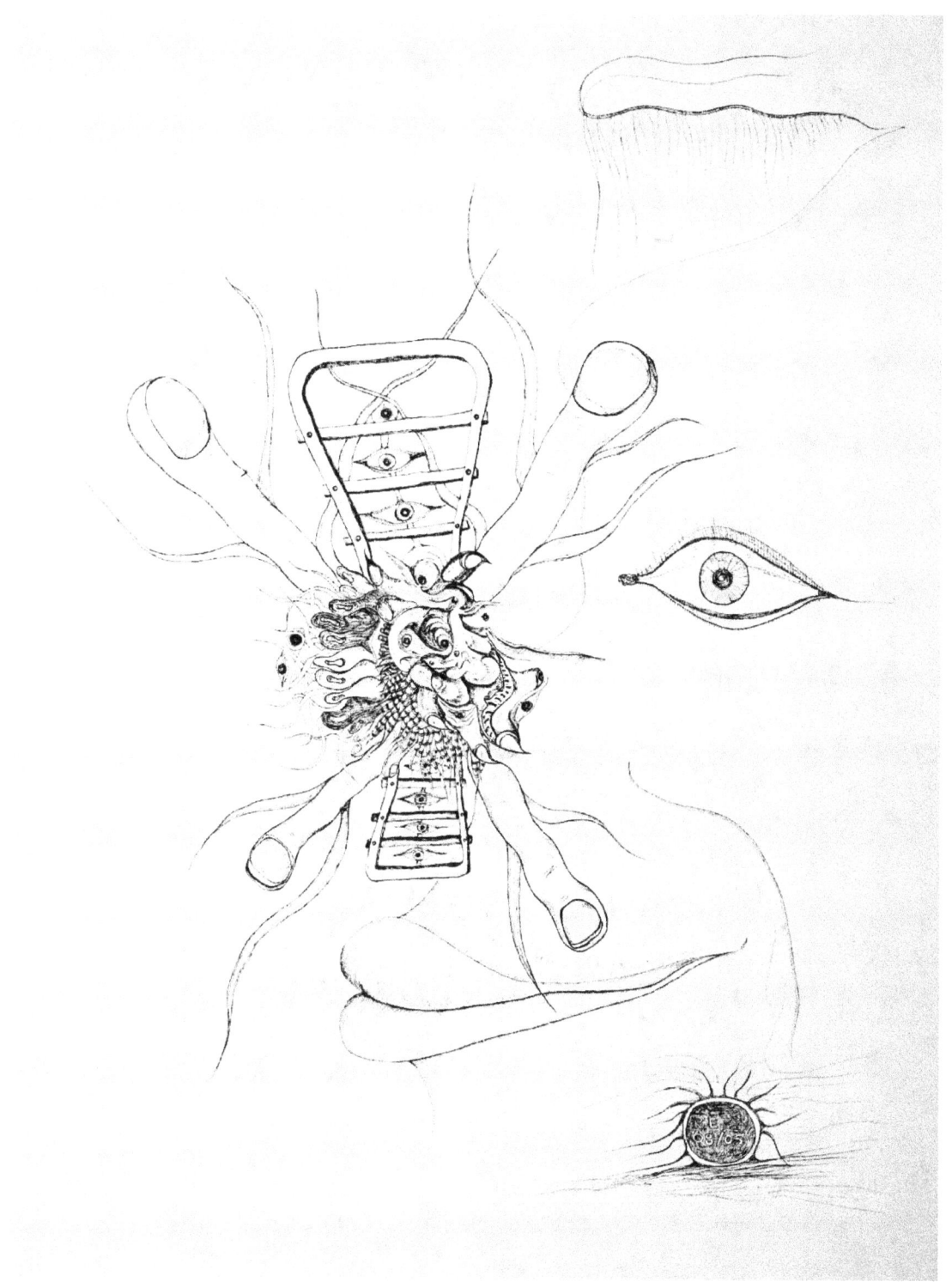

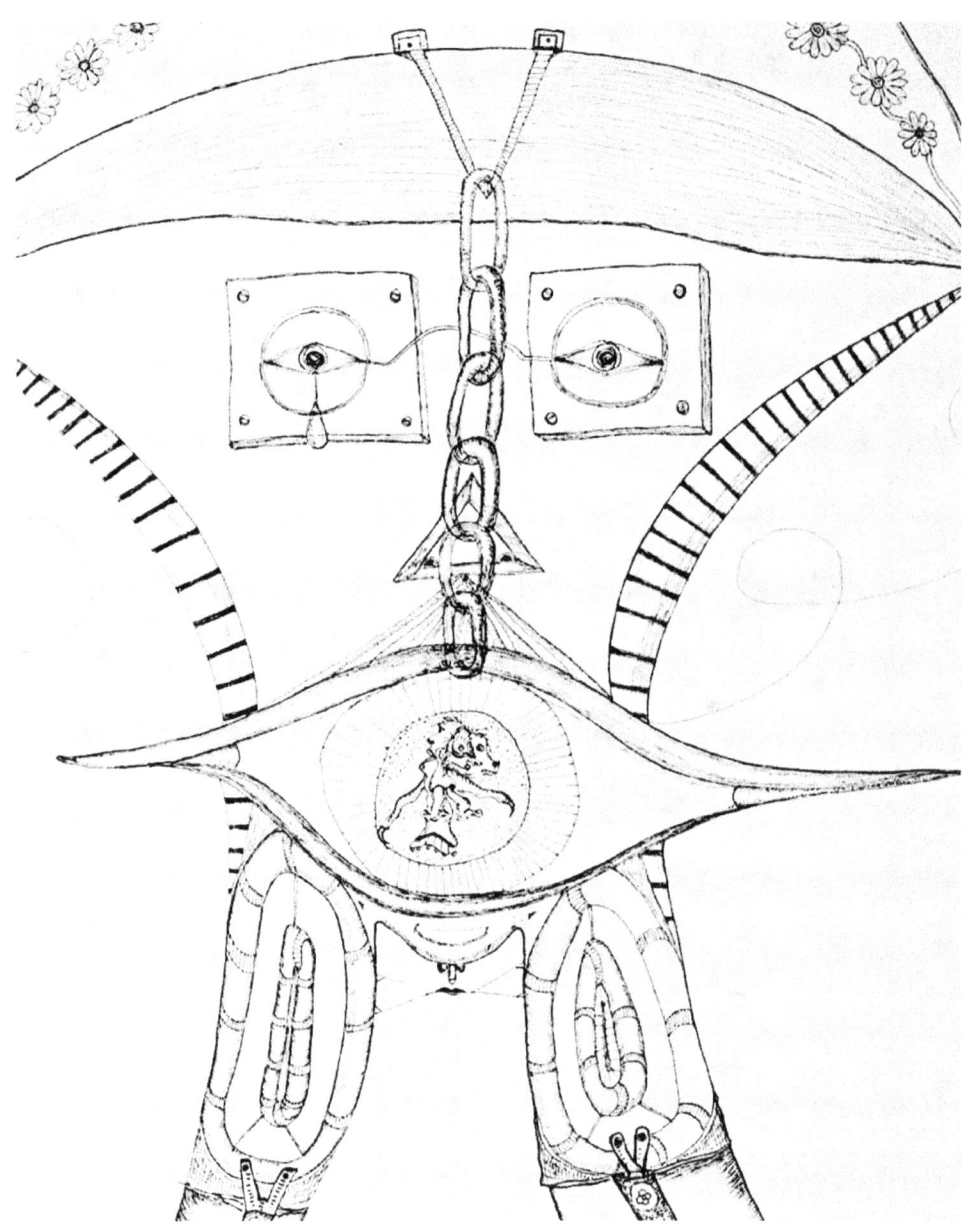

Above: Detail of *Dishonorable Discharge*

Opposite: *Dishonorable Discharge* (2005) -- Ink on paper - 30"x 22"

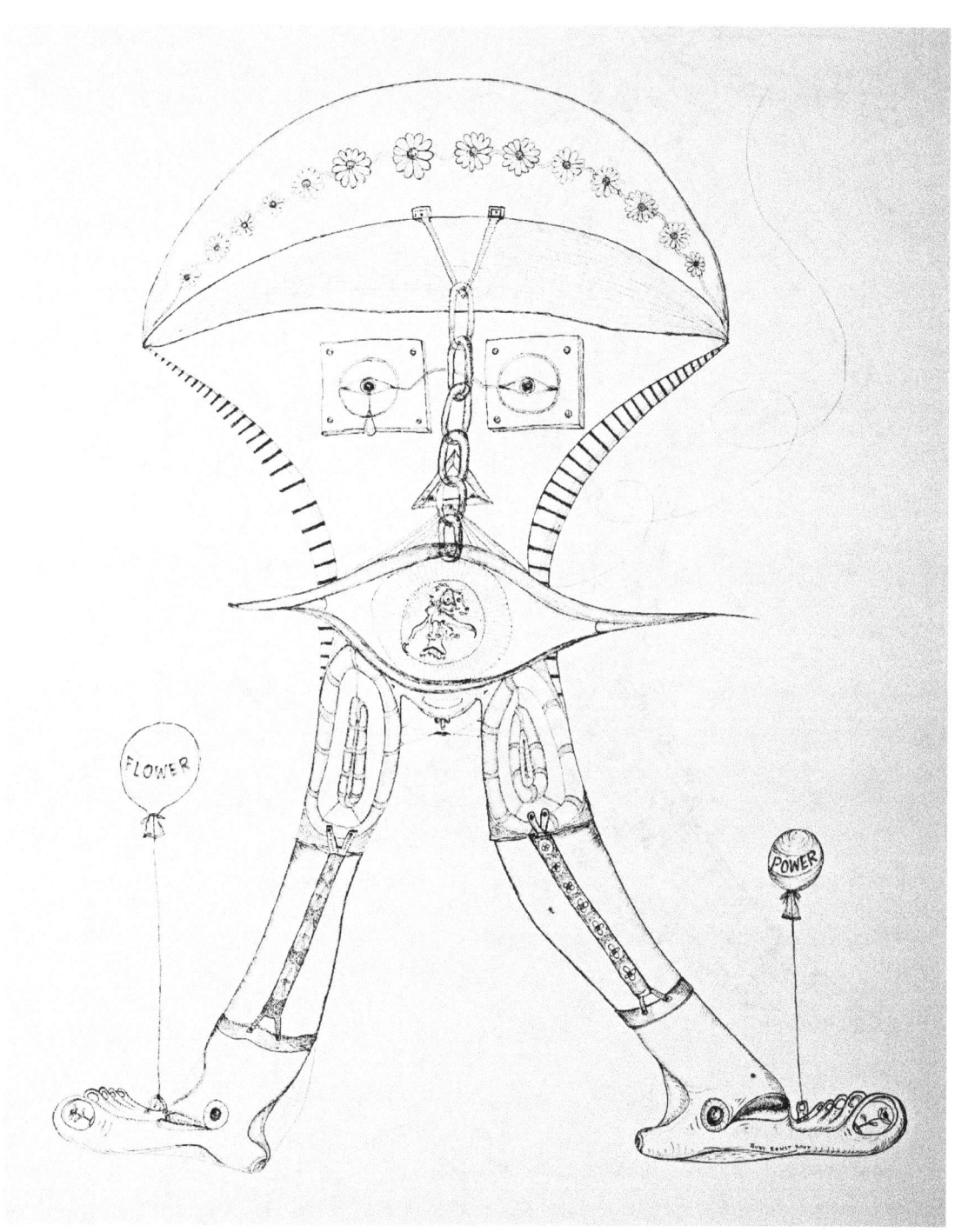

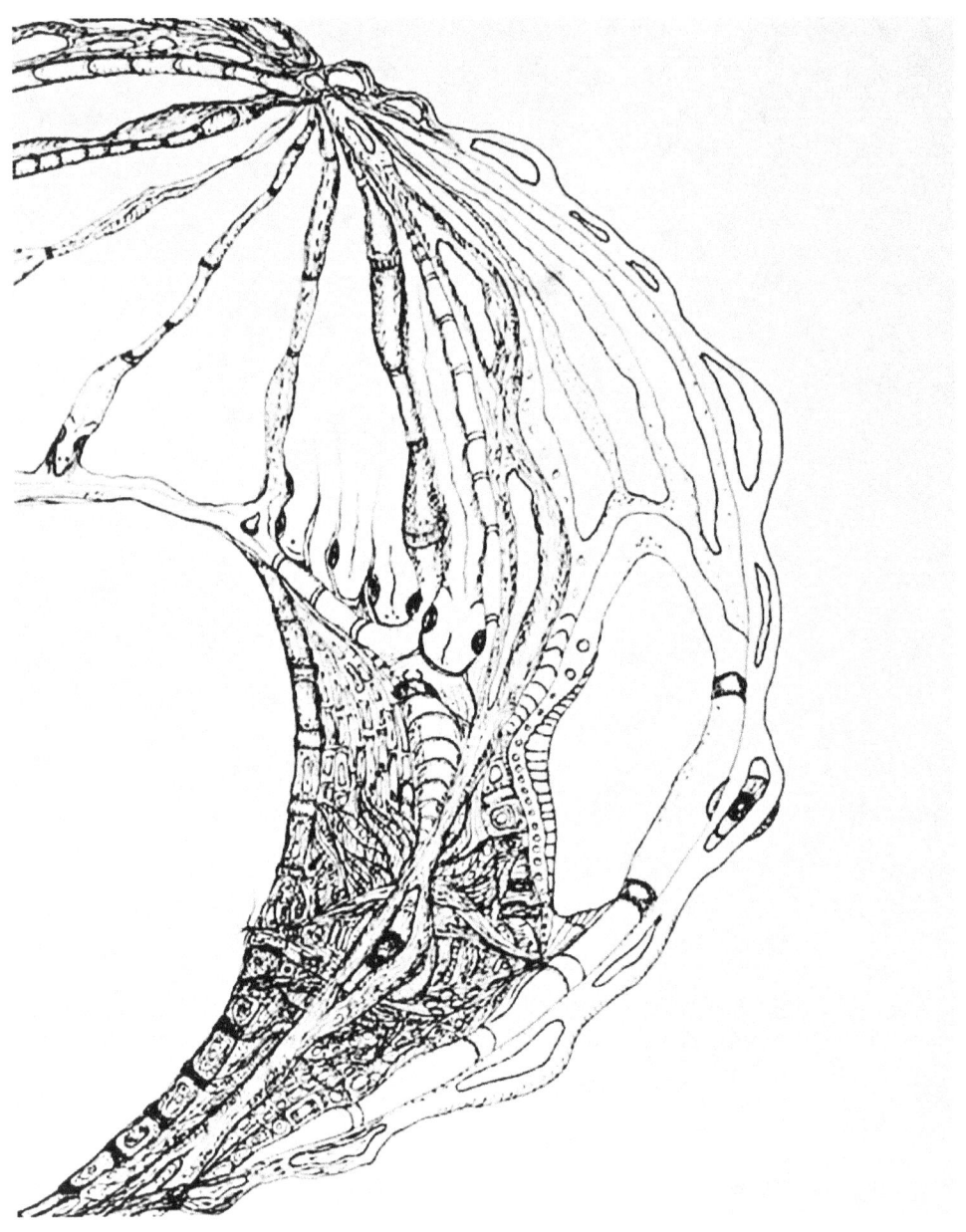

Above: Detail of *E.T.*

Opposite: *E.T.* (2005) -- Ink on paper - 30"x 22"

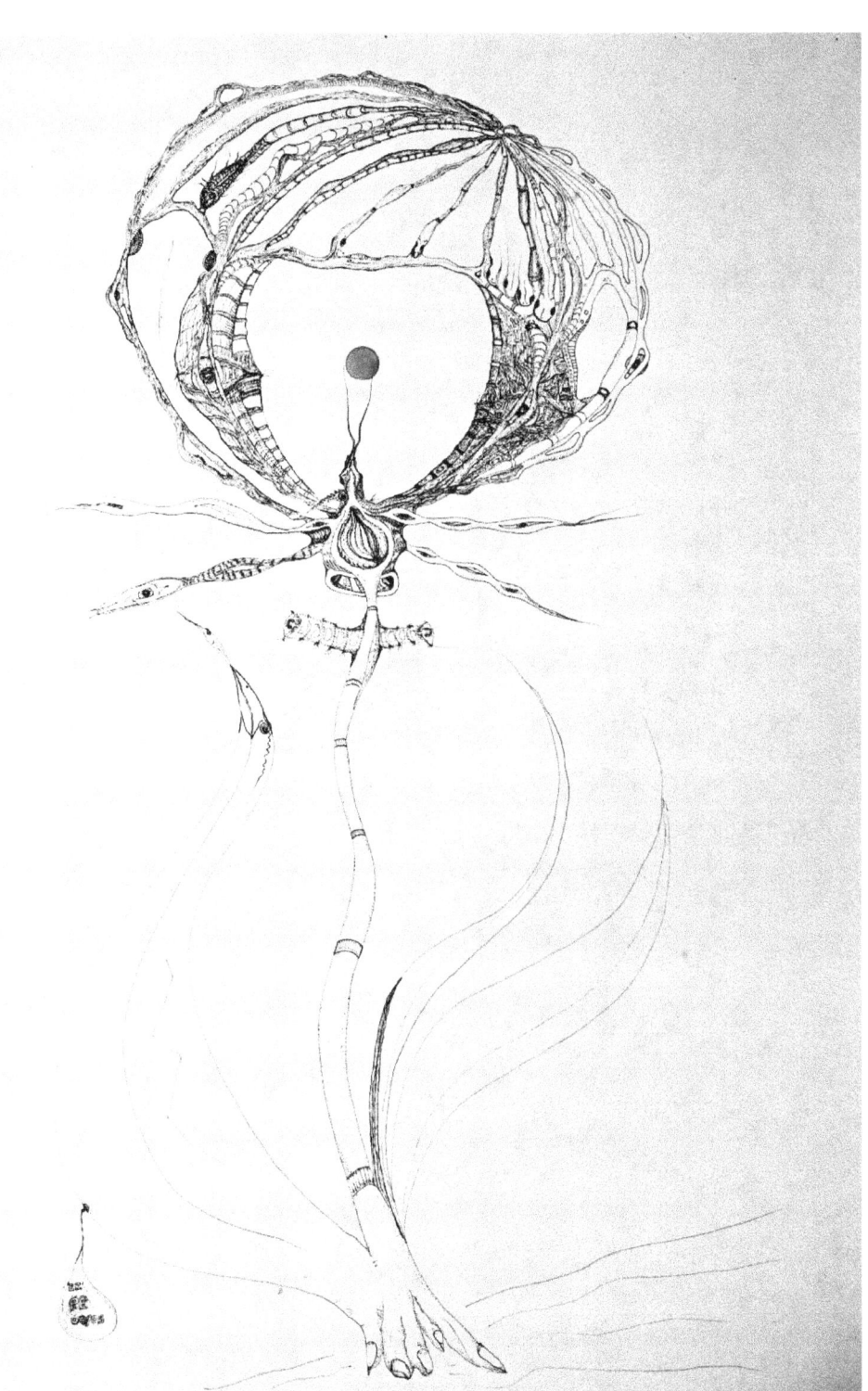

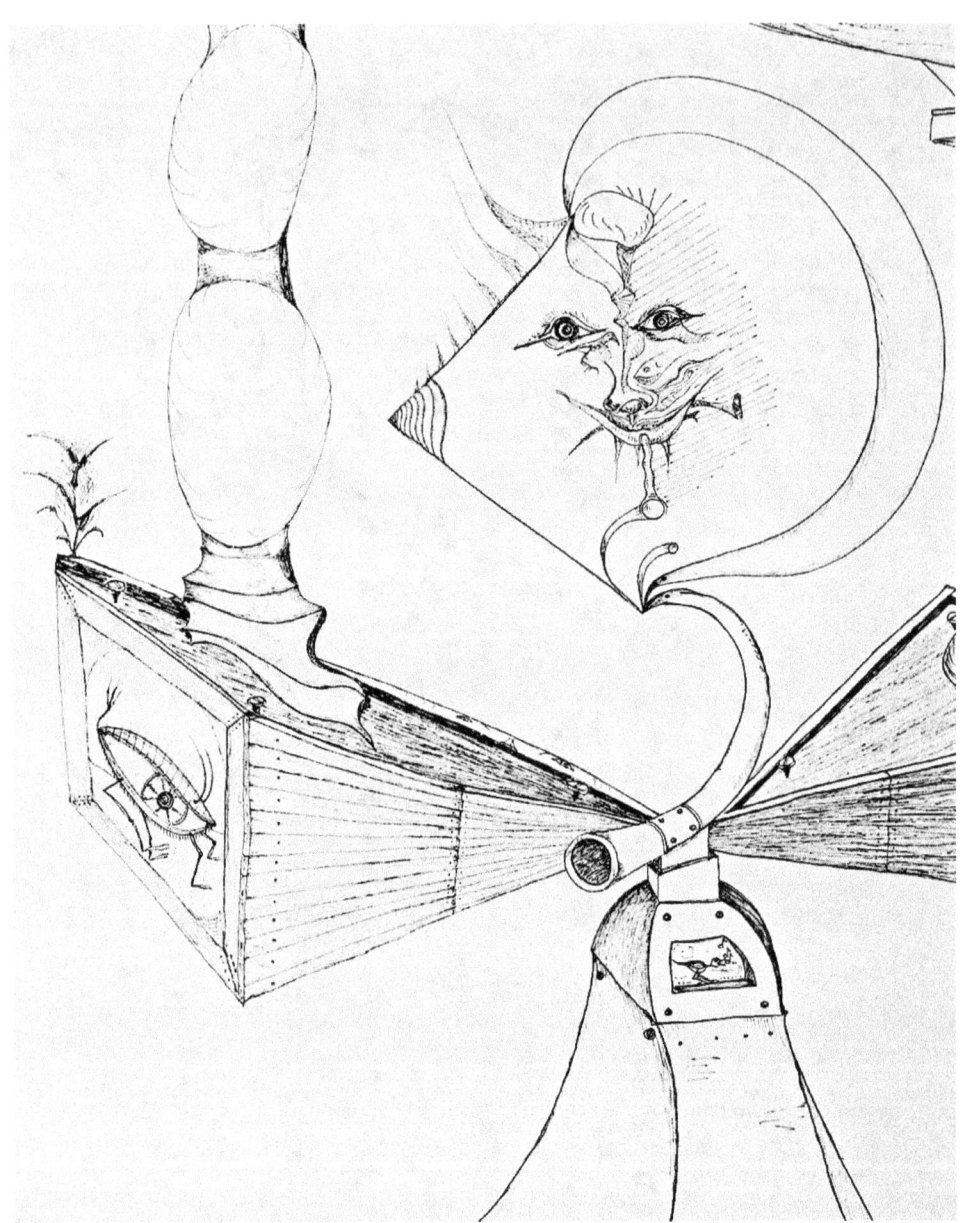

Above: Detail of *A Dream Come True*

Opposite: *A Dream Come True* (2008) -- Ink on paper - 30"x 22"

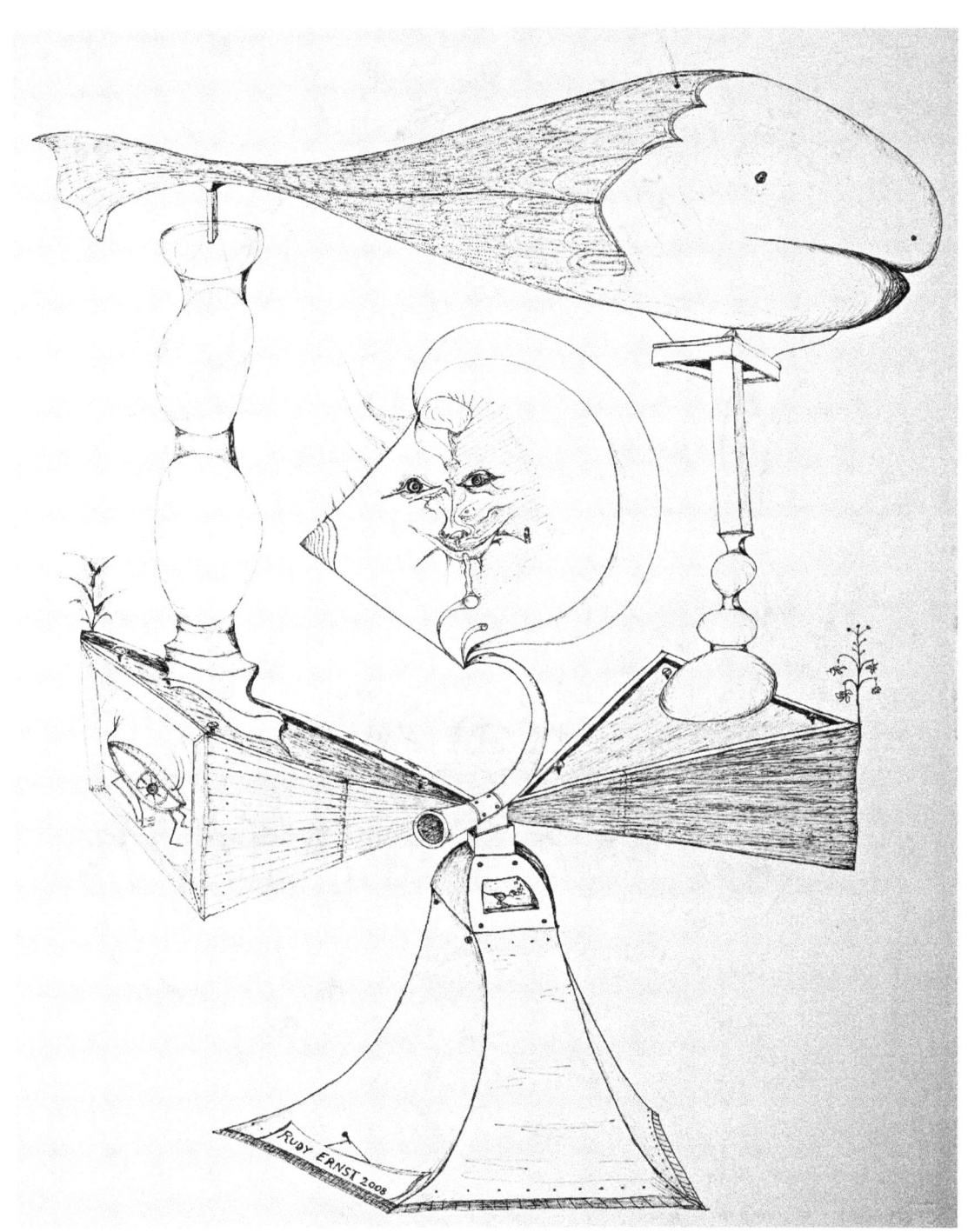

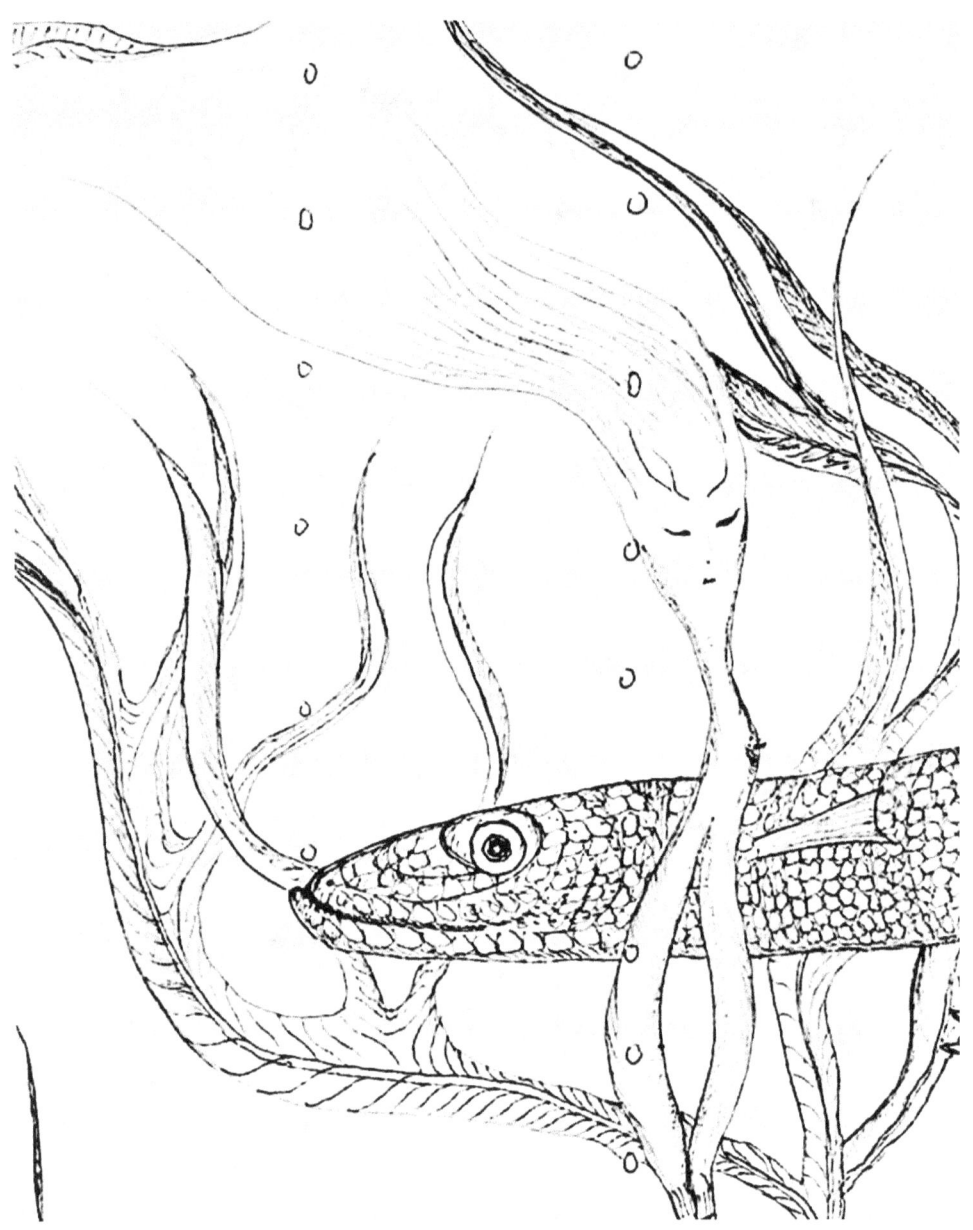

Above: Detail of *Wedding in St. John*

Opposite: *Wedding in St. John* (2006) -- Ink on paper - 22"x 30"

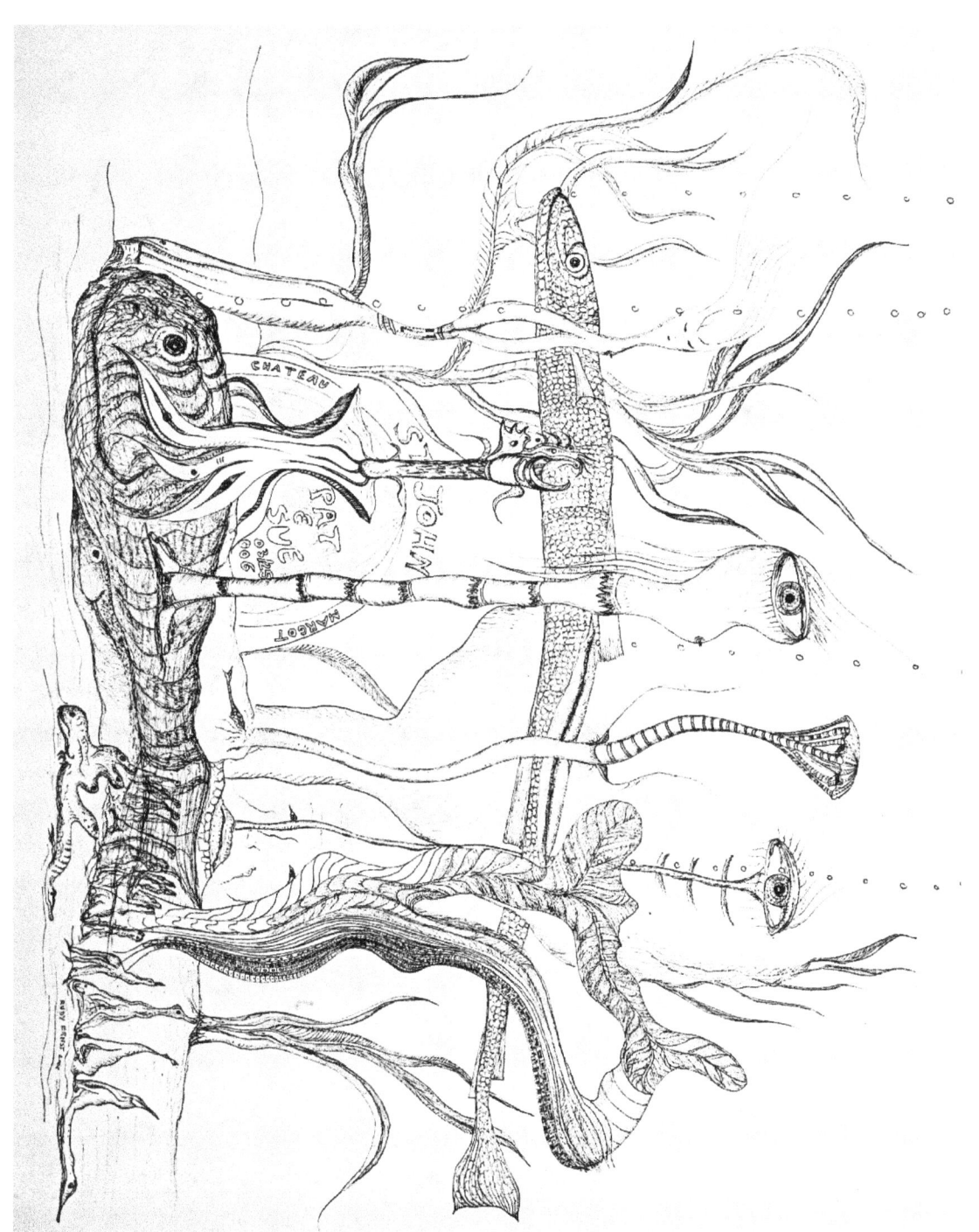

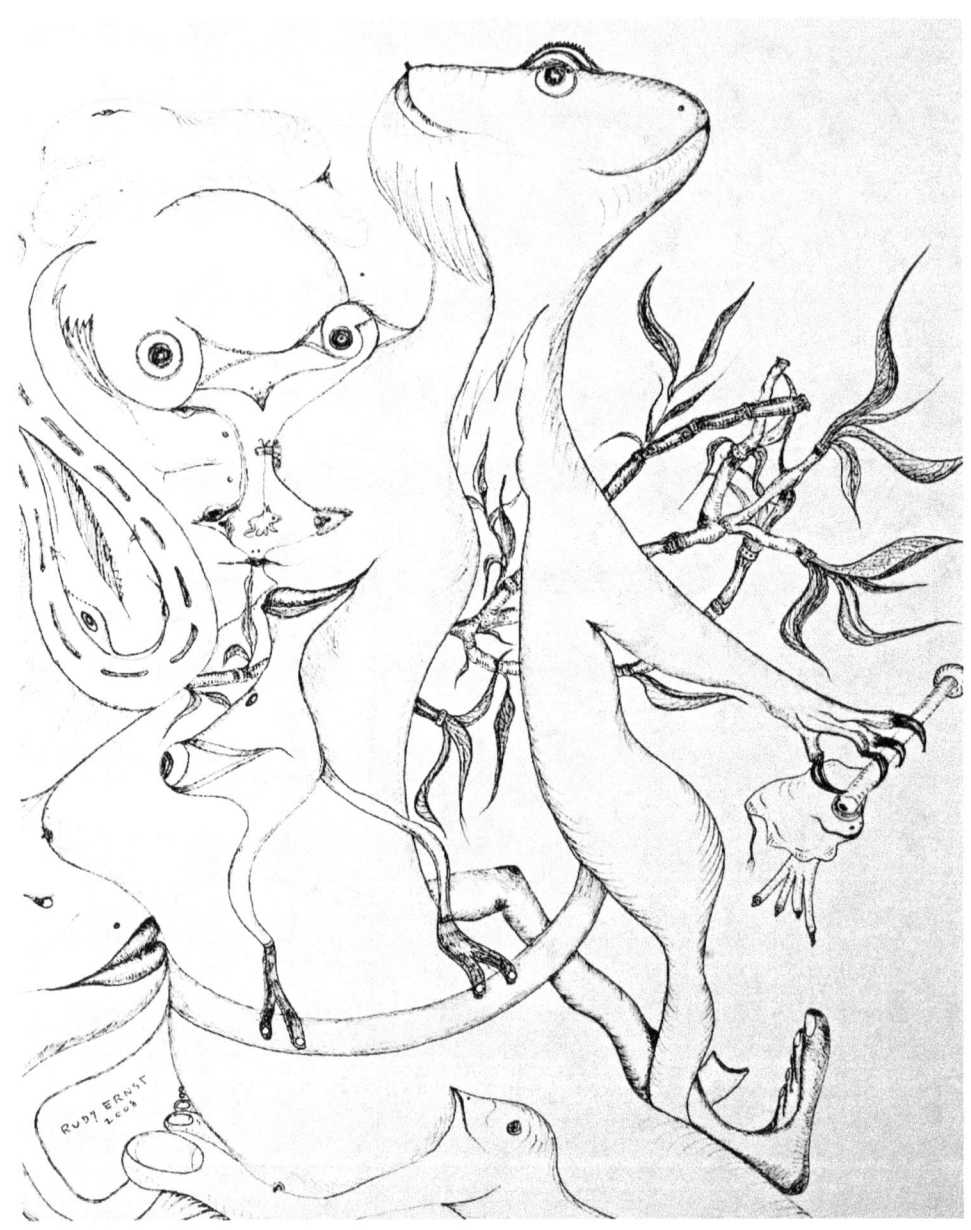

Above: Detail of *Before the (Brain) Storm*

Opposite: *Before the (Brain) Storm* (2008) - Ink on paper - 22"x 30"

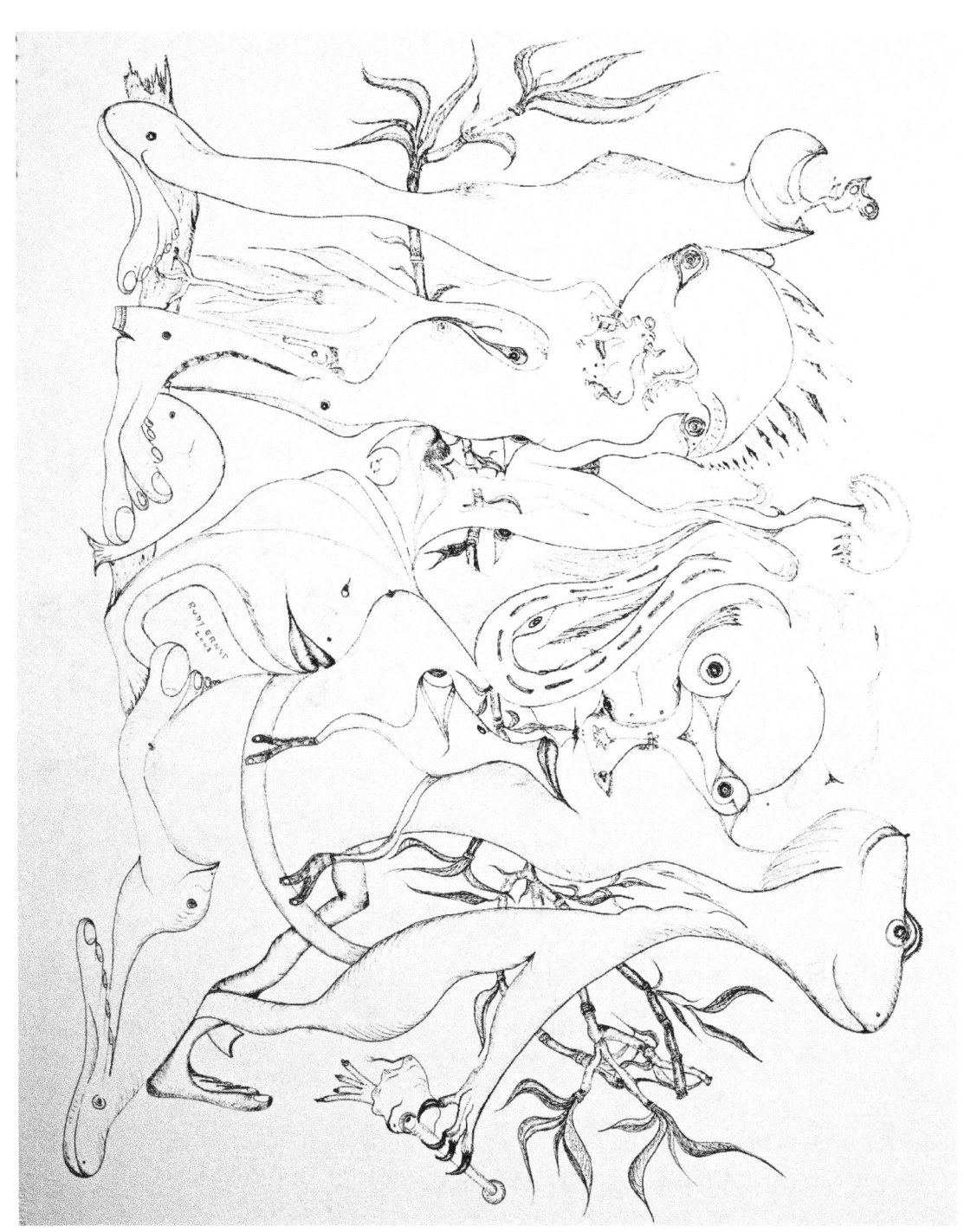

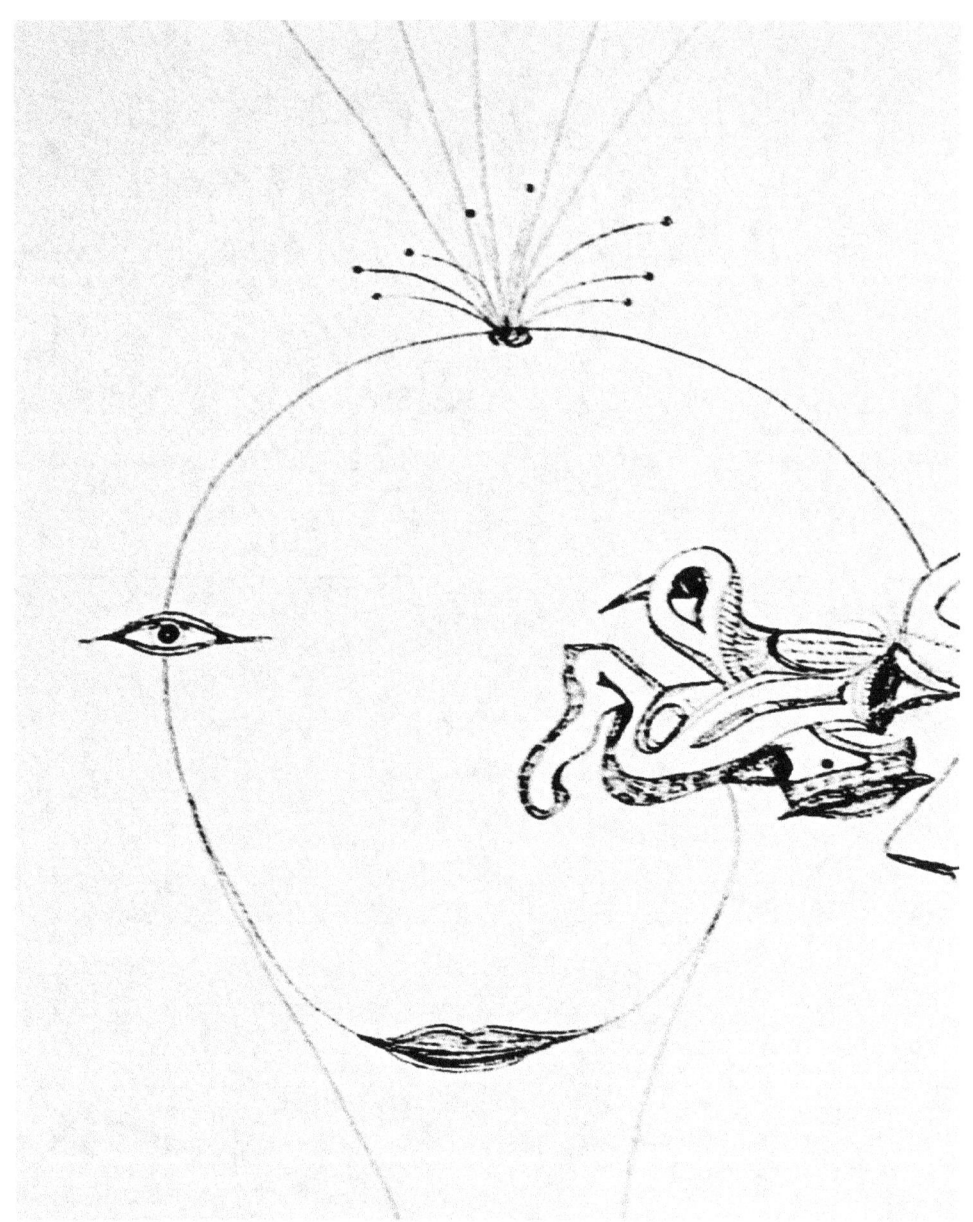

Above: Detail of *Lady Chatterly*

Opposite: *Lady Chatterly* (2005) - Ink on paper - 30"x 22"

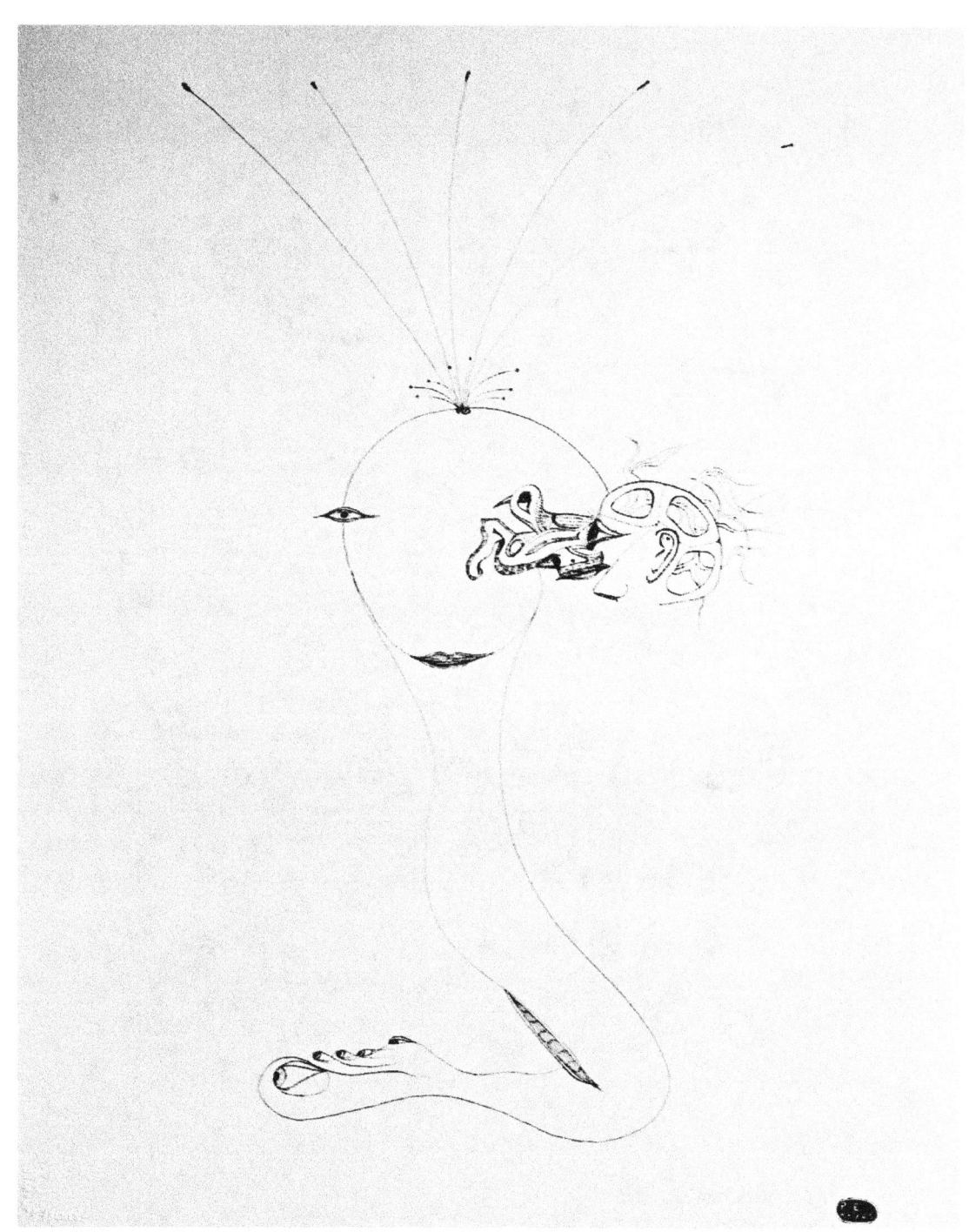

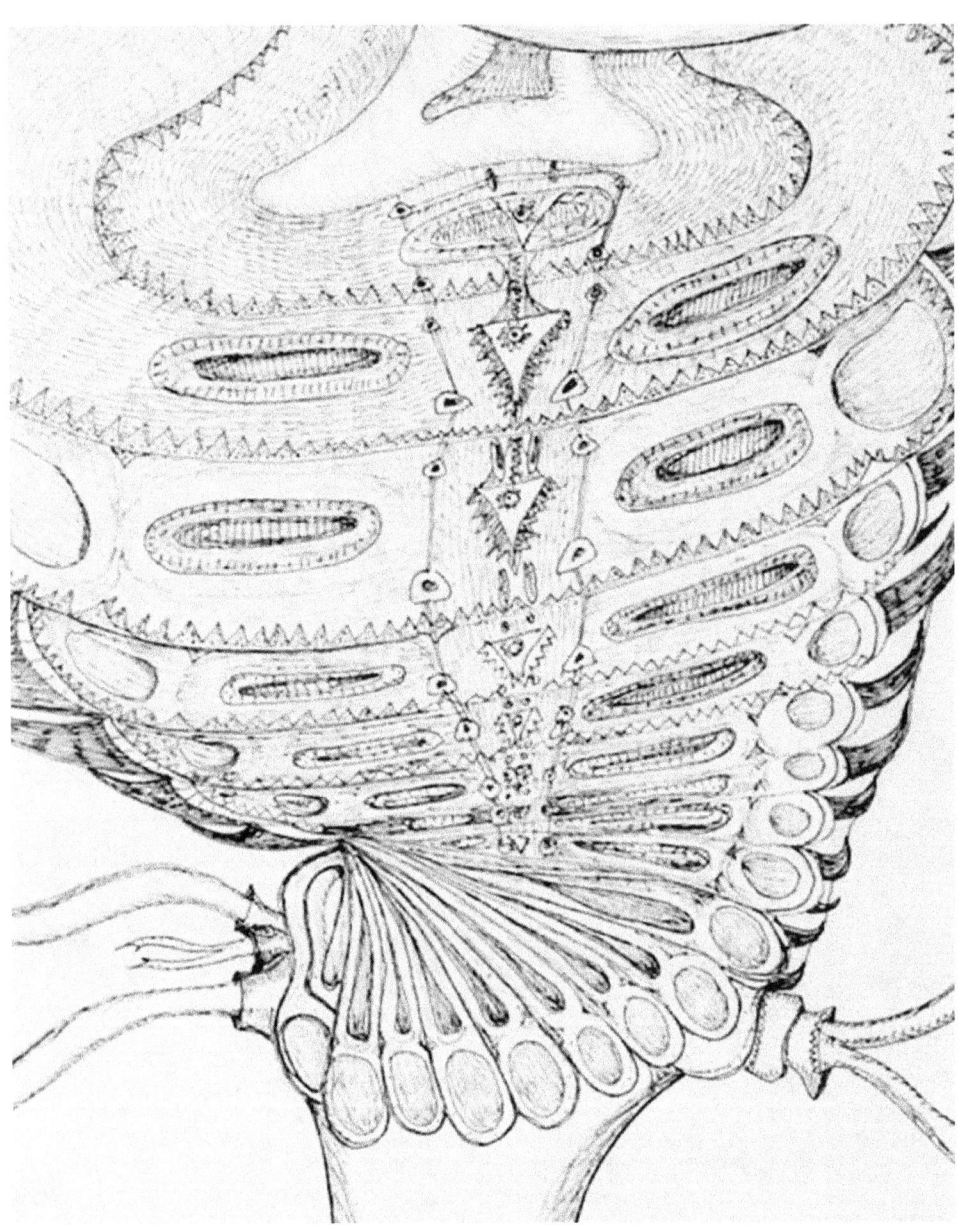

Above: Detail of *Imitation Lobster*

Opposite: *Imitation Lobster* (2008) - Ink on paper - 30"x 22"

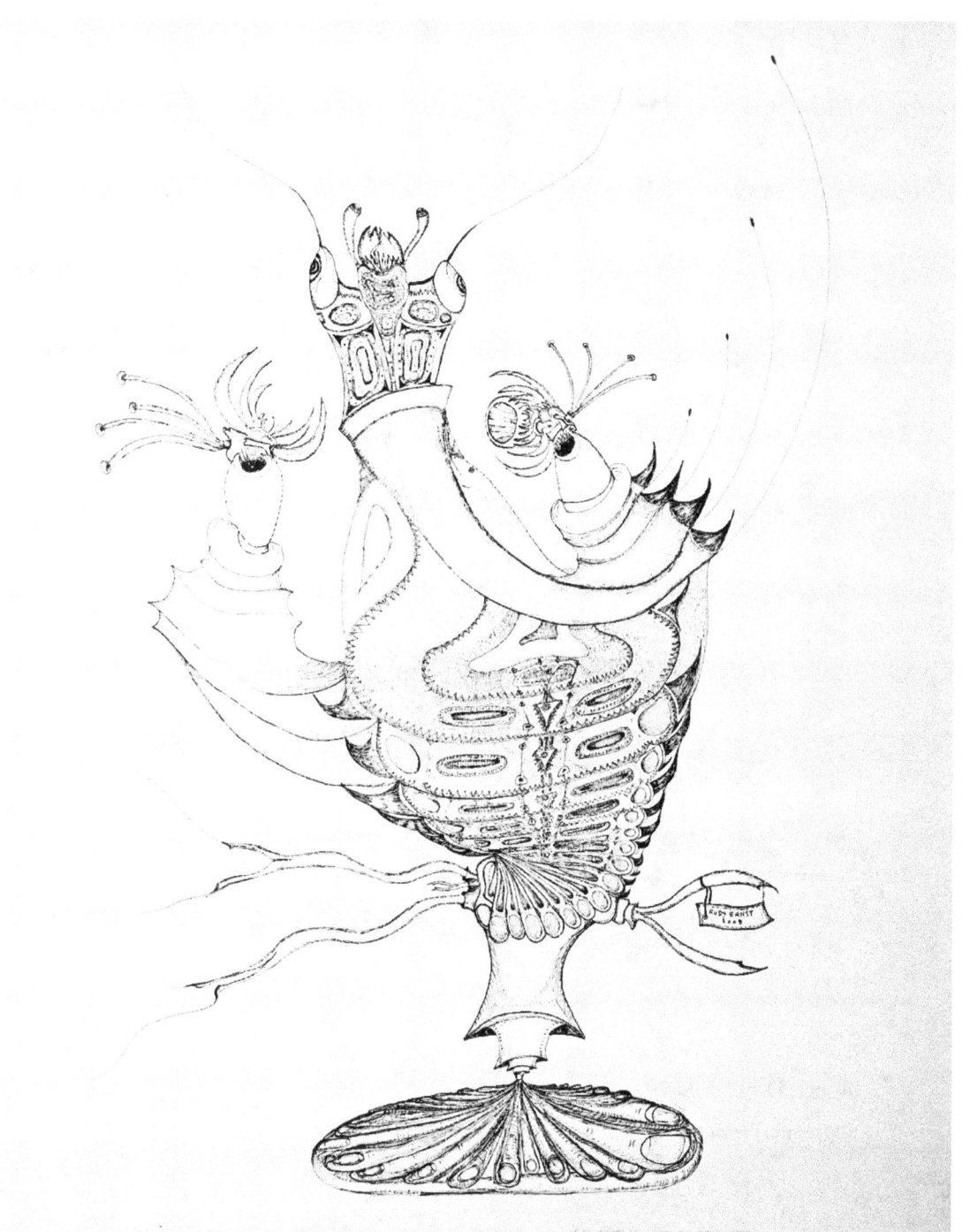

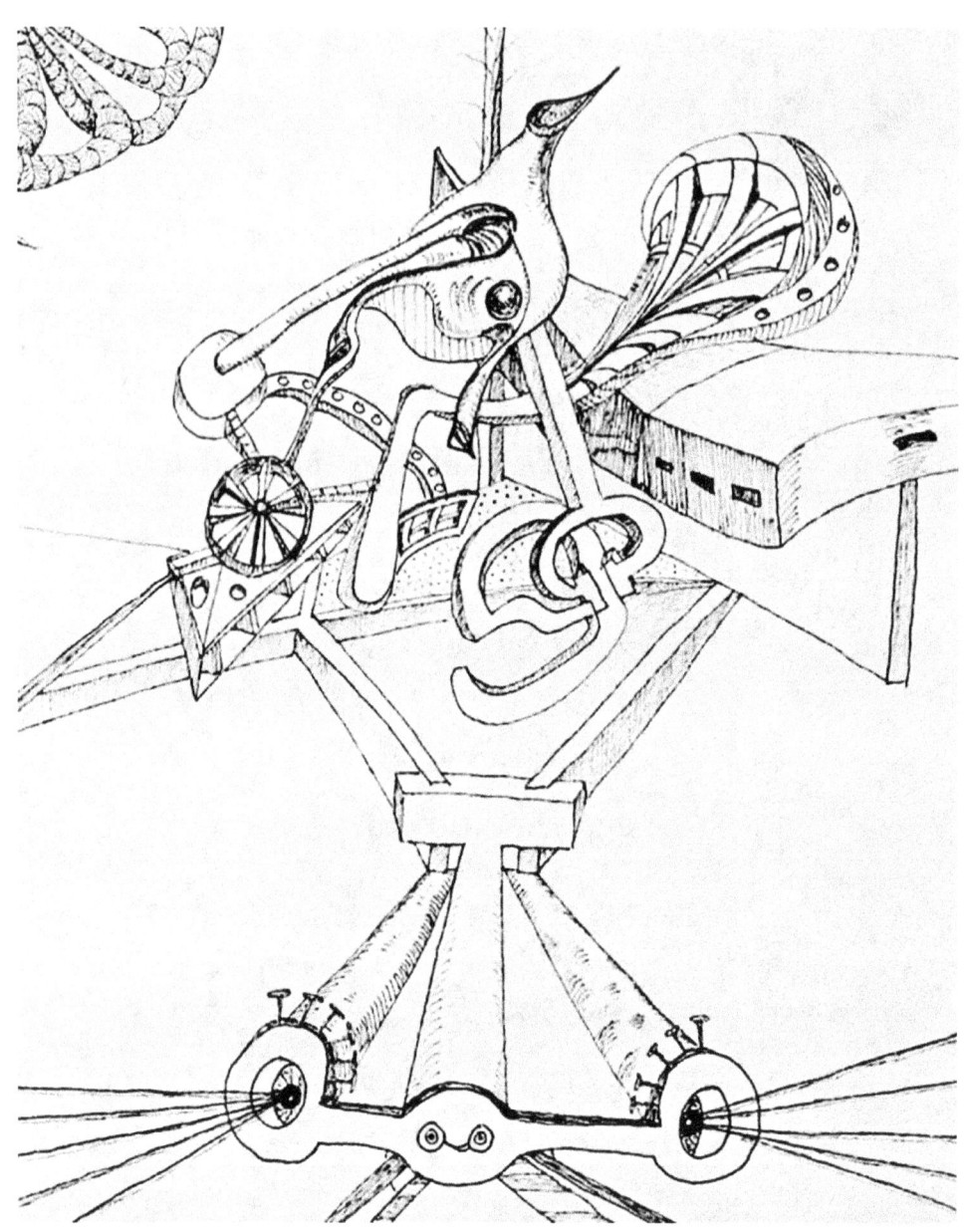

Above: Detail of *Equilibrium*

Opposite: *Equilibrium* (2005) – Ink on paper – 22"x 30"

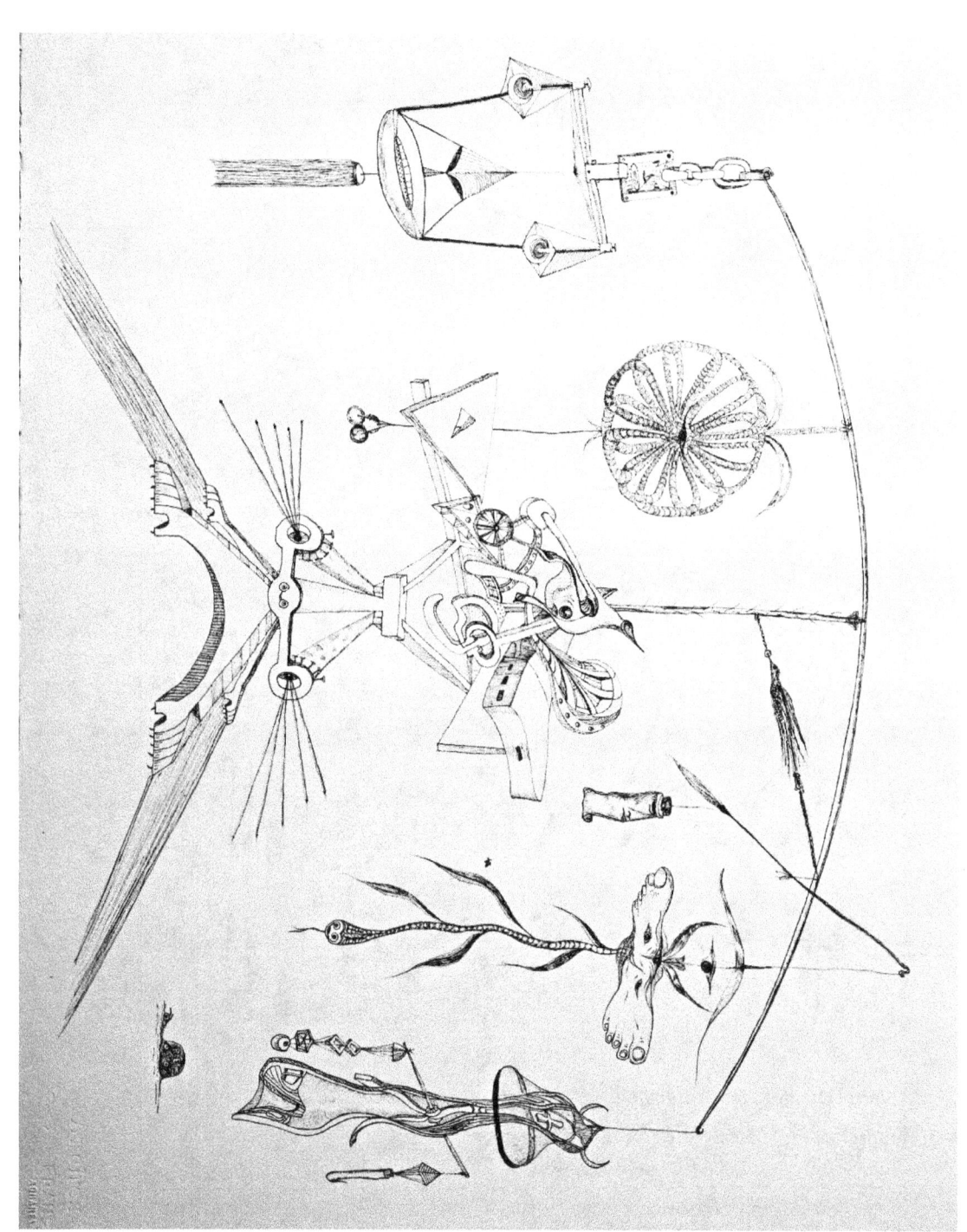

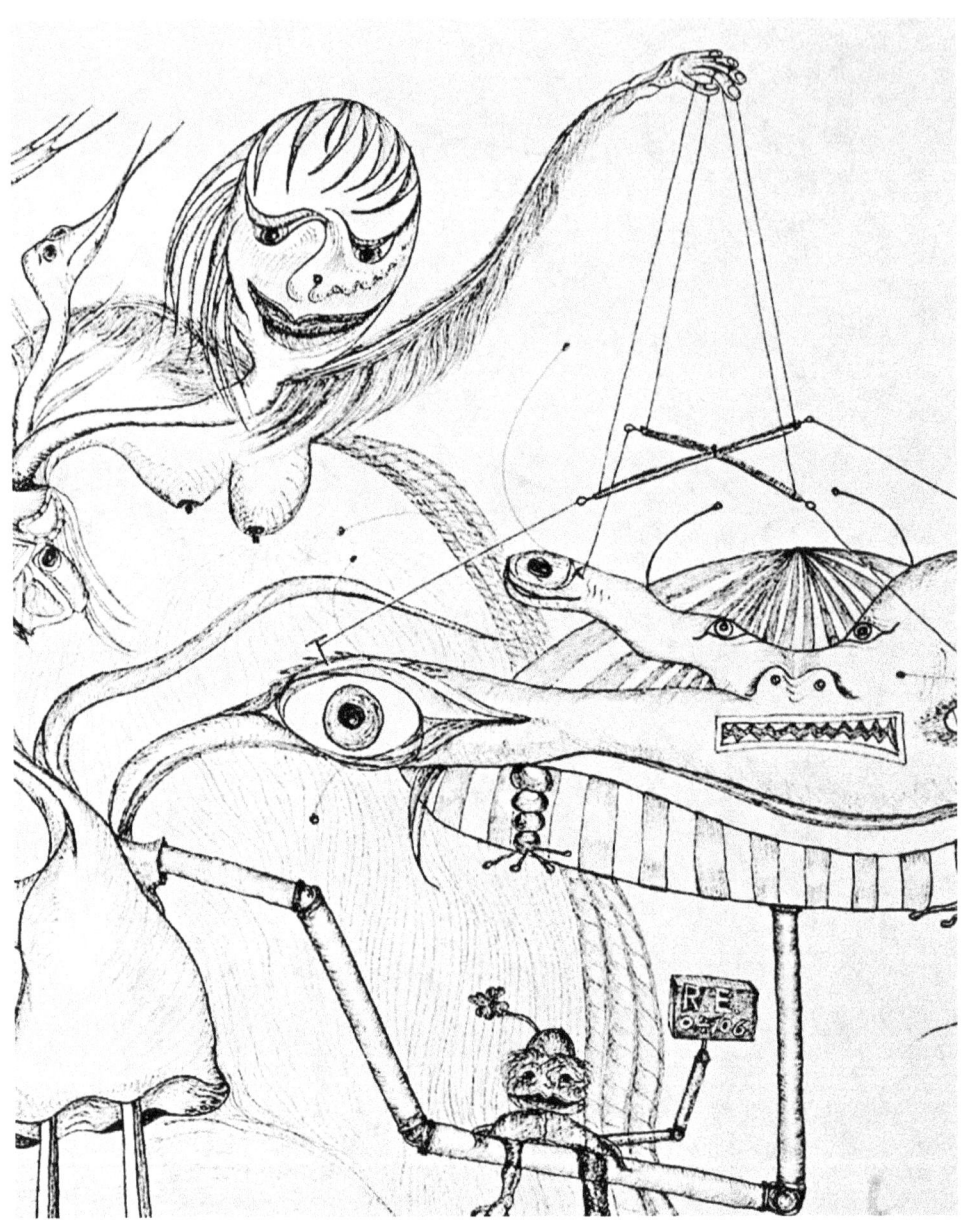

Above: Detail of *Past Midnight*

Opposite: *Past Midnight* (2006) - Ink on paper – 22"x 30"

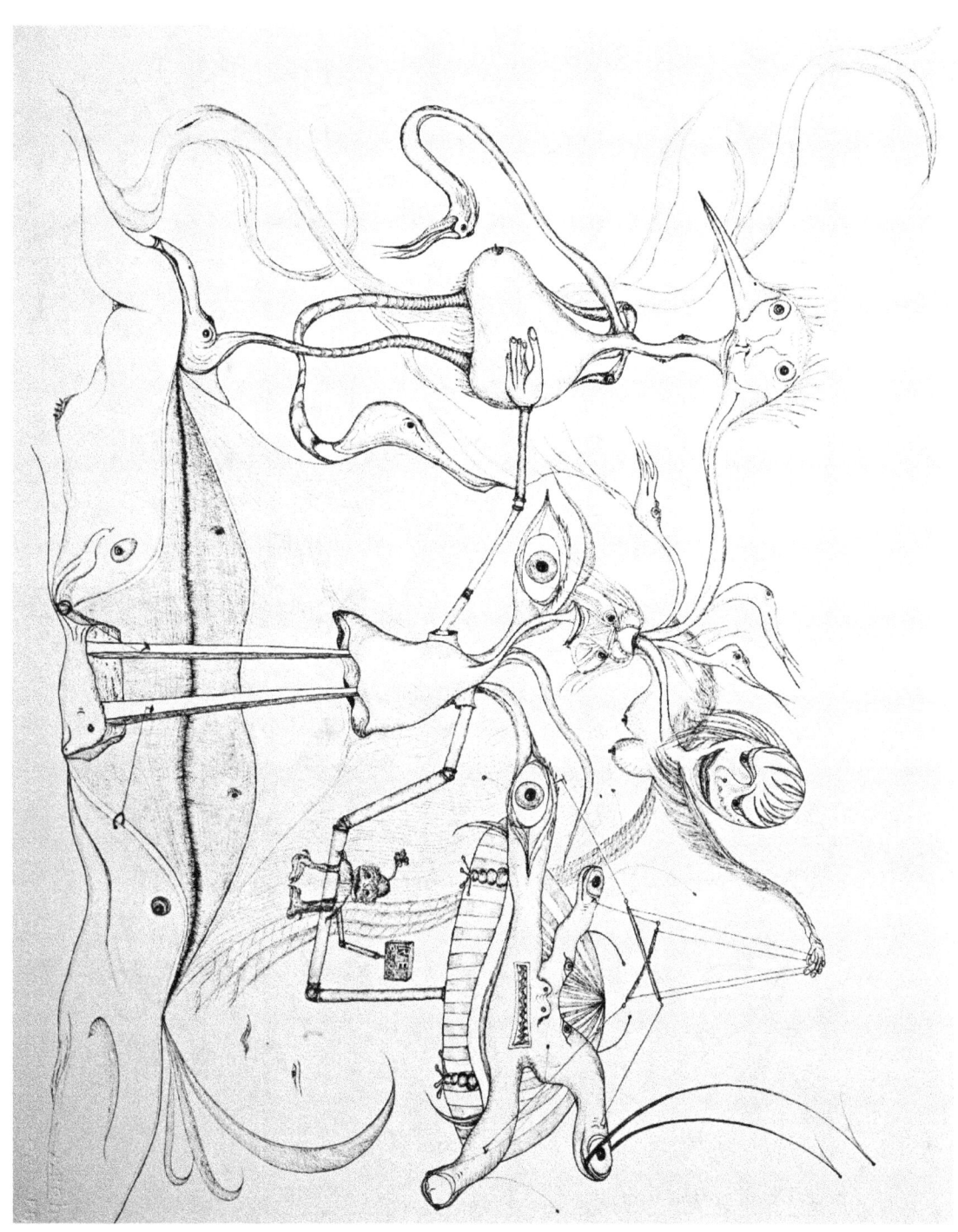

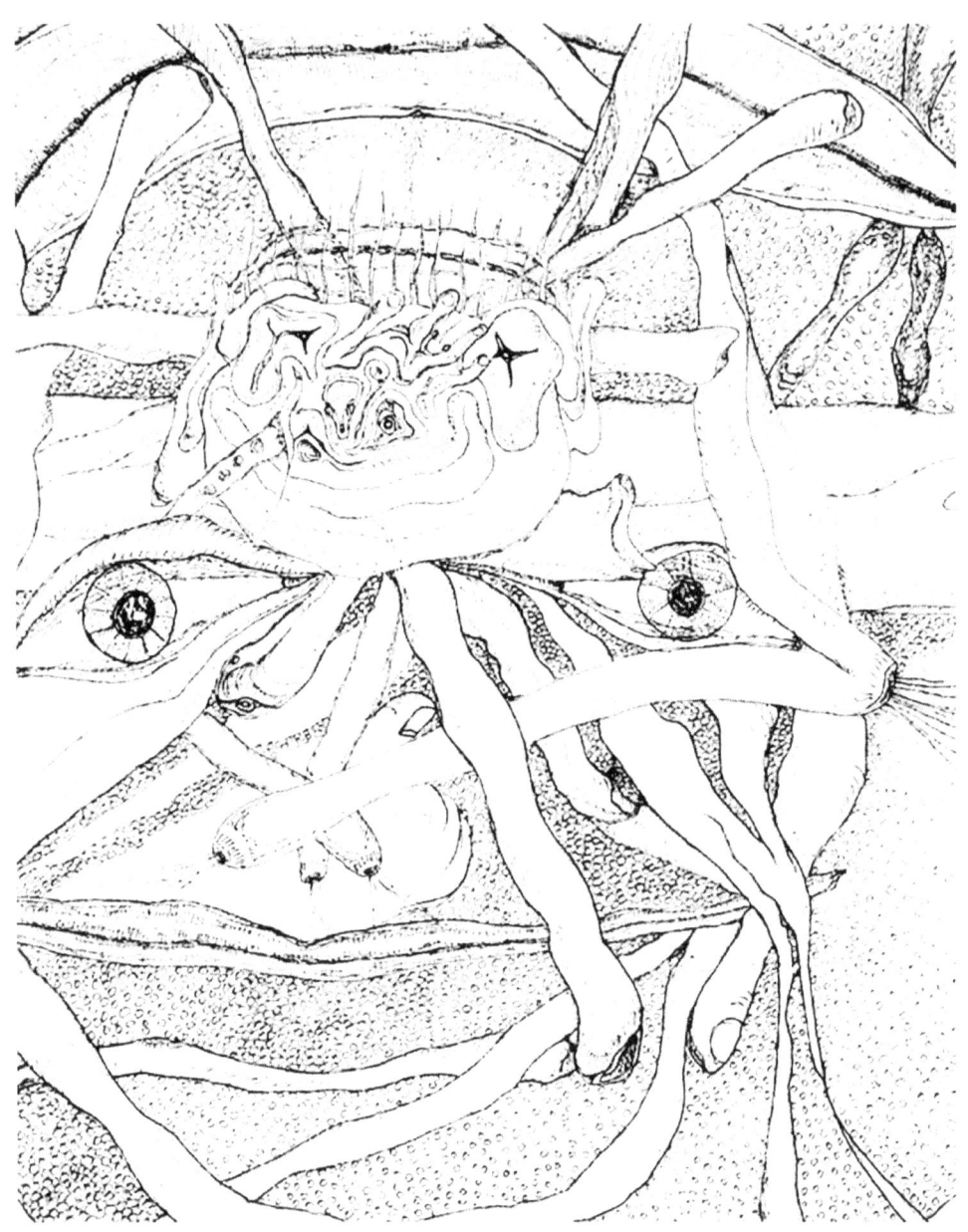

Above: Detail of *Walkathon*

Opposite: *Walkathon* (2005) - Ink on paper – 22"x 30"

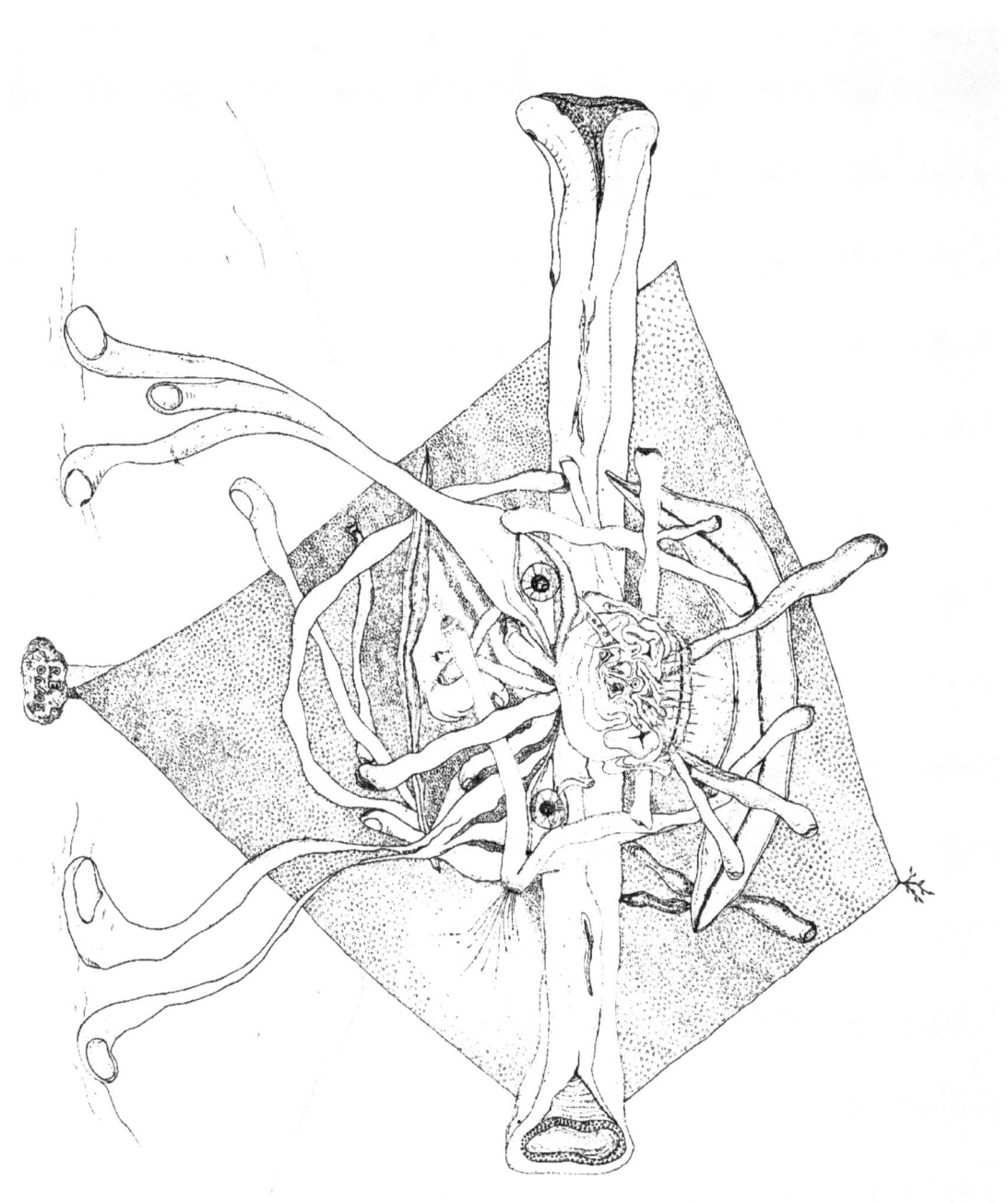

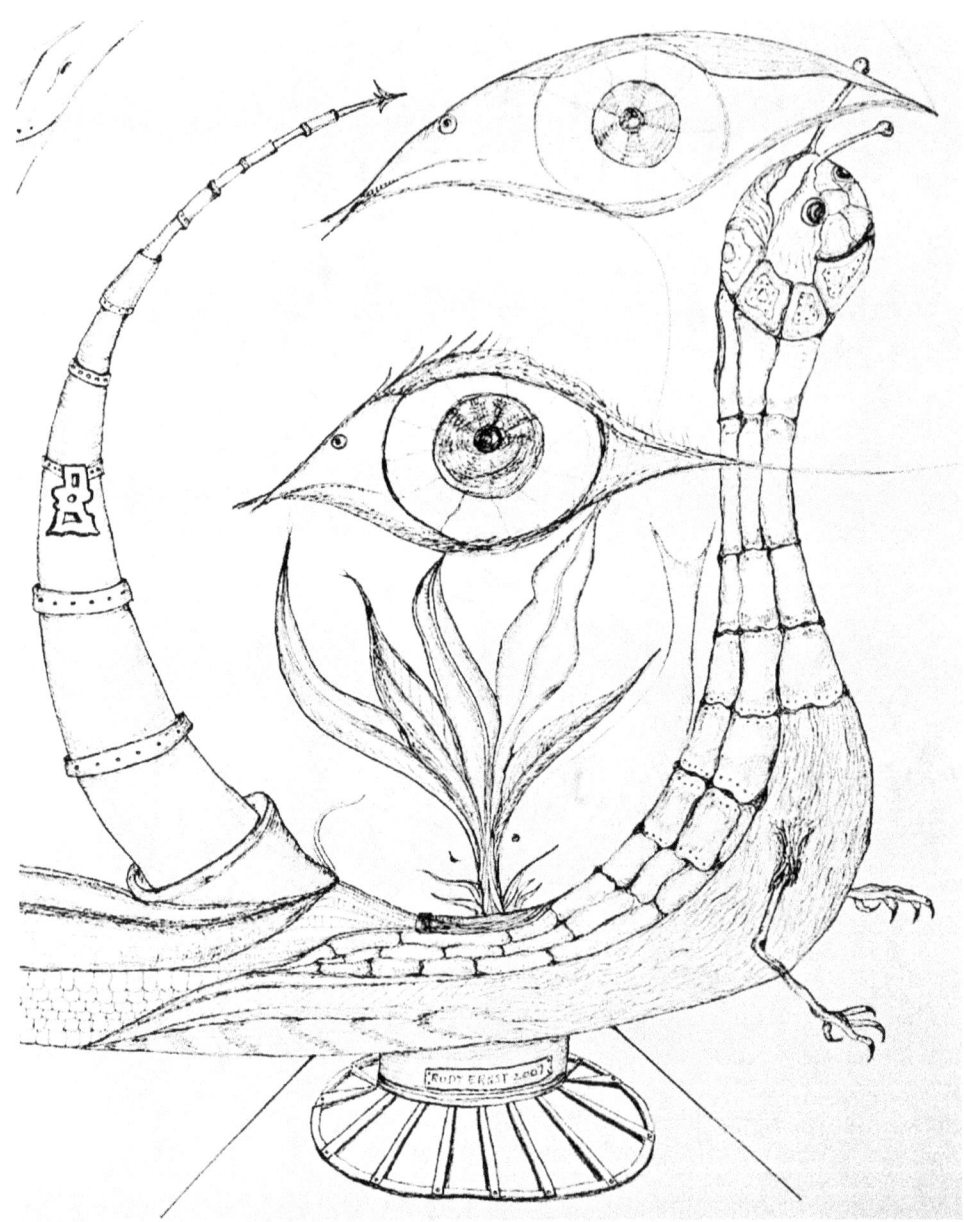

Above: Detail of *Eye-vory*

Opposite: *Eye-vory* (2007) - Ink on paper – 22"x 30"

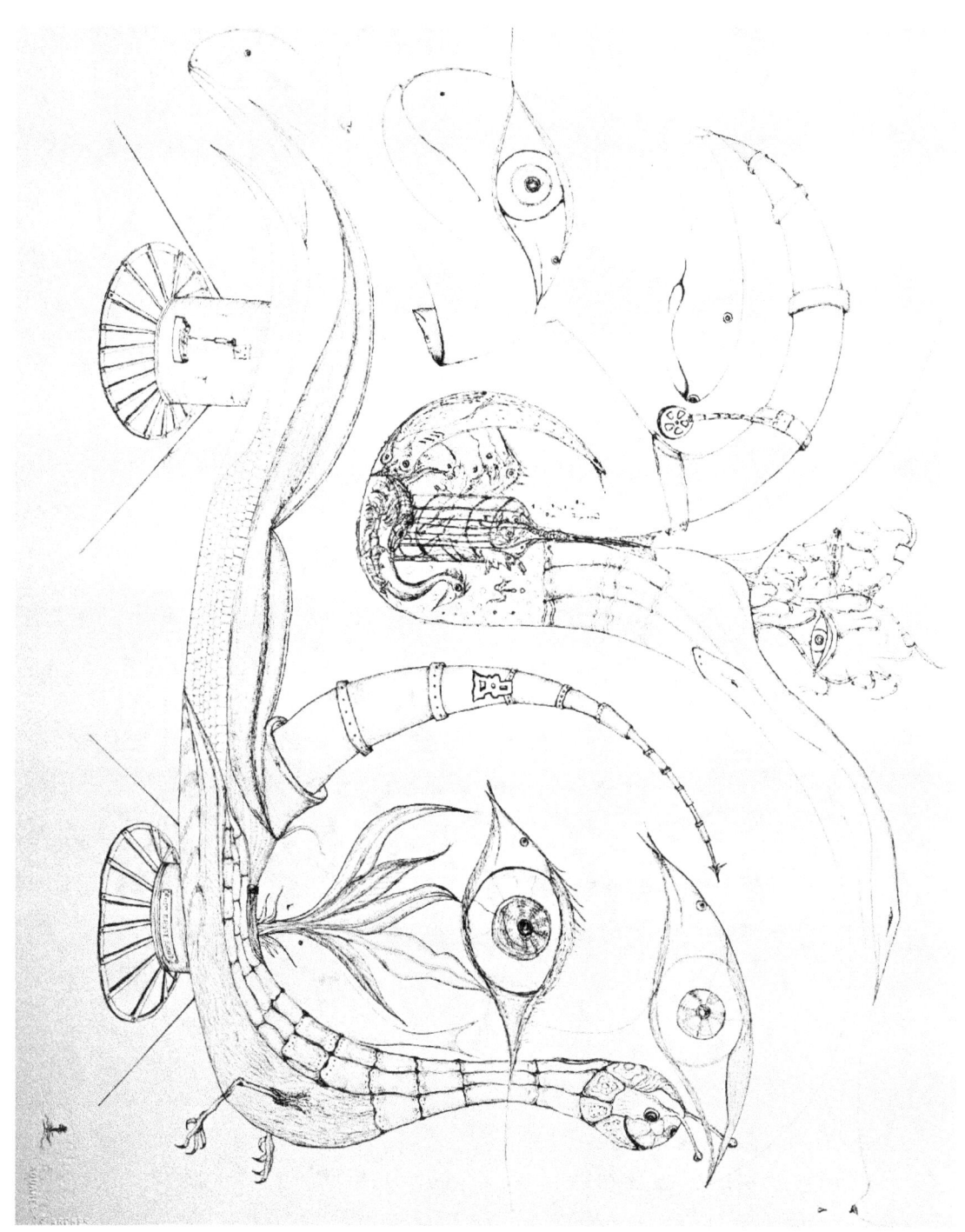

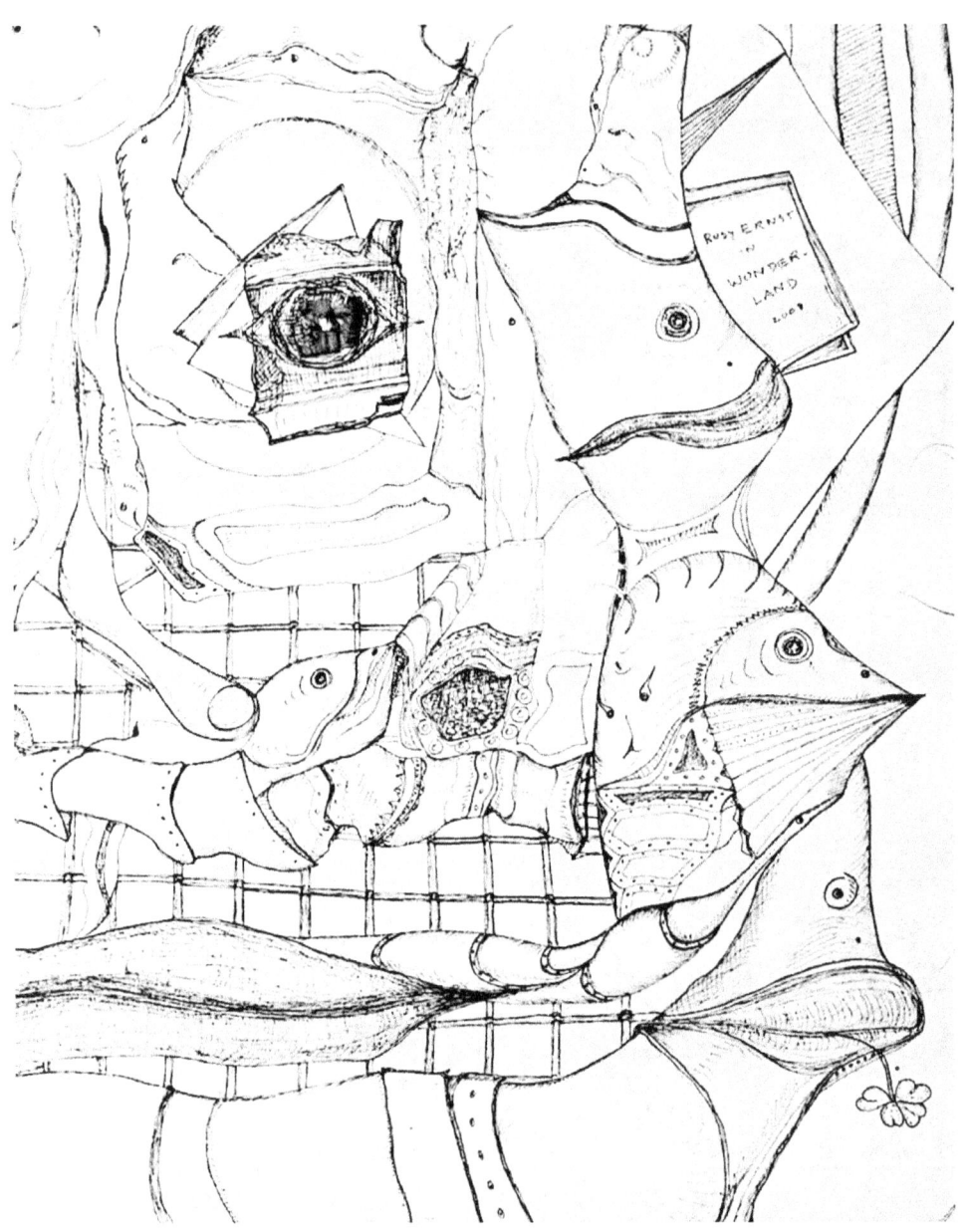

Above: Detail of *Rudy in Wonderland*

Opposite: *Rudy in Wonderland* (2008) – Ink on paper – 30"x 22"

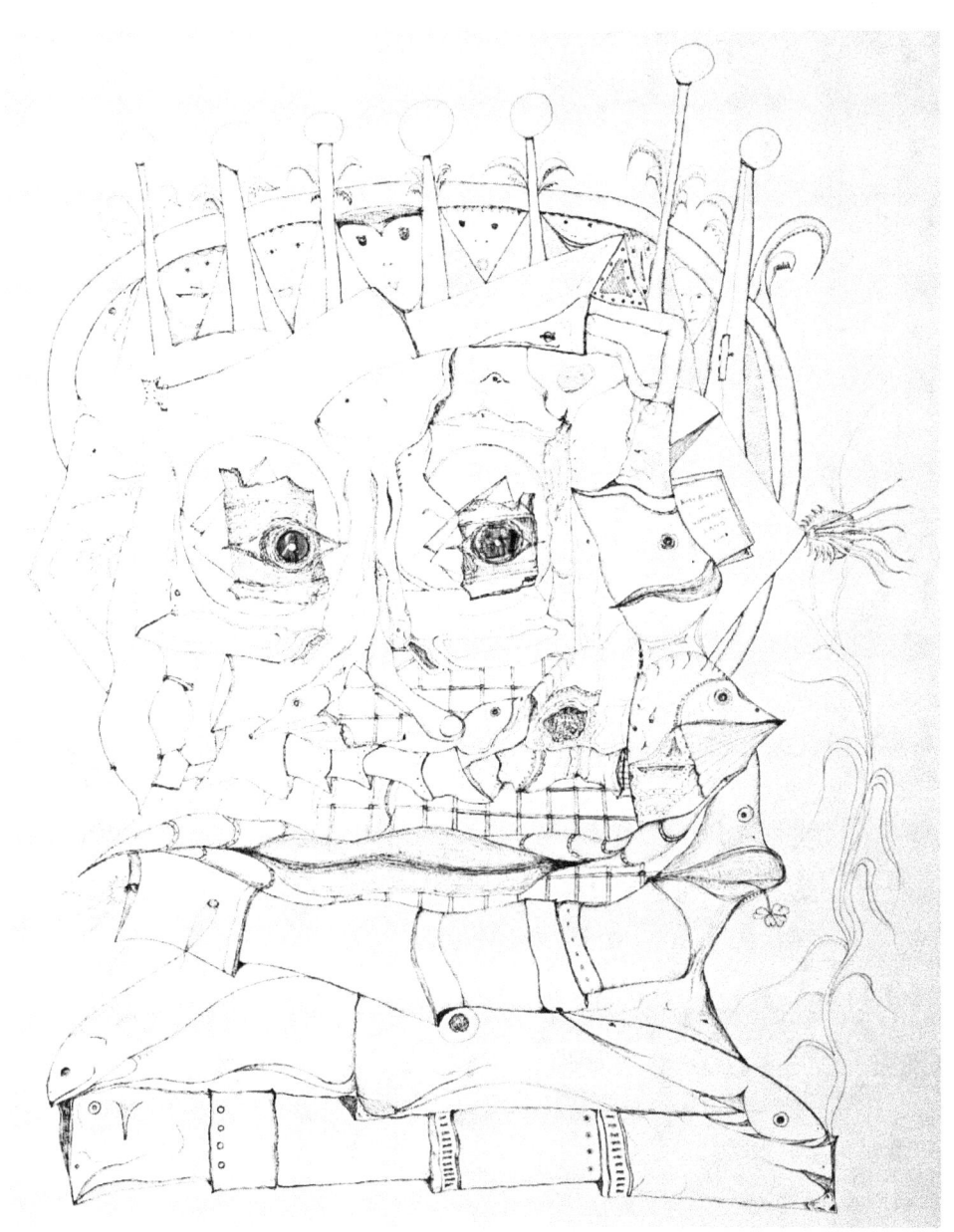

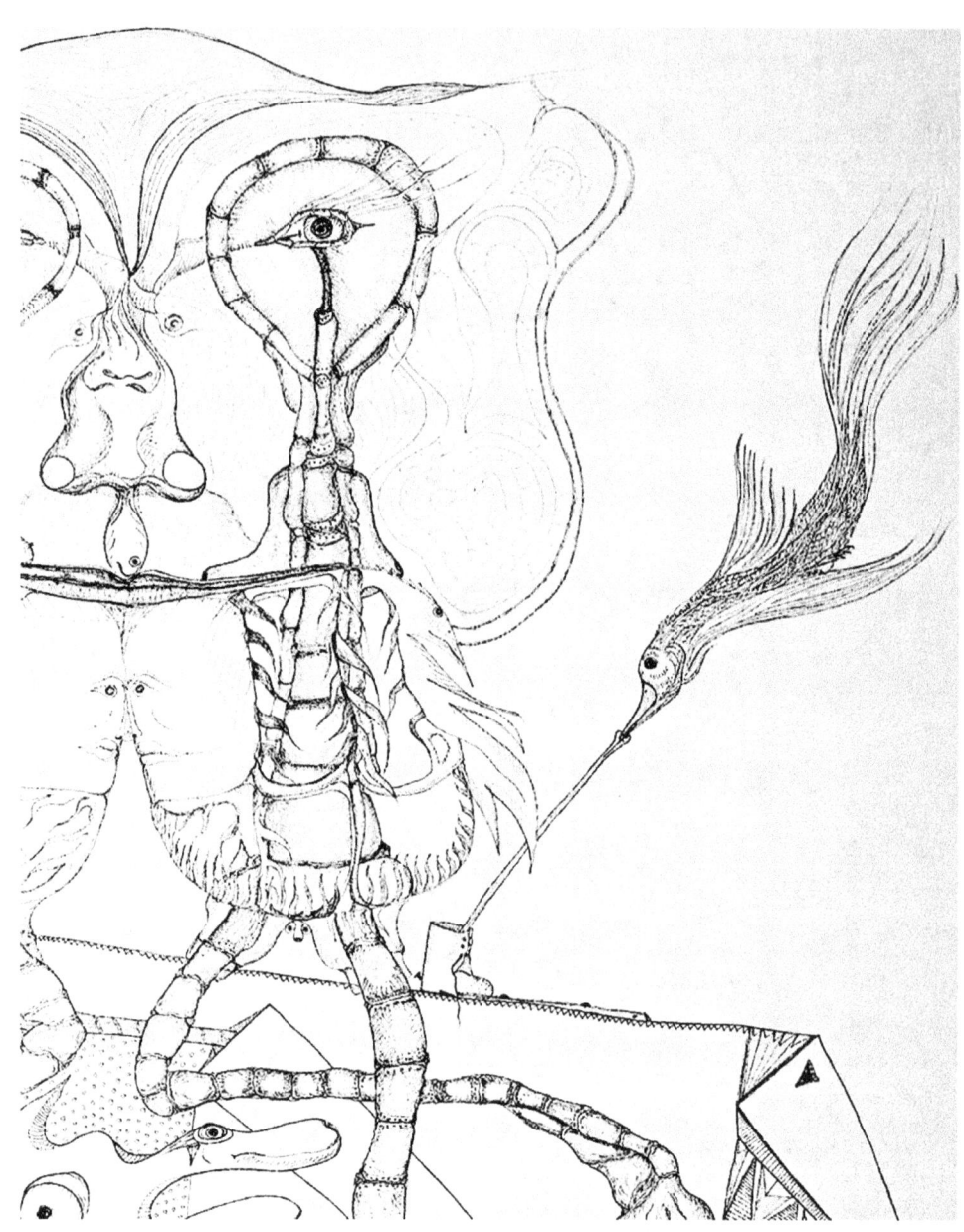

Above: Detail of *Still Holding On*

Opposite: *Still Holding On* (2006) – Ink on paper – 30"x 22"

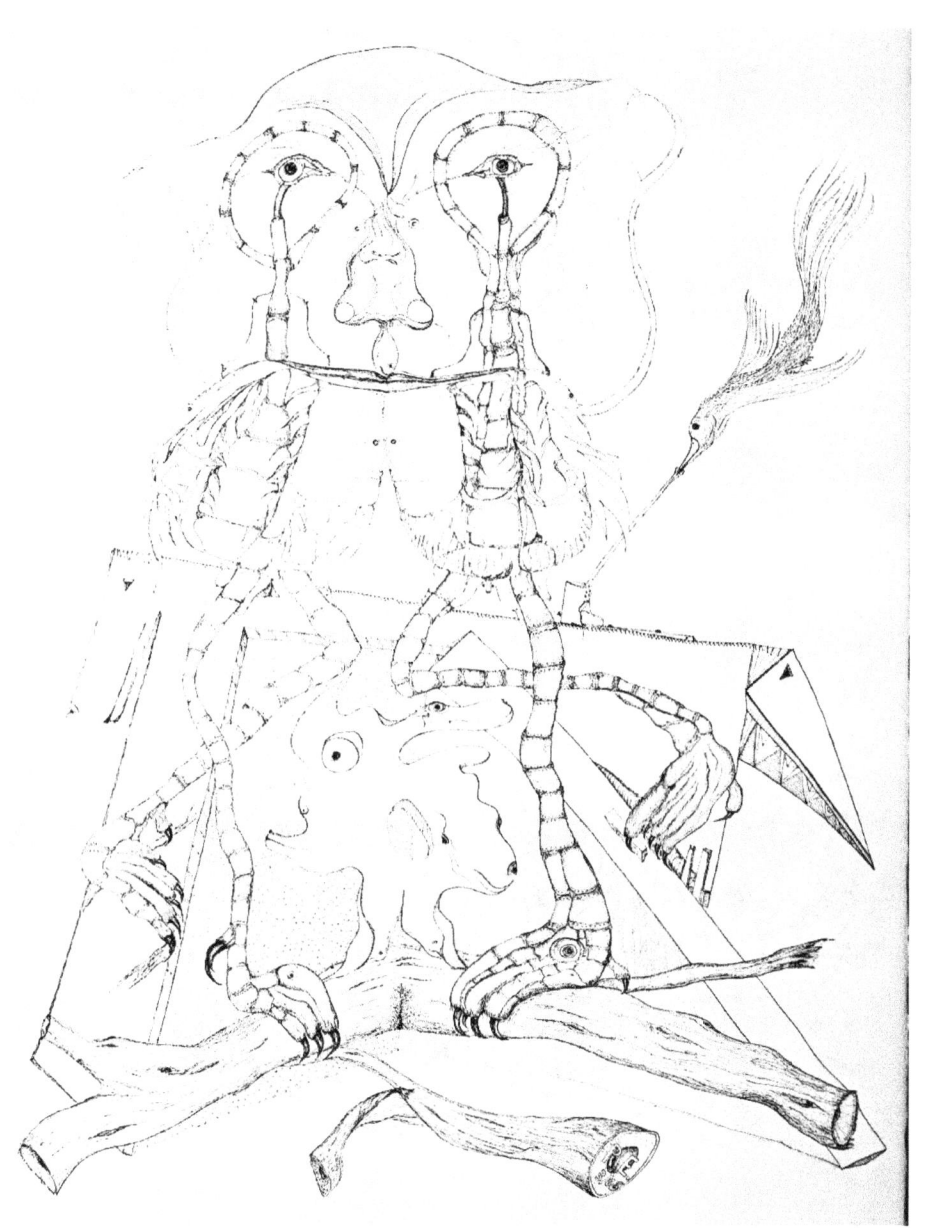

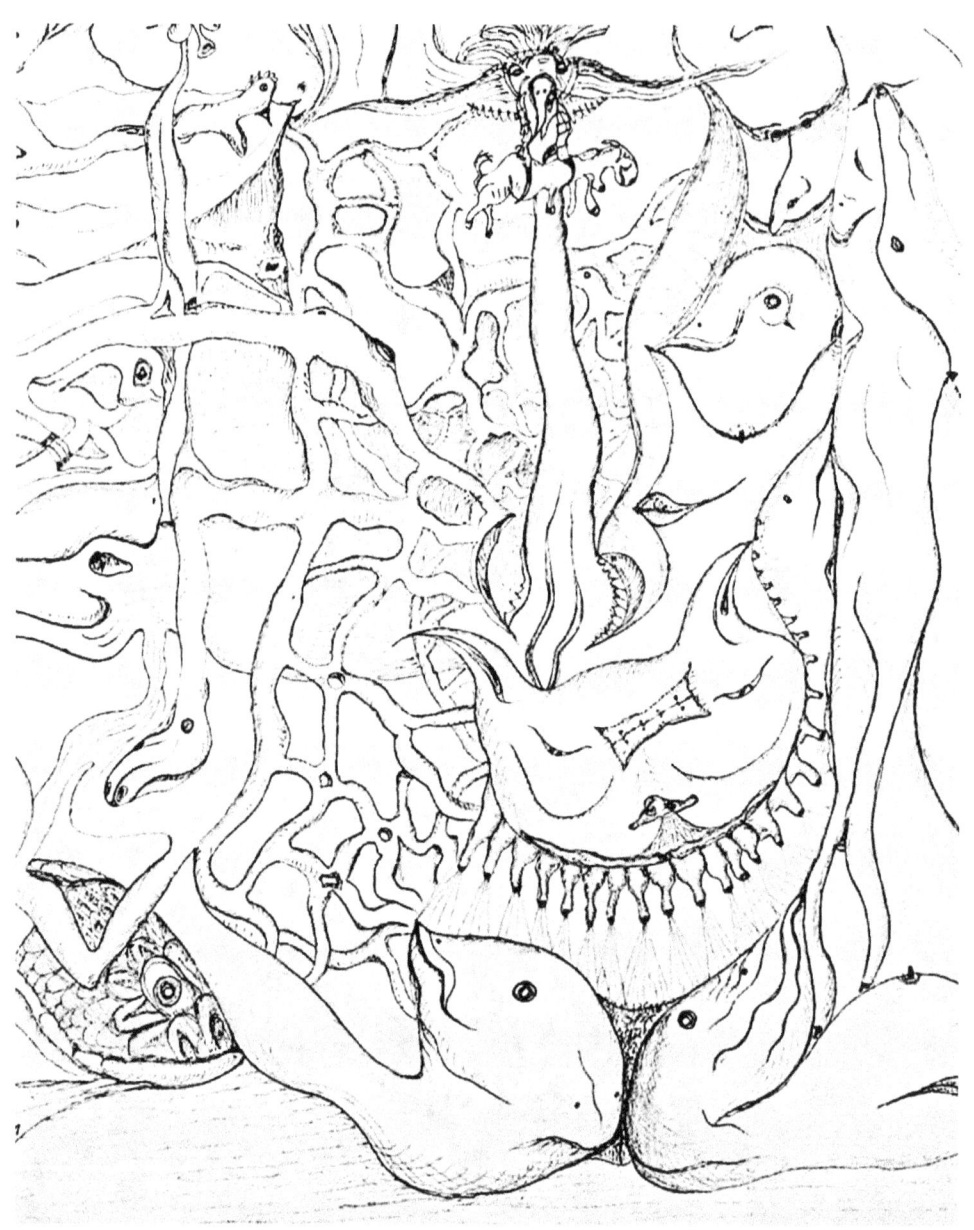

Above: Detail of *Arrowhead*

Opposite: *Arrowhead* (2007) – Ink on paper – 22"x 30"

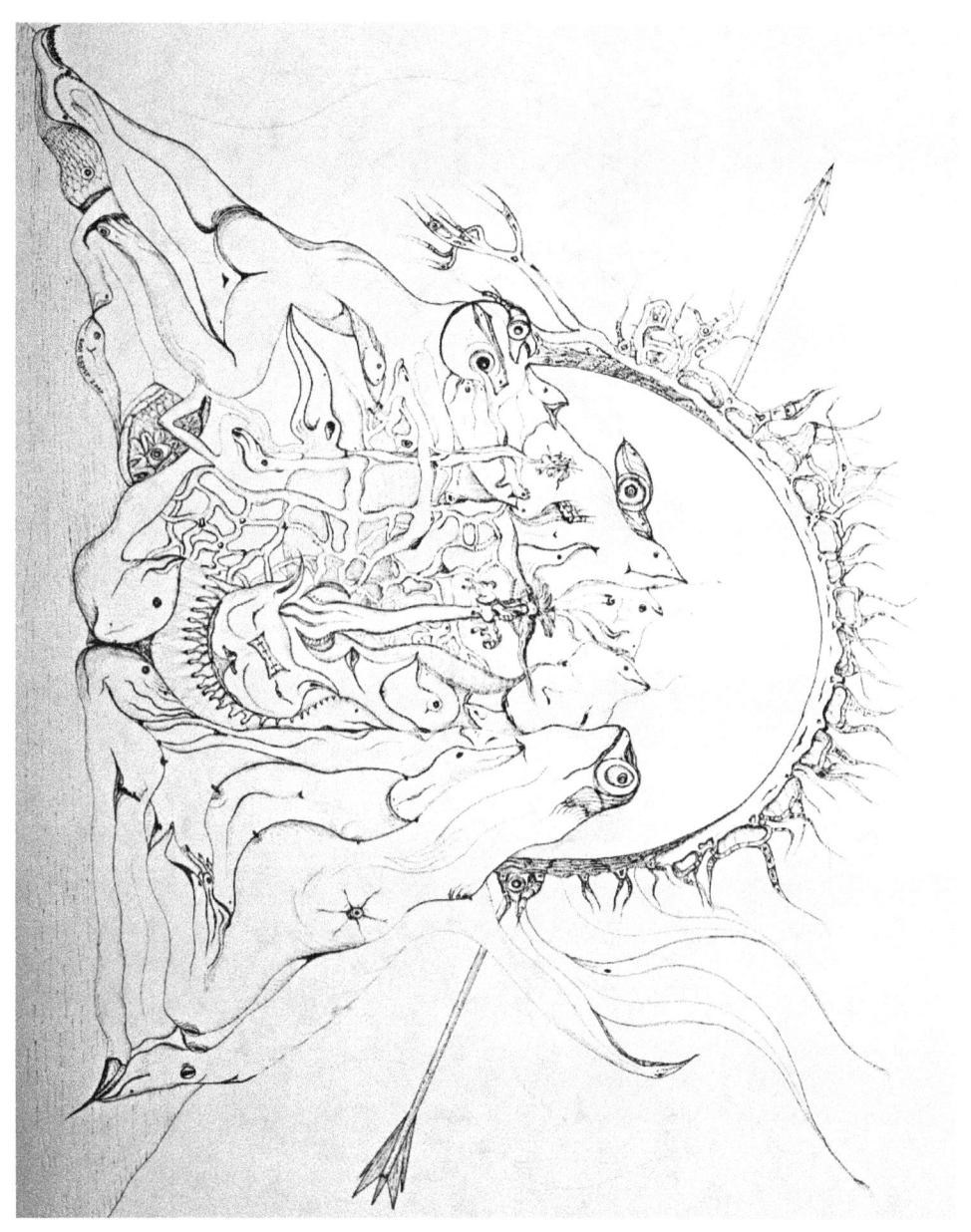

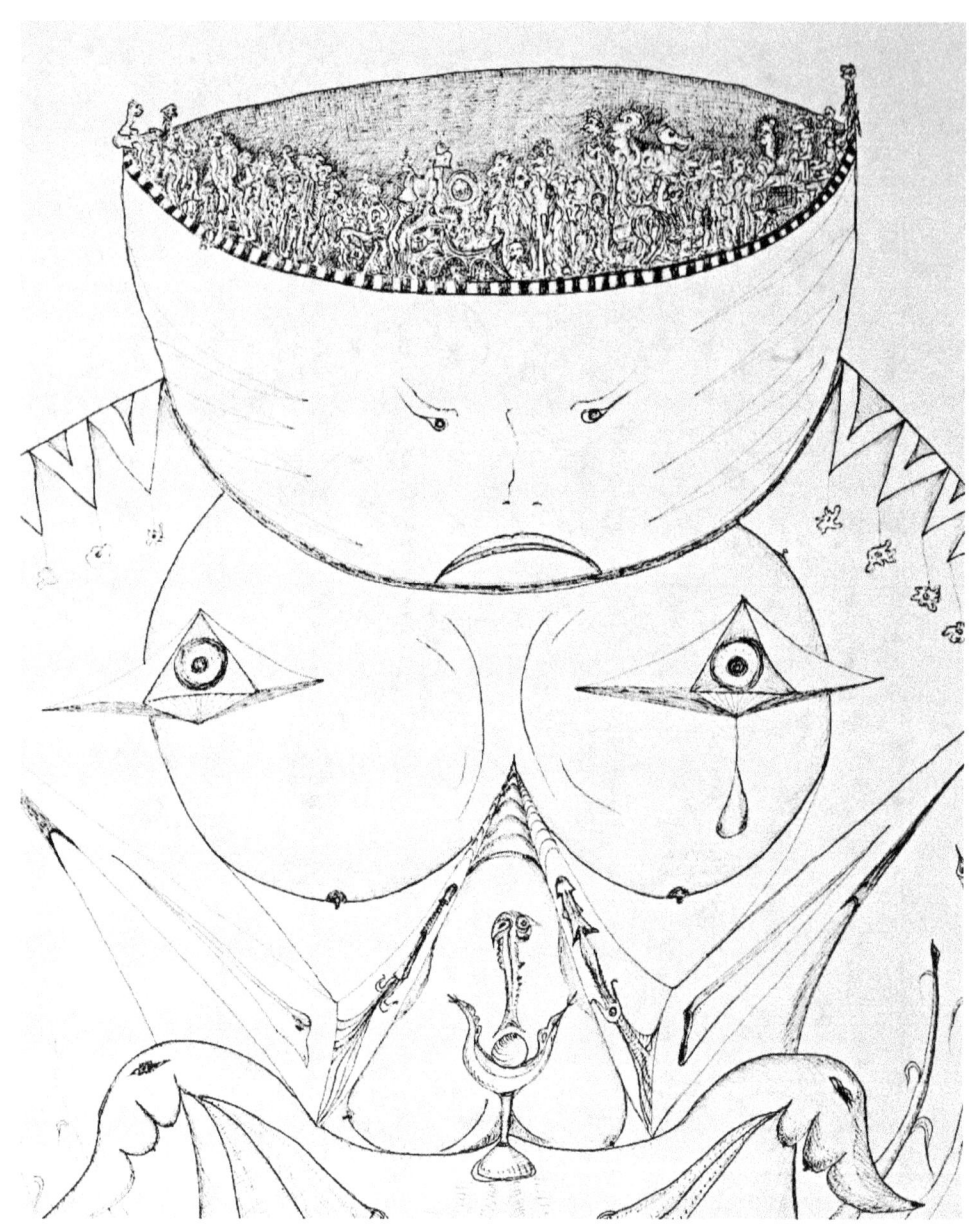

Above: Detail of *Mindful*

Opposite: *Mindful* (2008) – Ink on paper – 30"x 22"

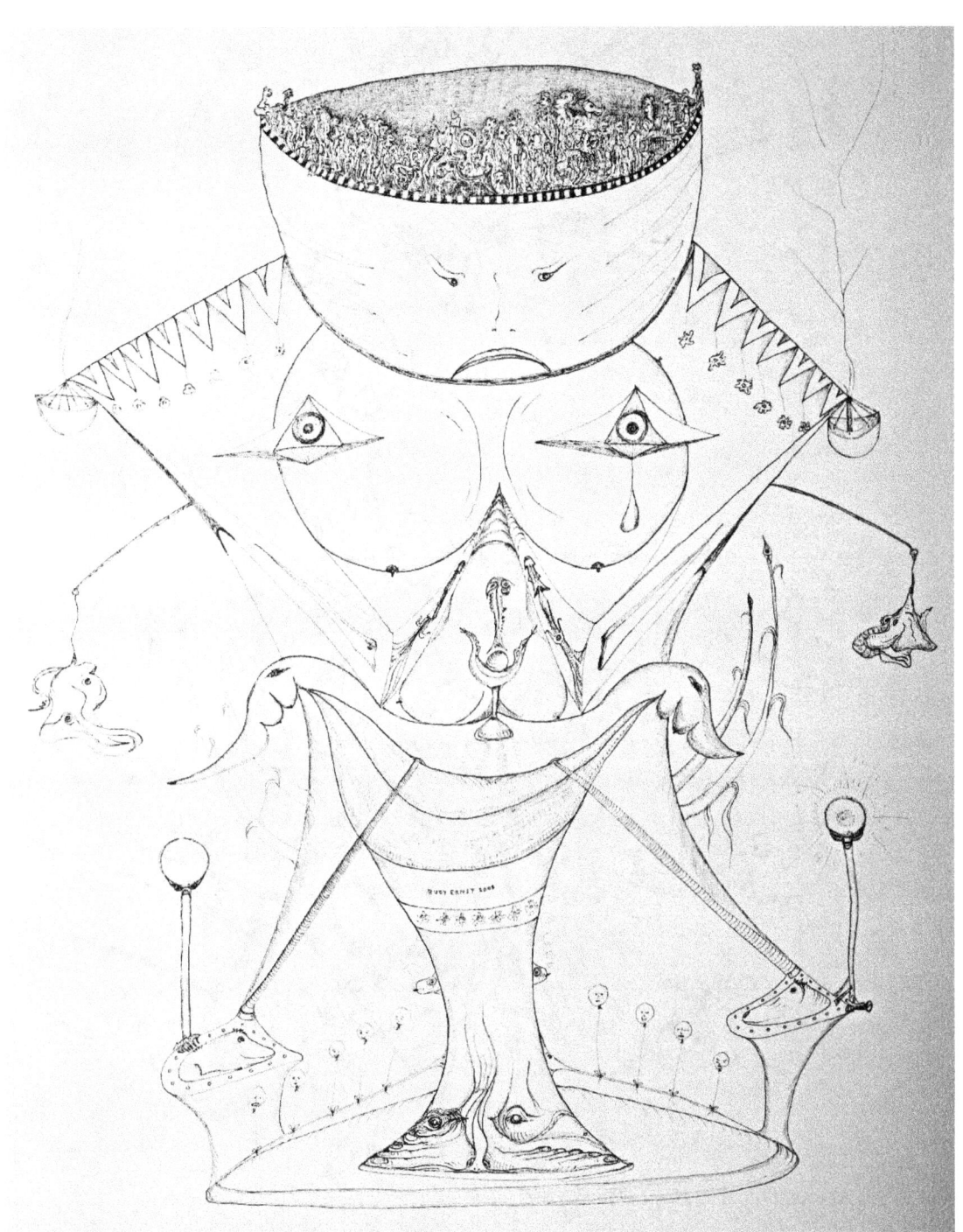

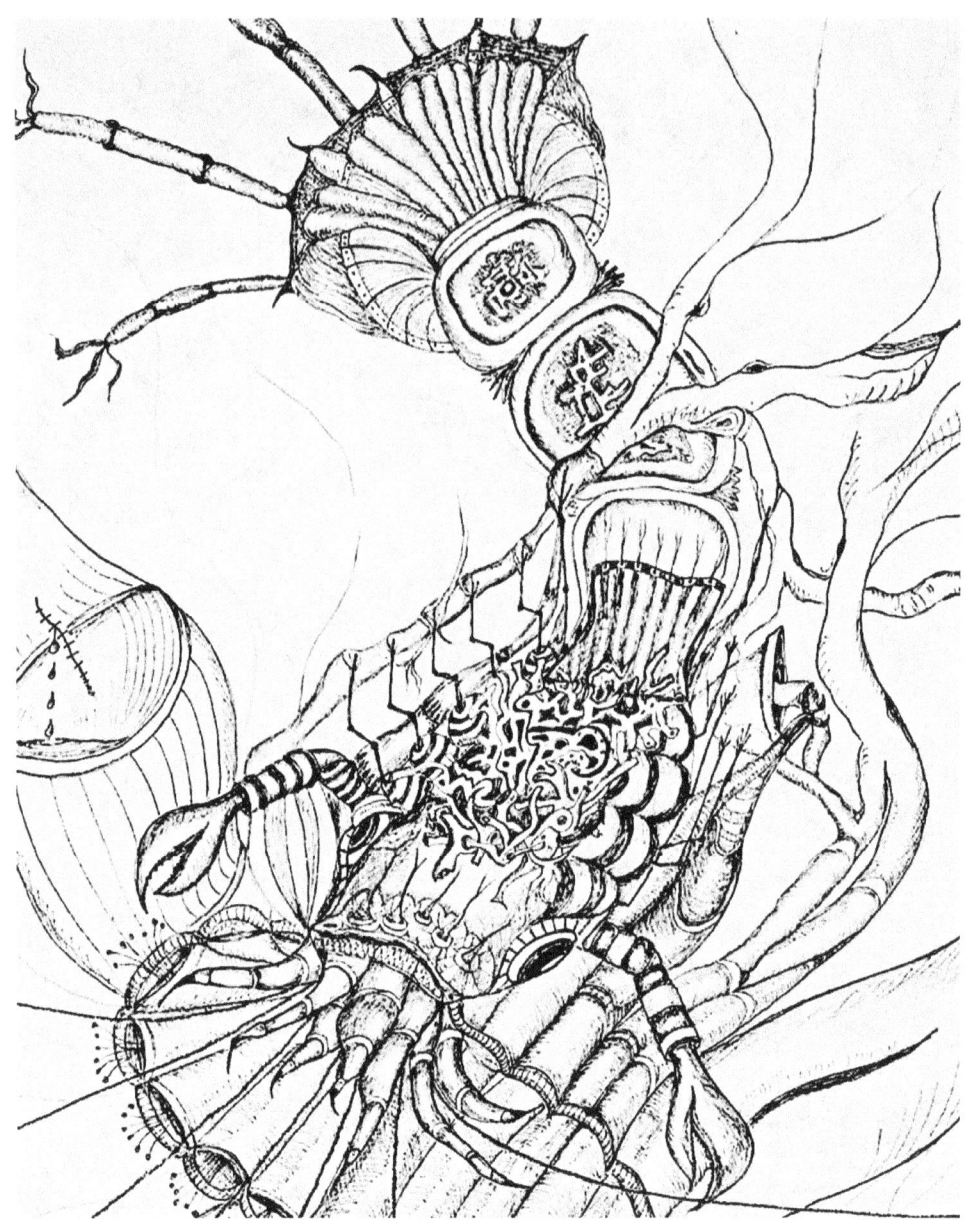

Above: Detail of *Home Run*

Opposite: *Home Run* (2007) – Ink on paper – 30"x 22"

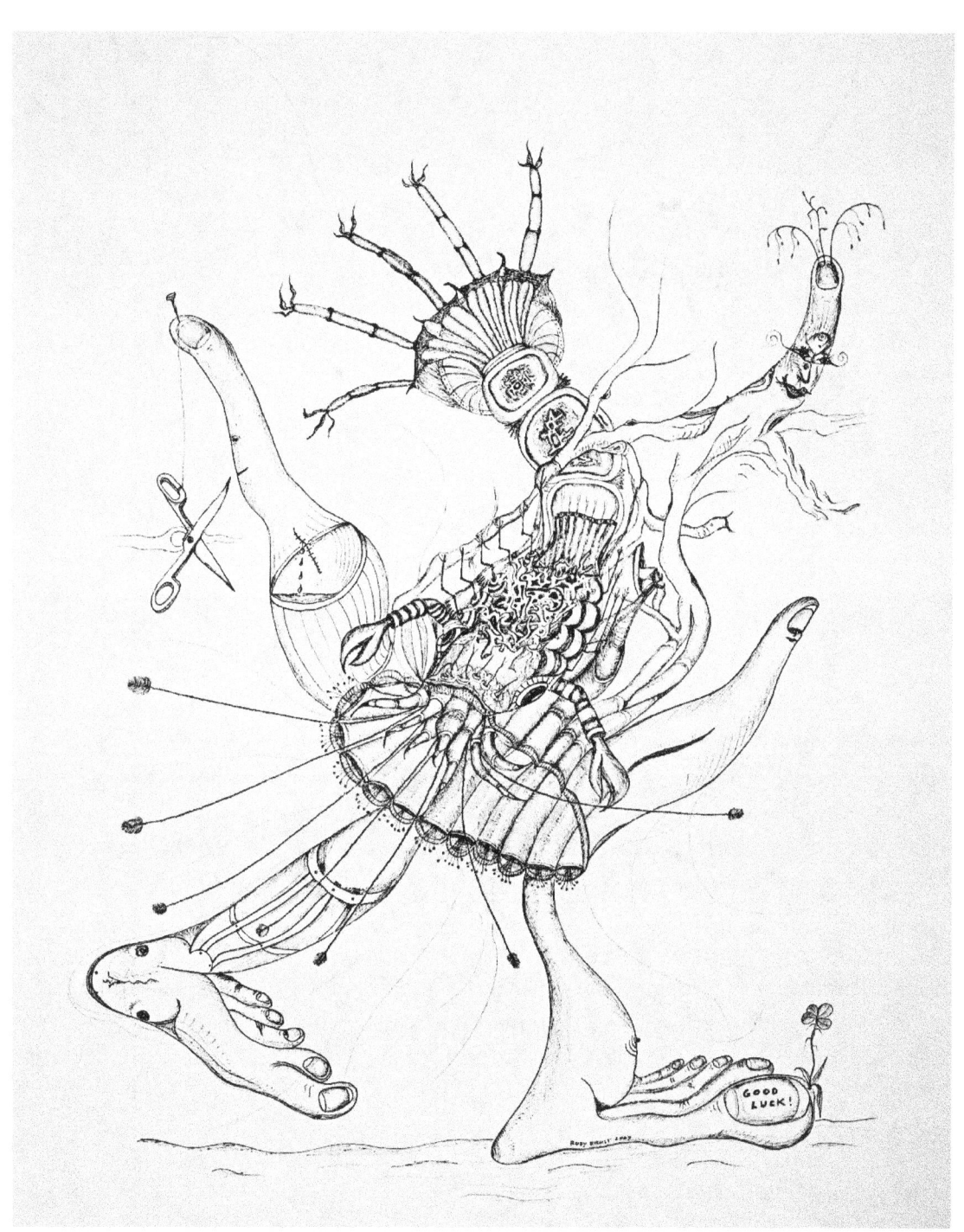

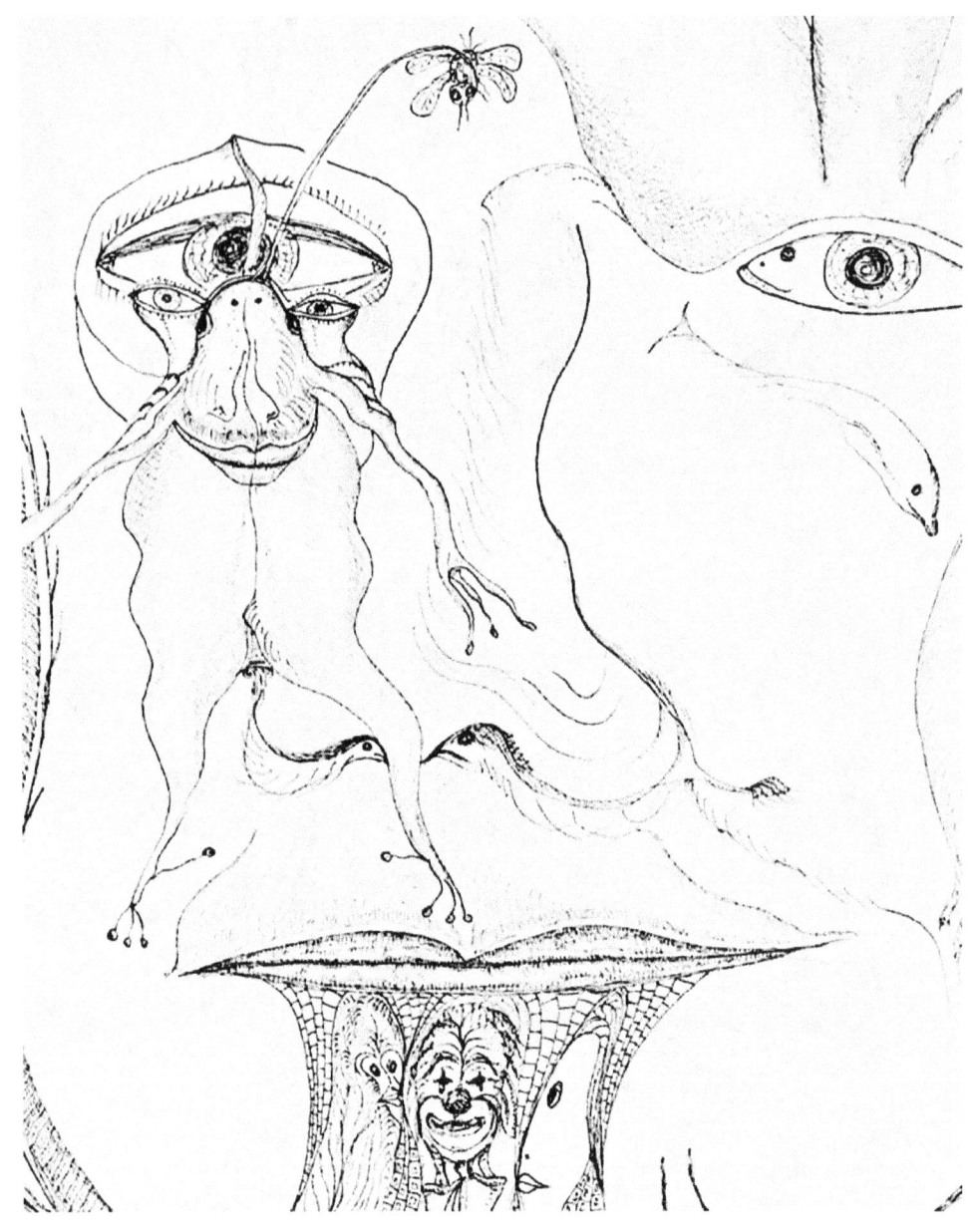

Above: Detail of *Finger Licking Good*

Opposite: *Finger Licking Good* (2006)) - Ink on paper - 30"x 22"

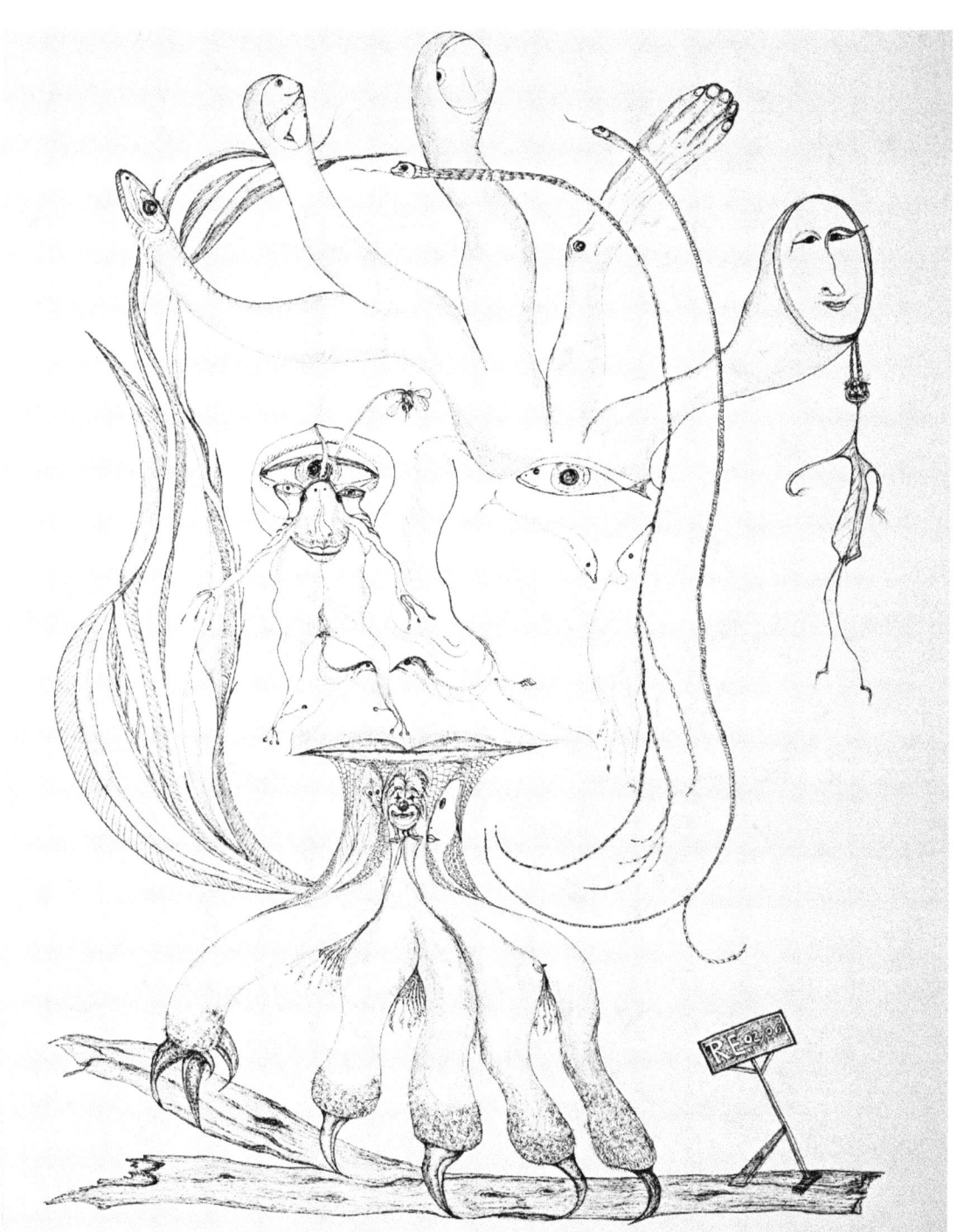

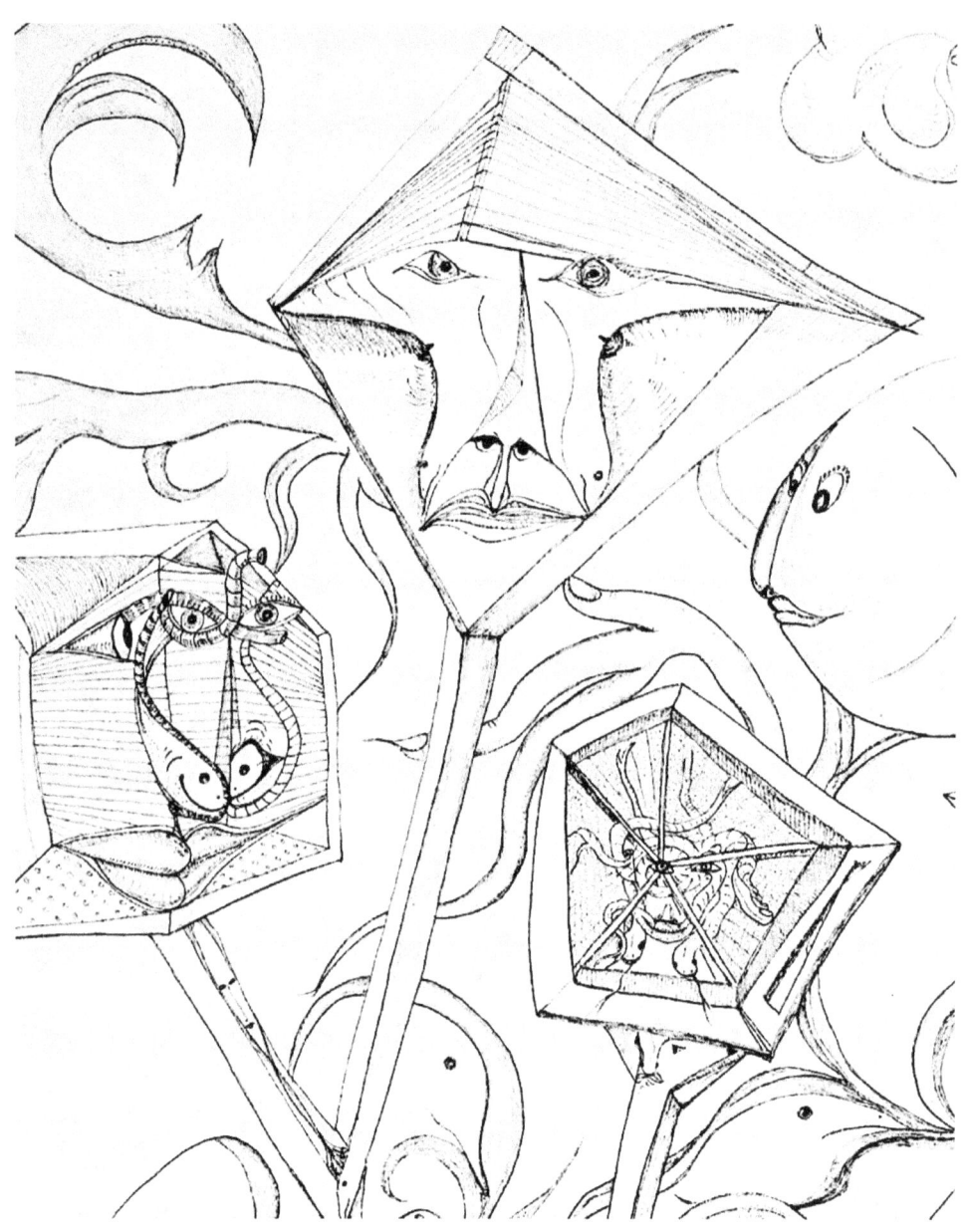

Above: Detail of *Dangerous Toys*

Opposite: *Dangerous Toys* (2006) – Ink on paper – 30"x 22"

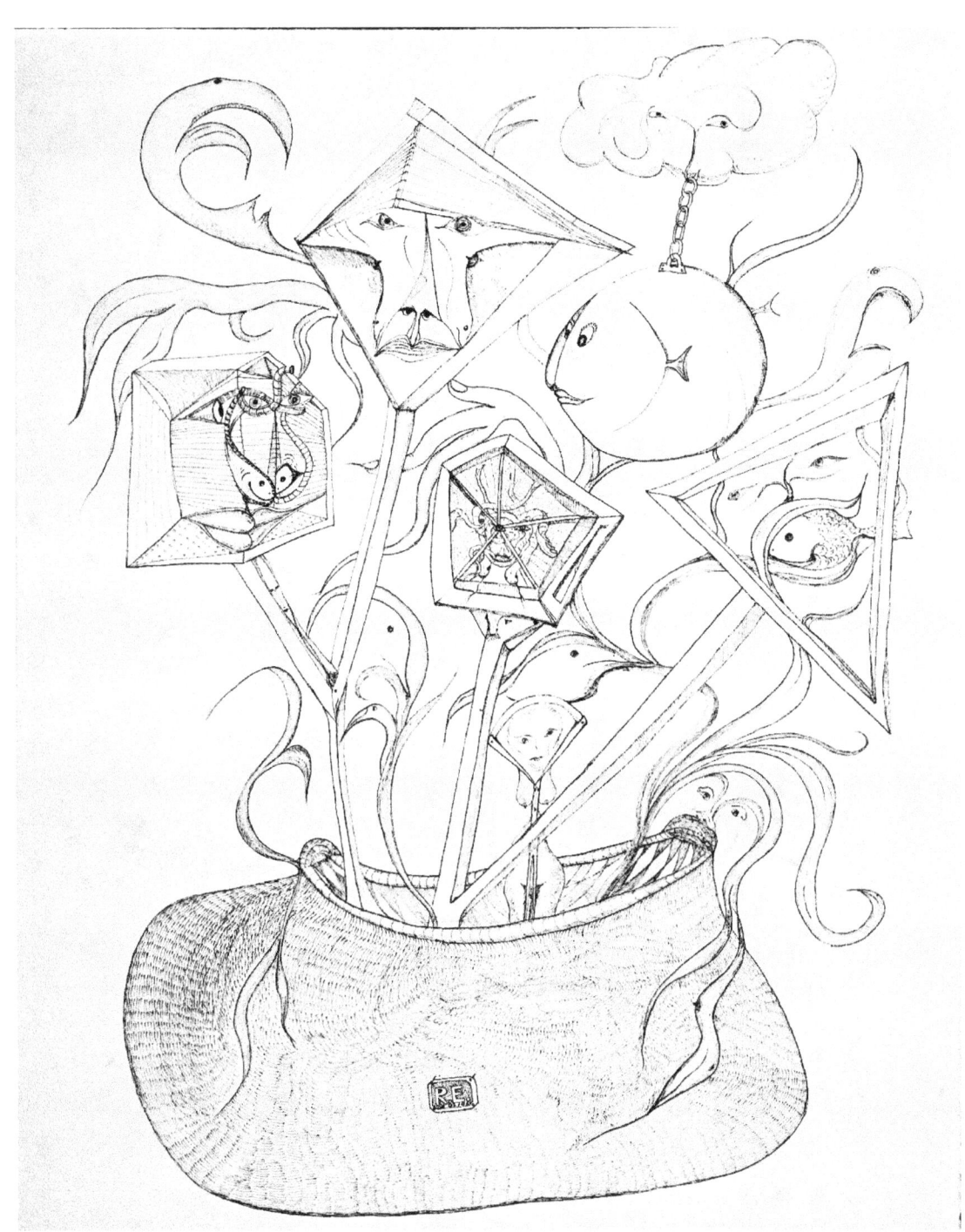

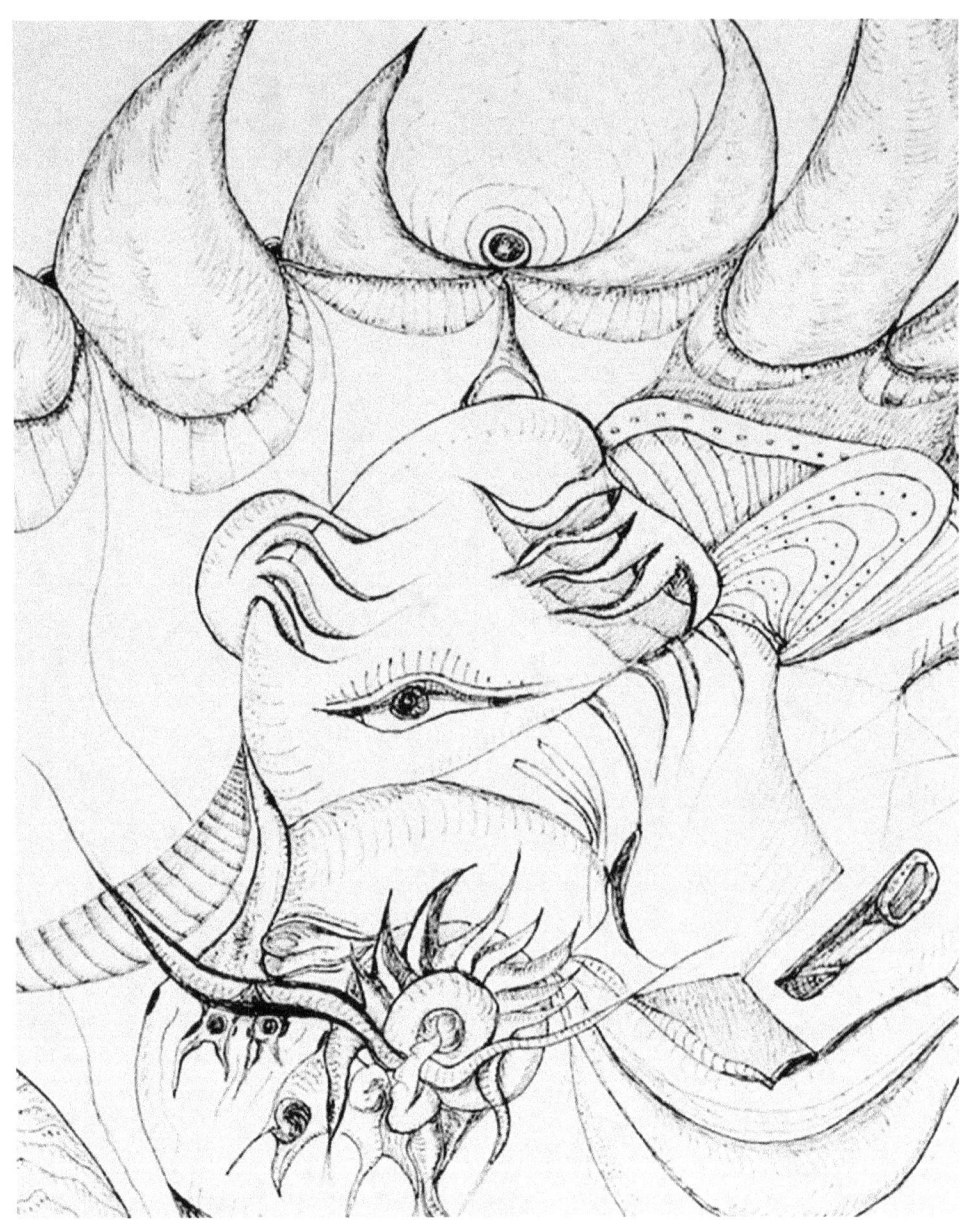

Above: Detail of *Cornudo*

Opposite: *Cornudo* (2005) – Ink on paper – 22"x 30"

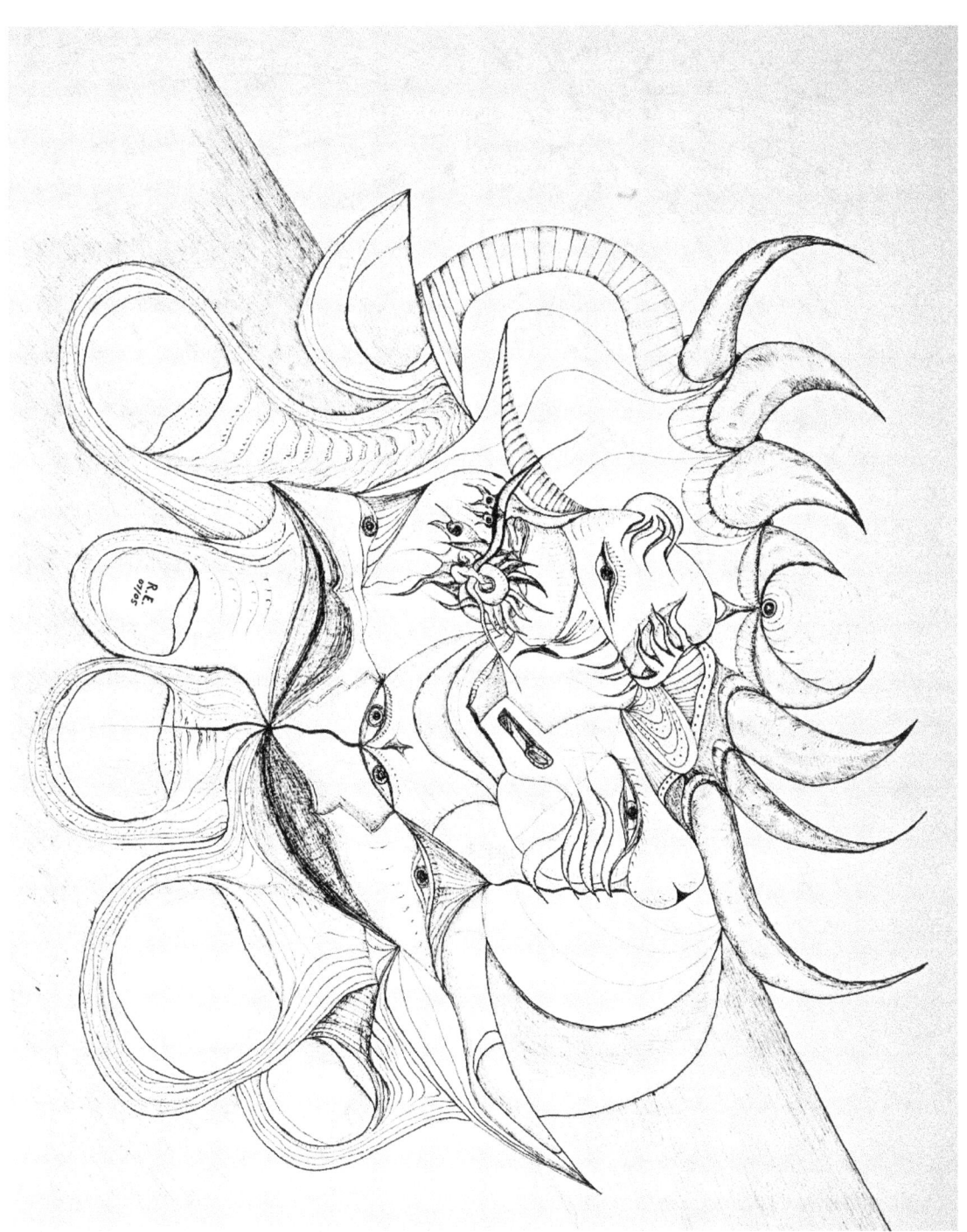

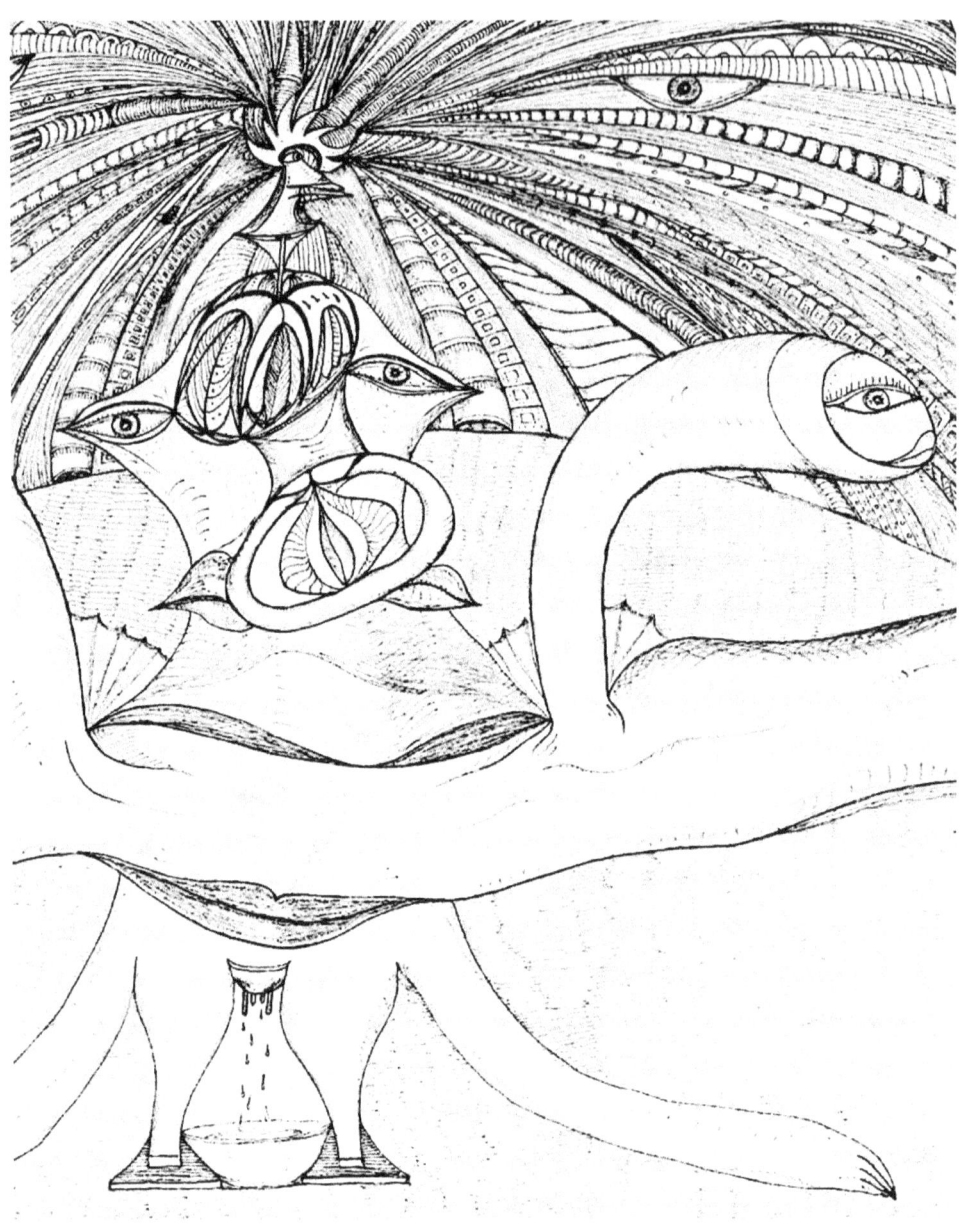

Above: Detail of *Distillation*

Opposite: *Distillation* (2005) - Ink on paper – 22”x 30”

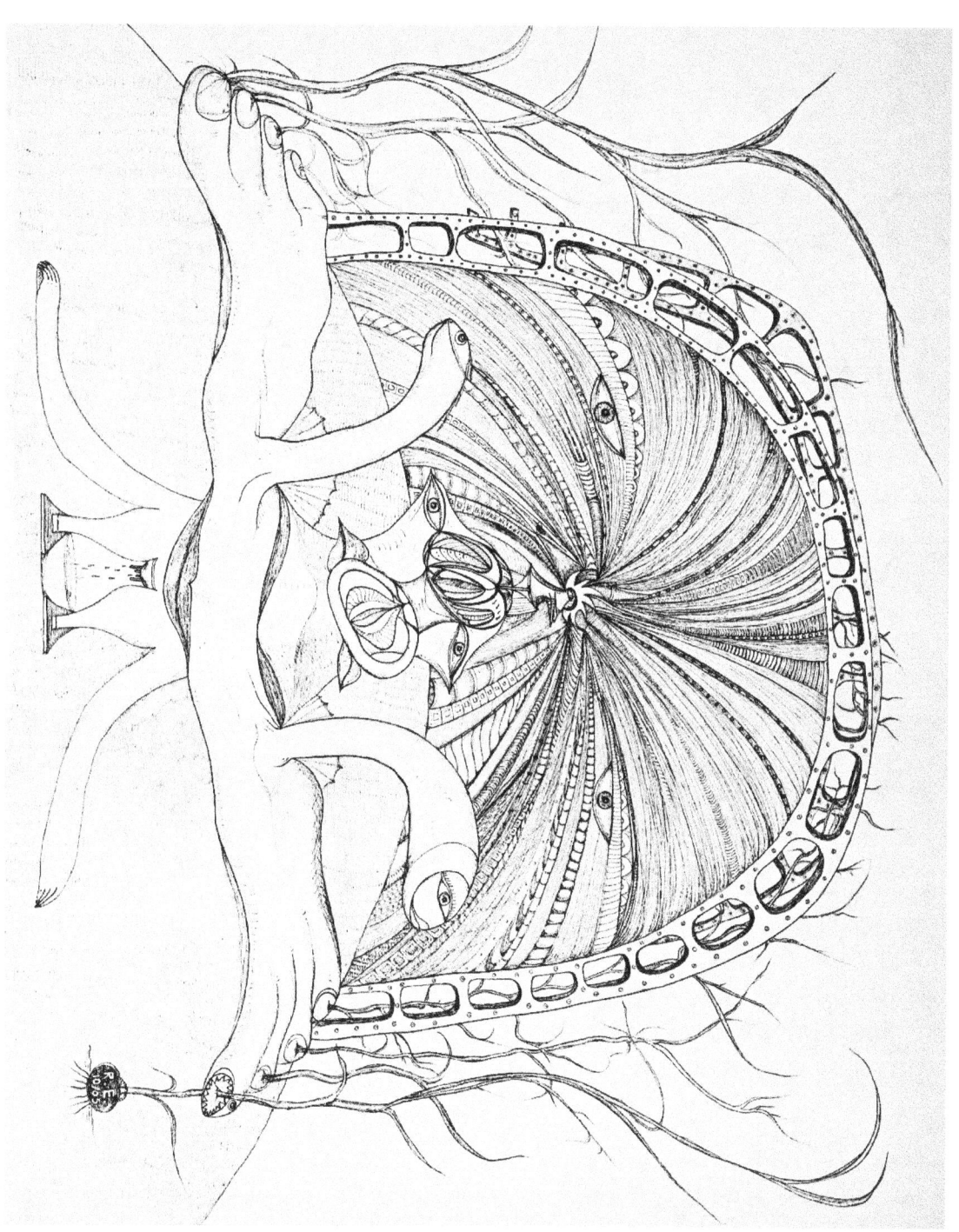

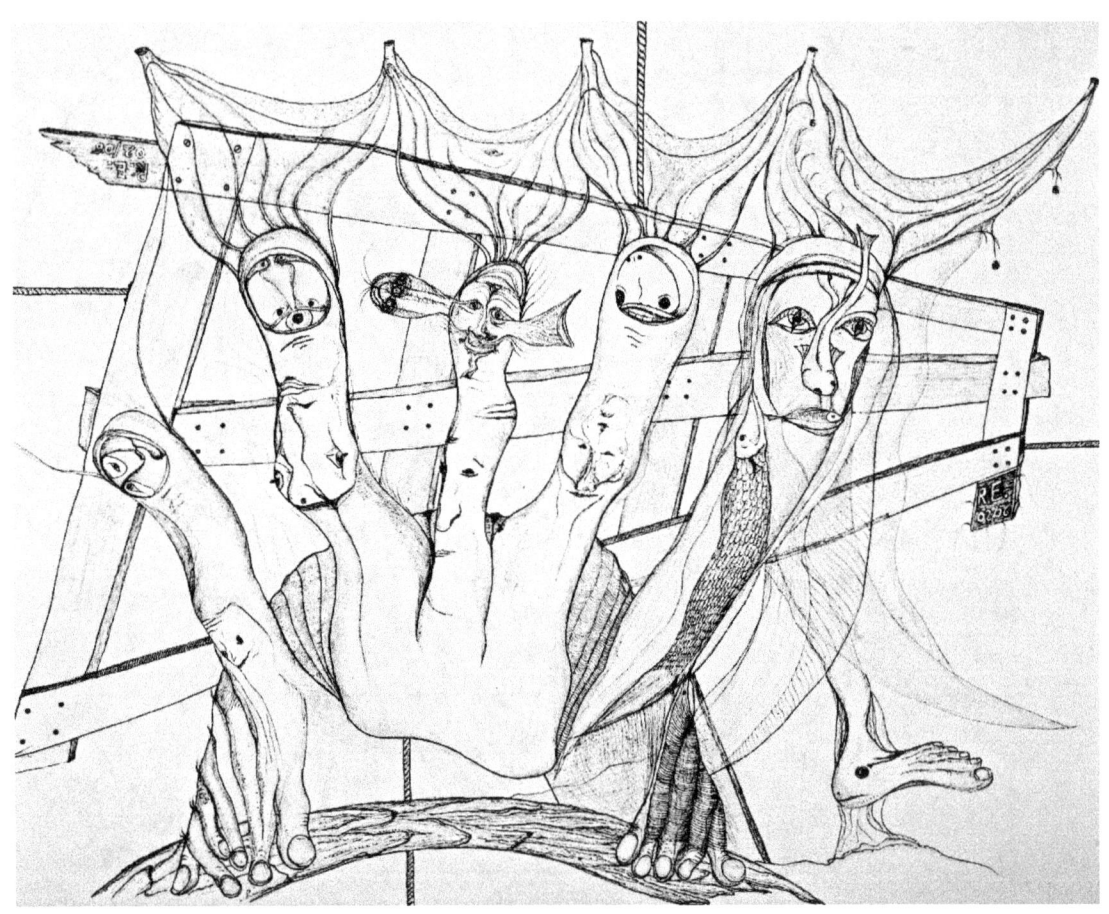

Above: Detail of *Mariners' Wives*

Opposite: *Mariners' Wives* (2006) - Ink on paper – 22"x 30"

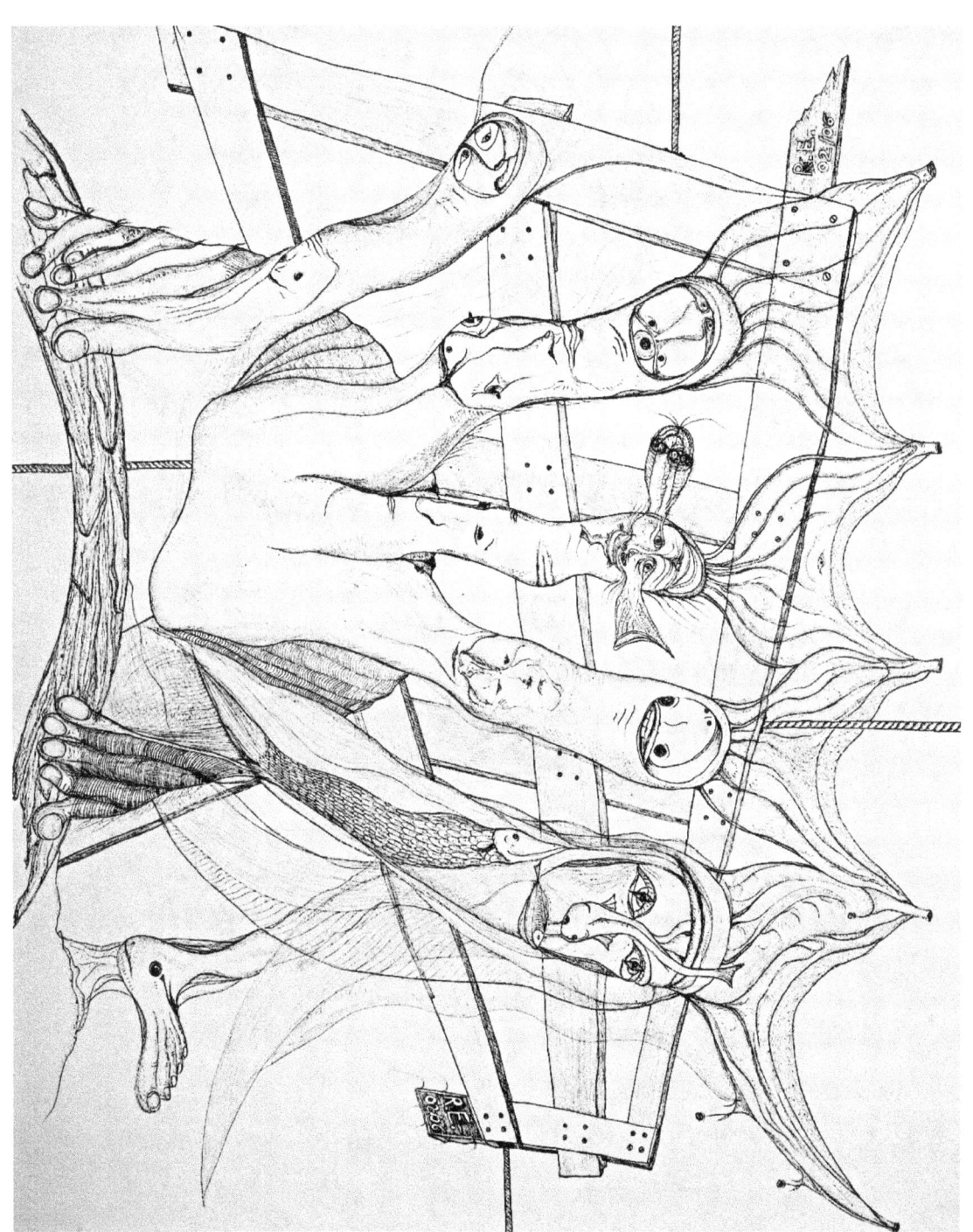

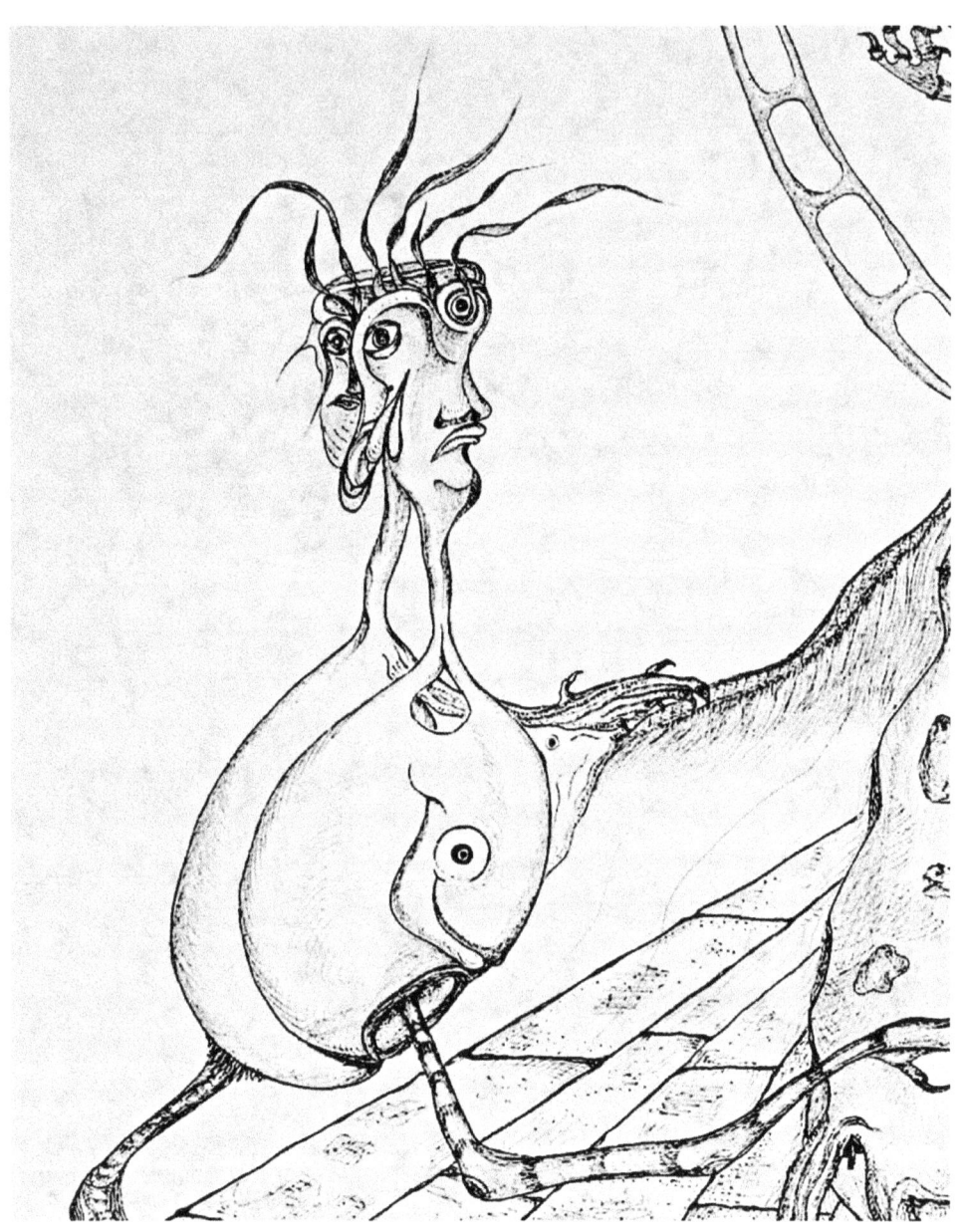

Above: Detail of *Reindeer Masquerade*

Opposite: *Reindeer Masquerade*   (2006) - Ink on paper – 22"x 30"

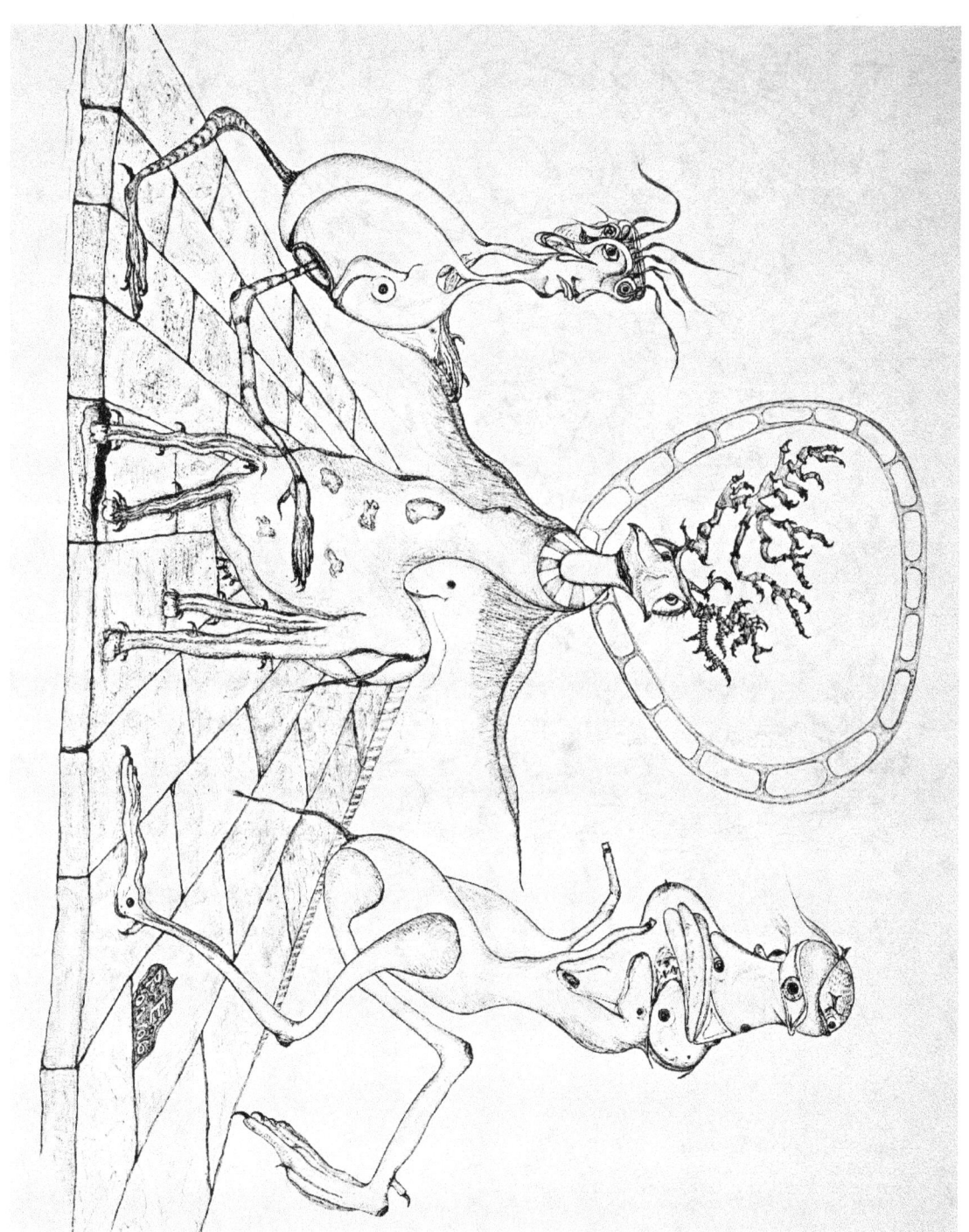

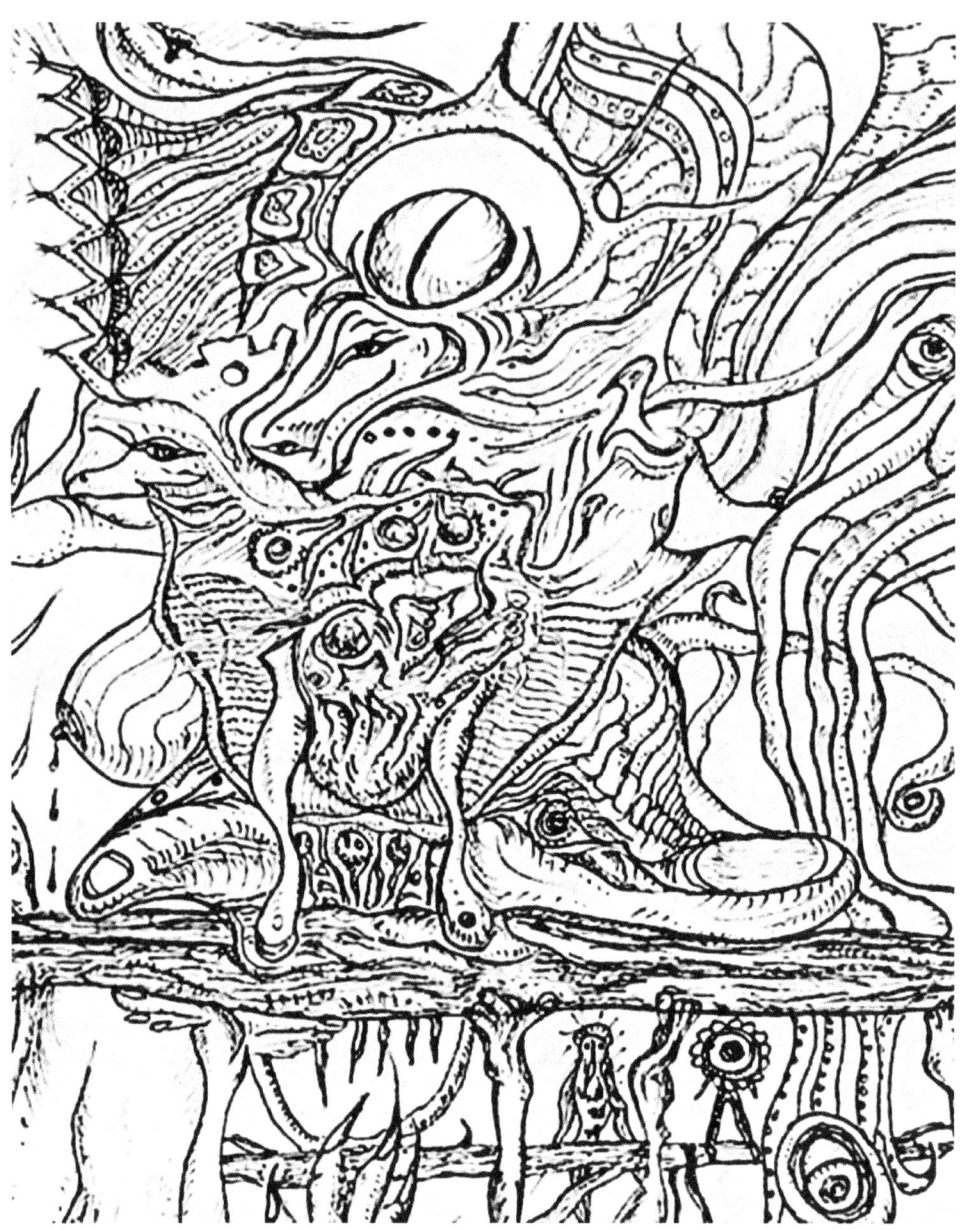

Above: Detail of *Swinging*

Opposite: *Swinging* (2005) – Ink on paper – 22"x 30"

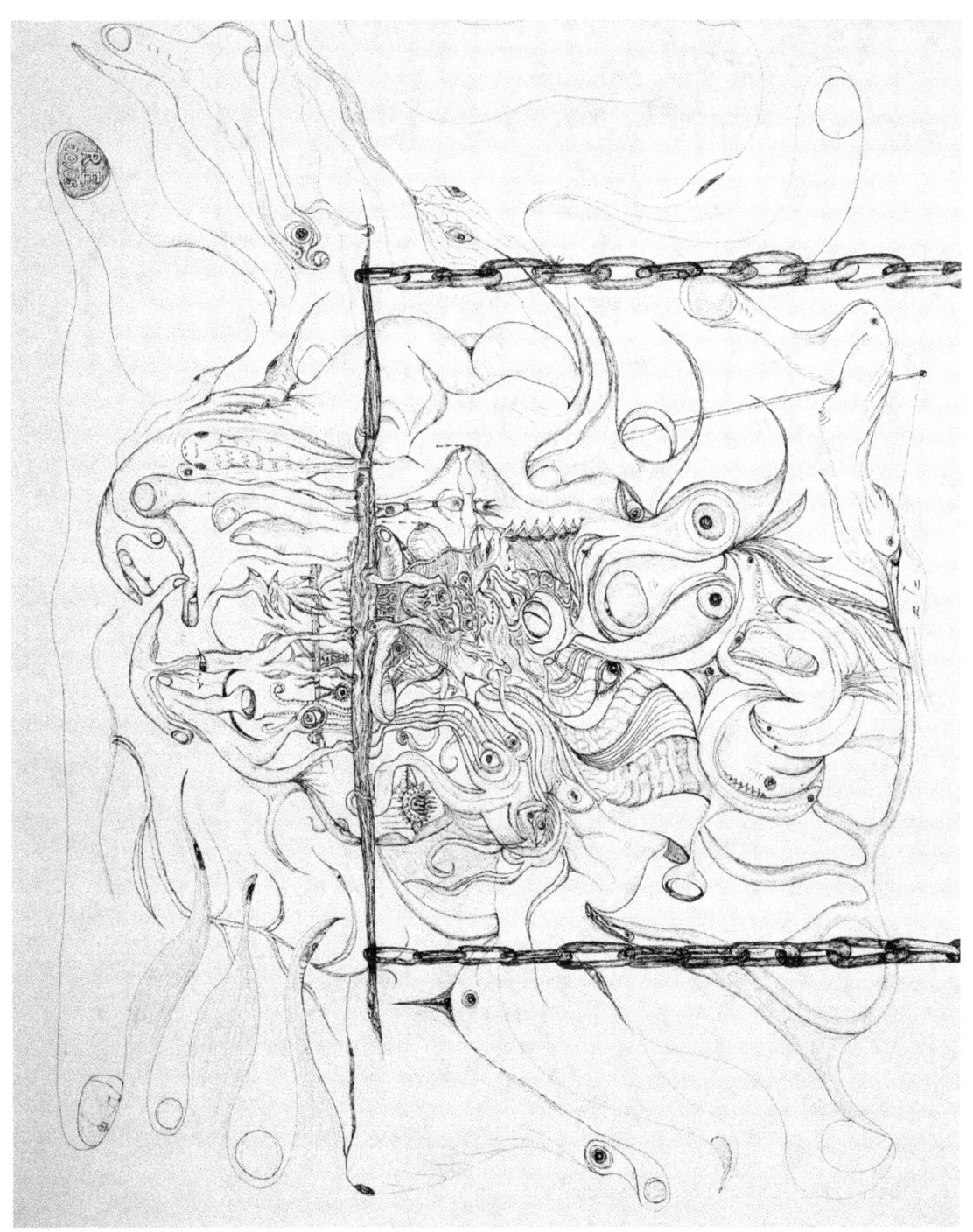

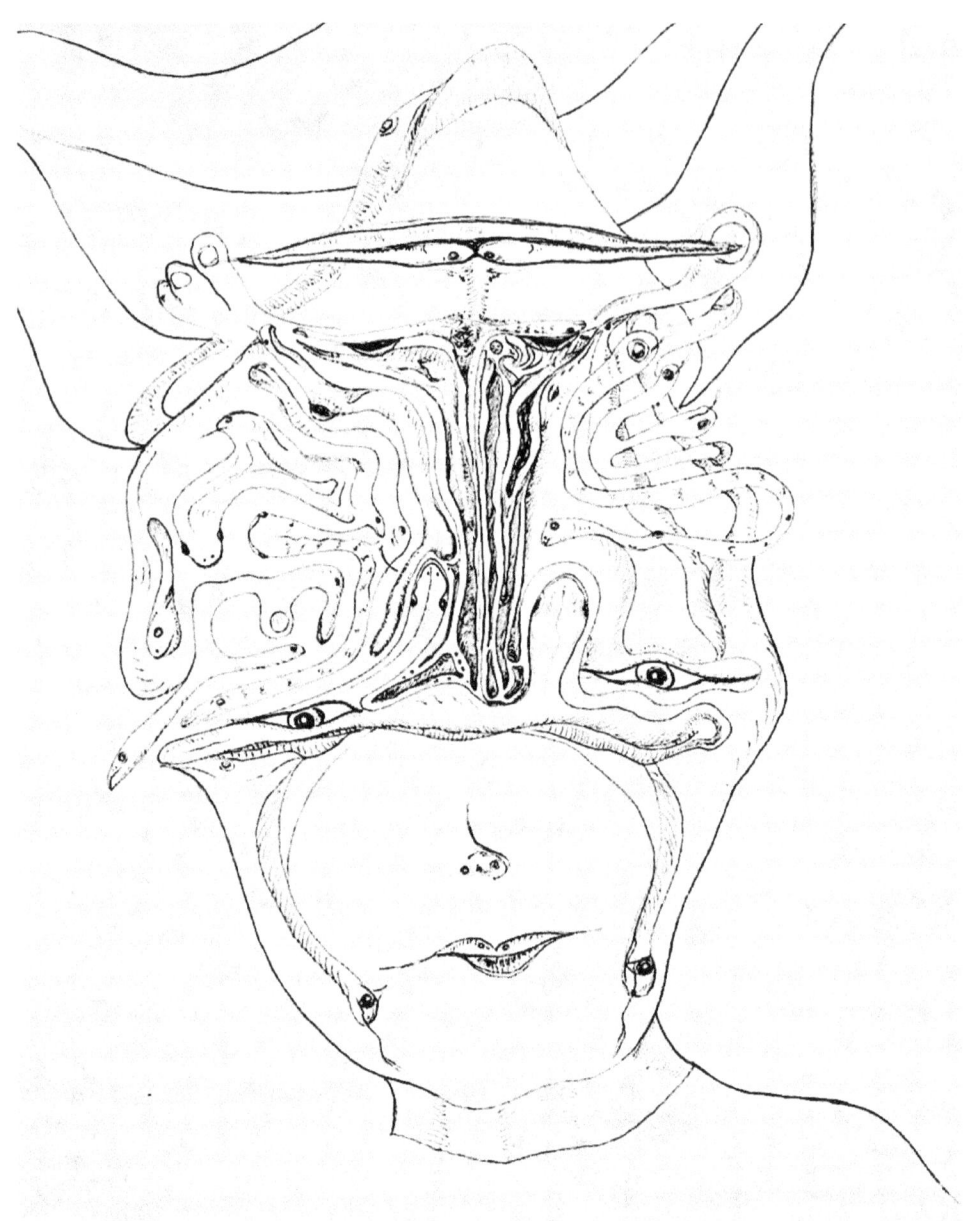

Above: Detail of *One Way or Another*

Opposite: *One Way or Another* (2006) – Ink on paper – 22"x 30"

Note: Turn this image around to see another picture

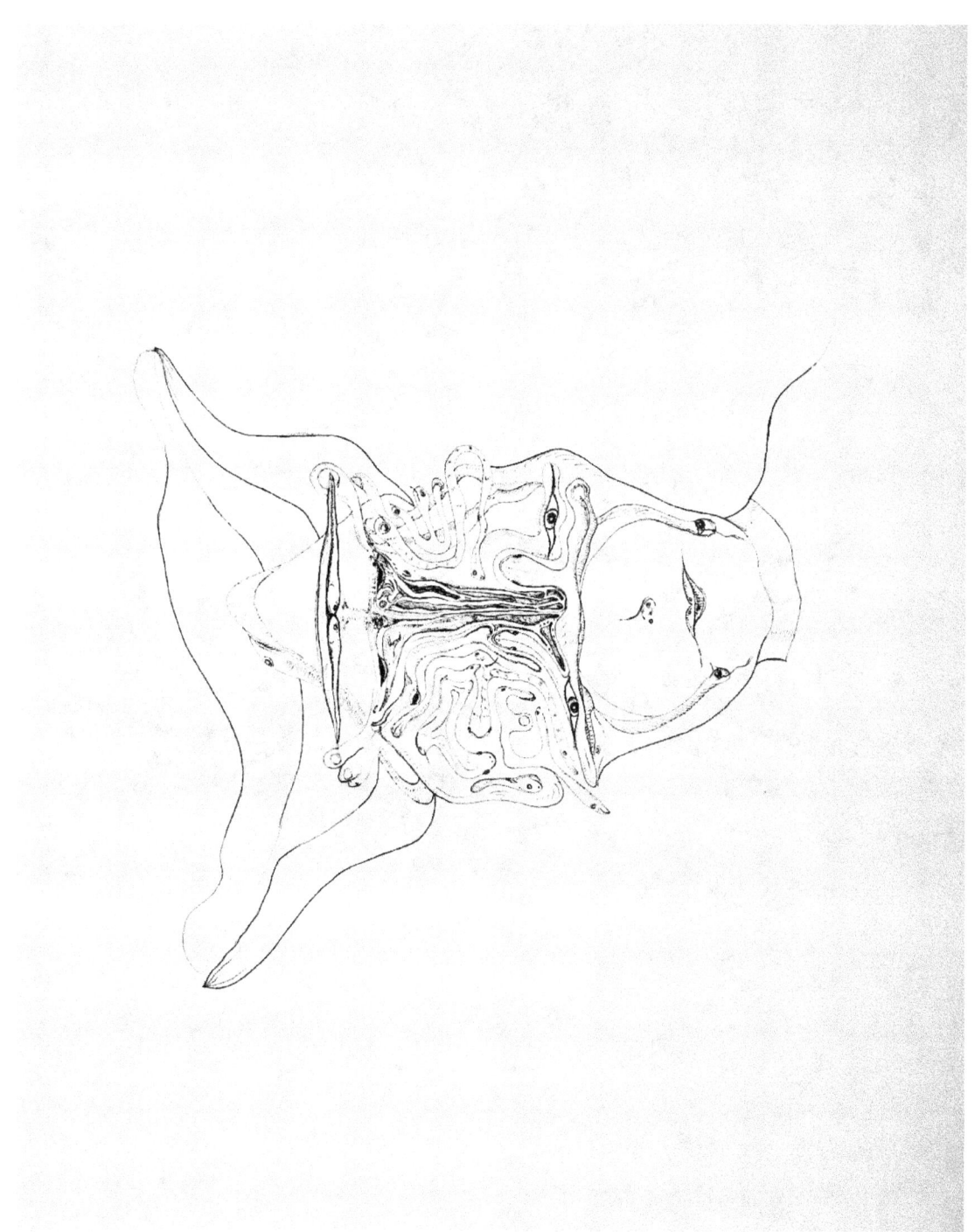

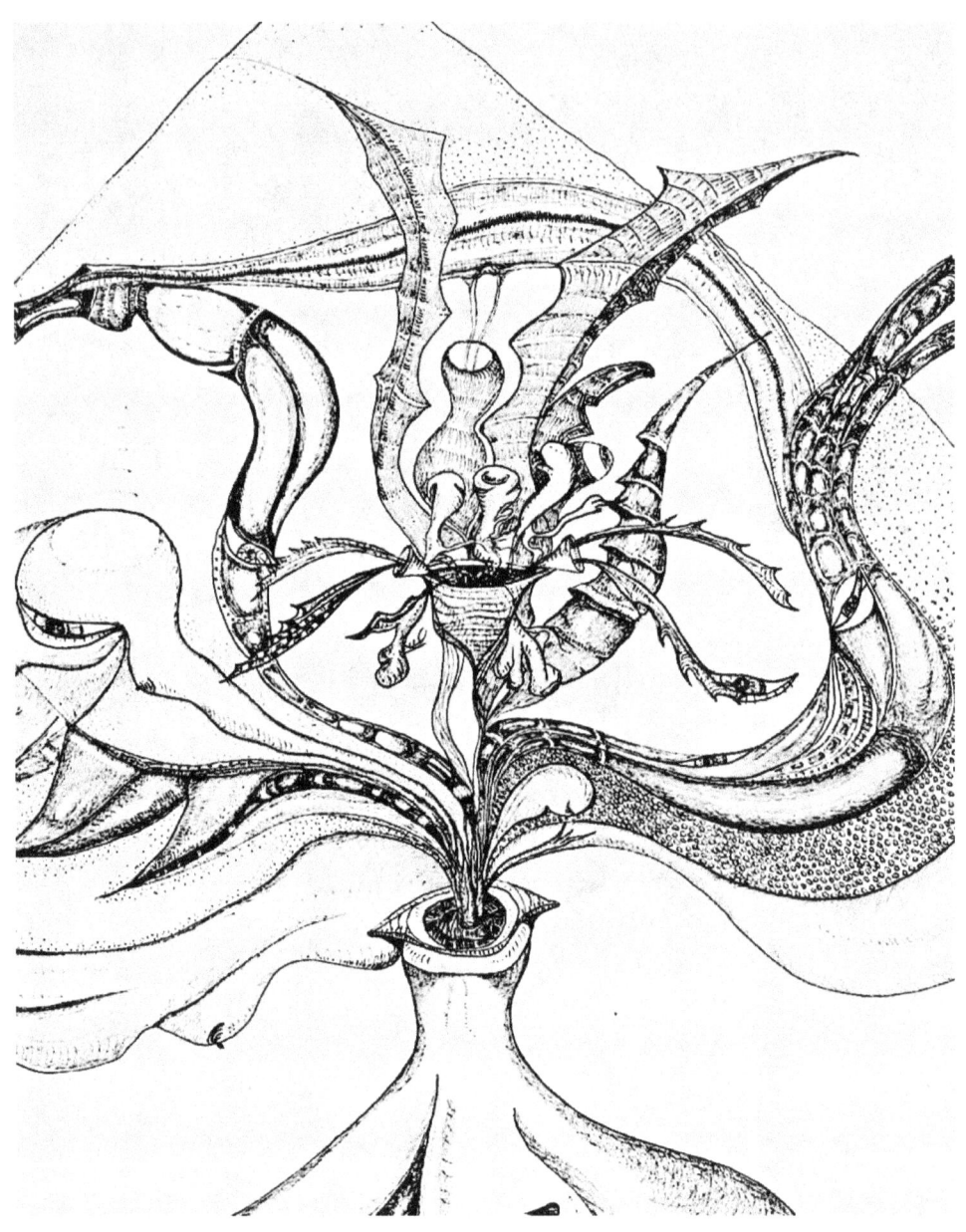

Above: Detail of *Reversible*

Opposite: *Reversible* (2005) – Ink on paper – 22"x 30"

Note: Turn this image around to see another picture

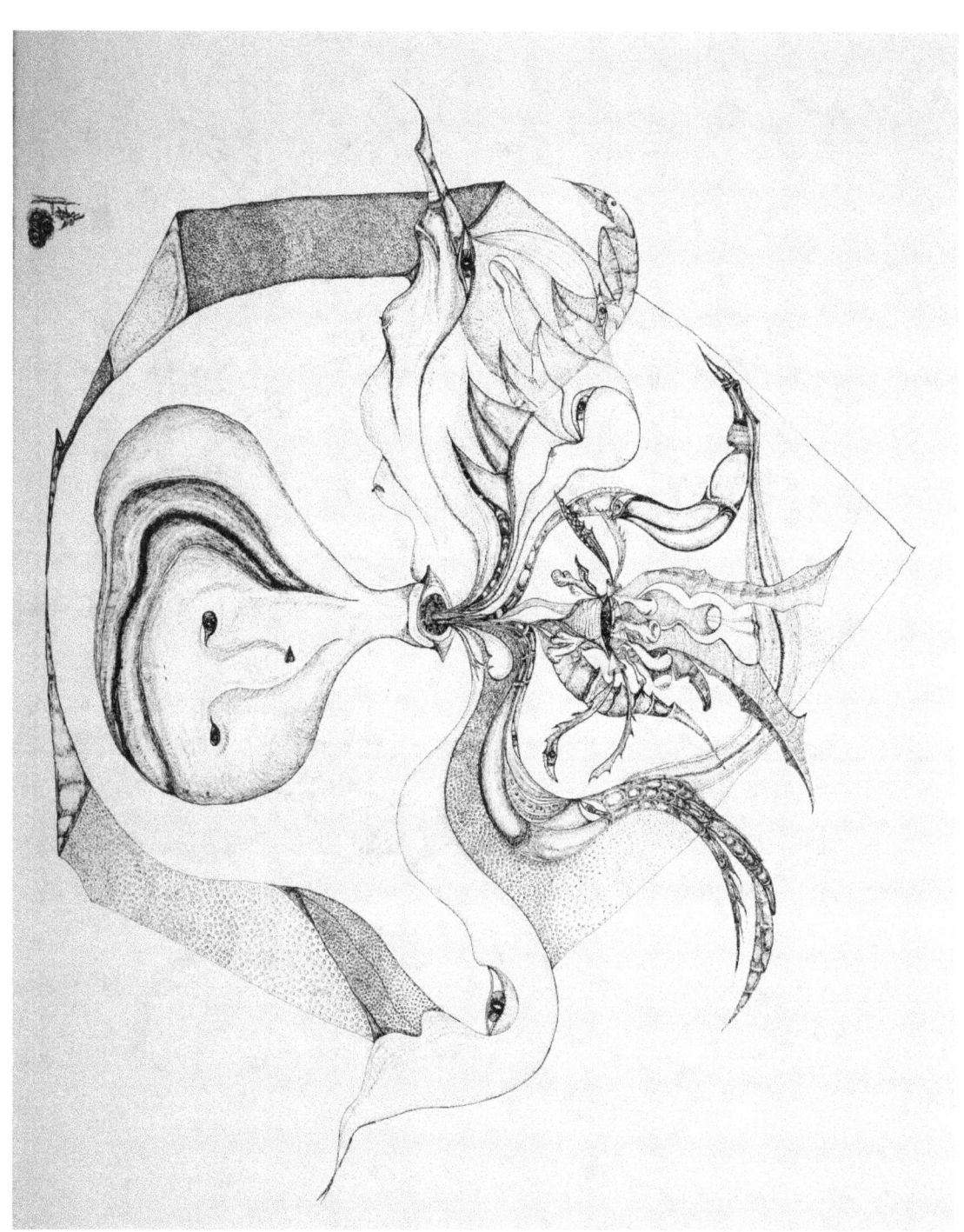

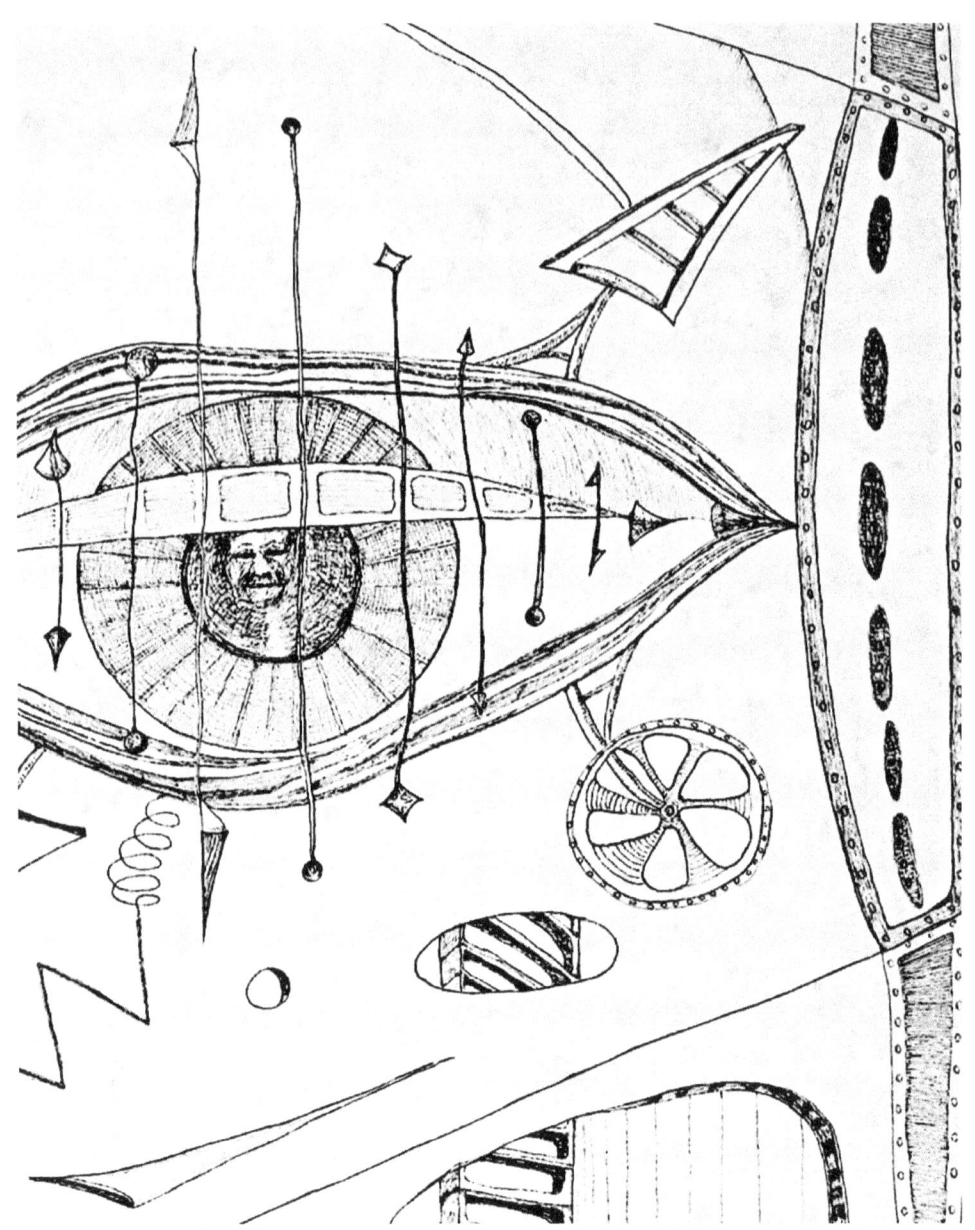

Above: Detail of *Self Portrait*

Opposite: *Self Portrait* (2005) - Ink on paper - 30"x 22"

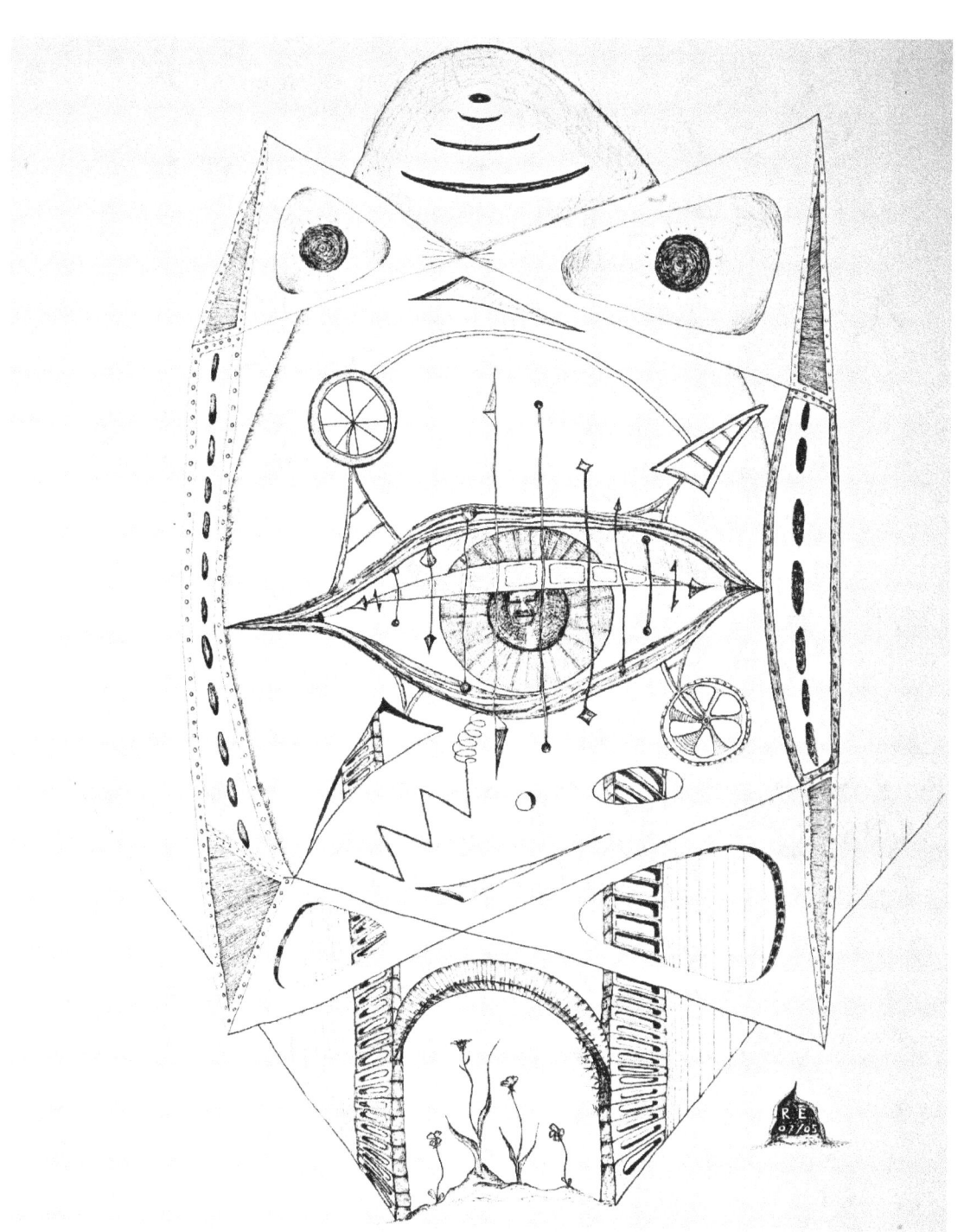

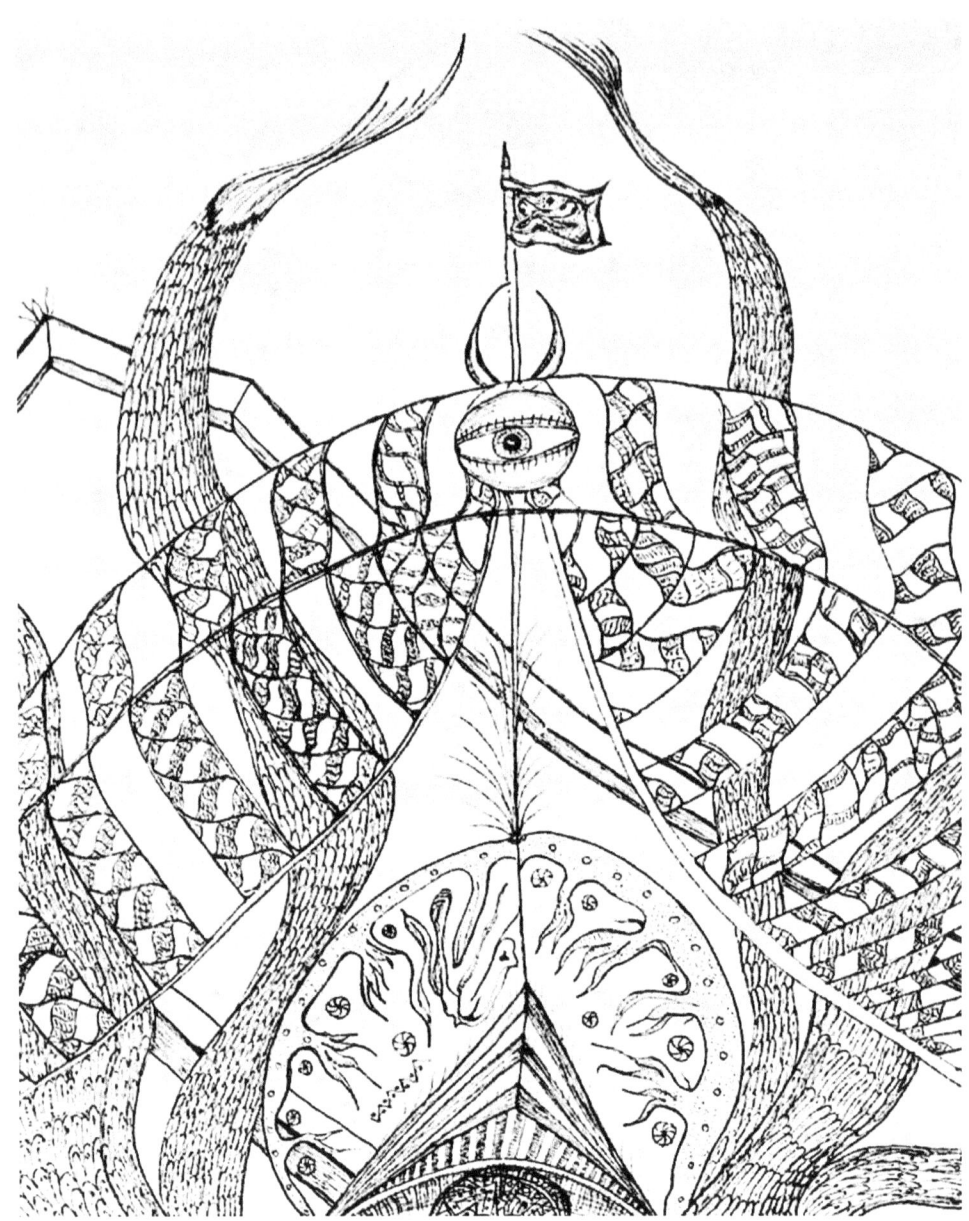

Above: Detail of *Watch Out!*

Opposite: *Watch Out!* (2005) - Ink on paper - 30"x 22"

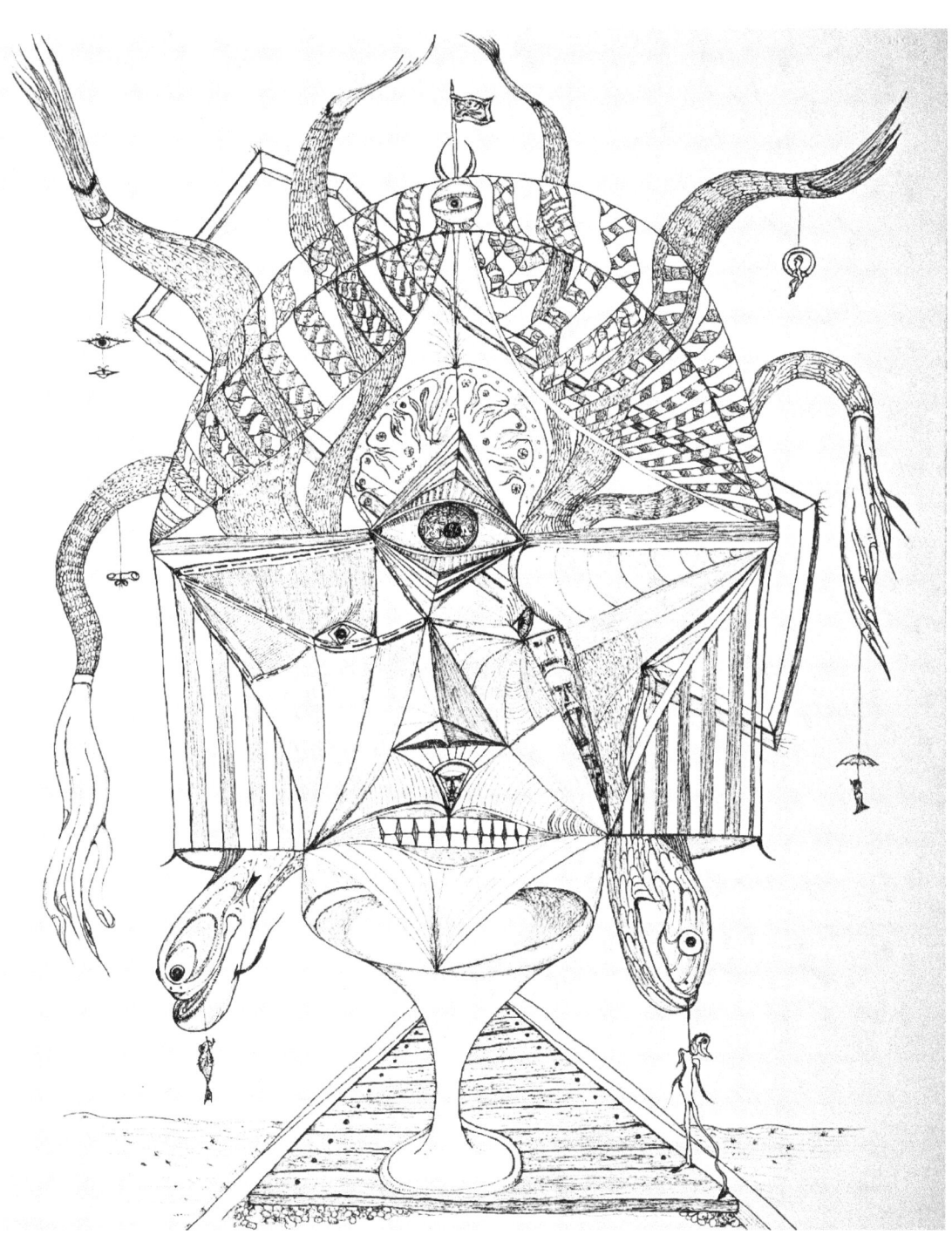

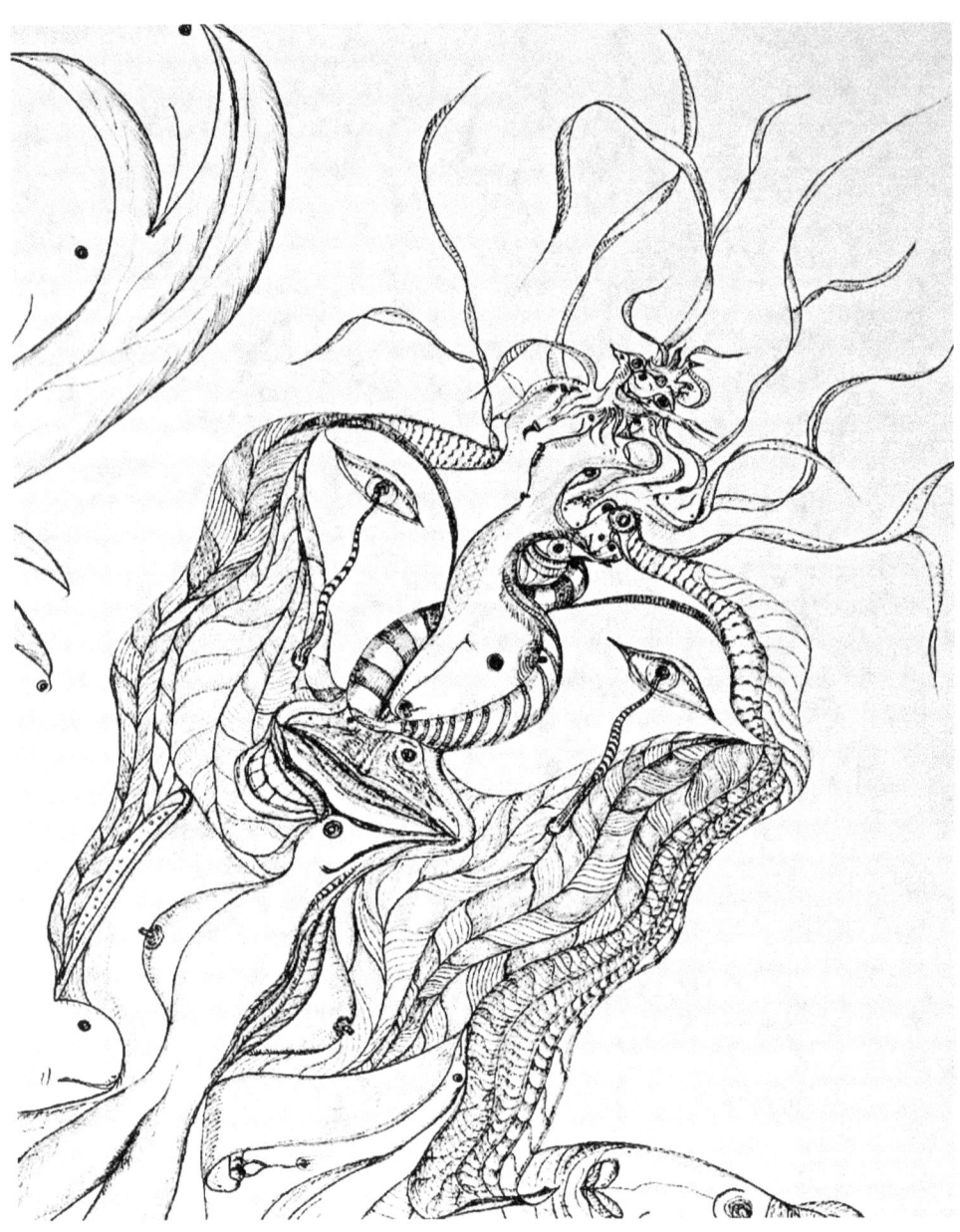

Above: Detail of *Lionesque*

Opposite: *Lionesque* (2006) – Ink on paper – 30"x 22"

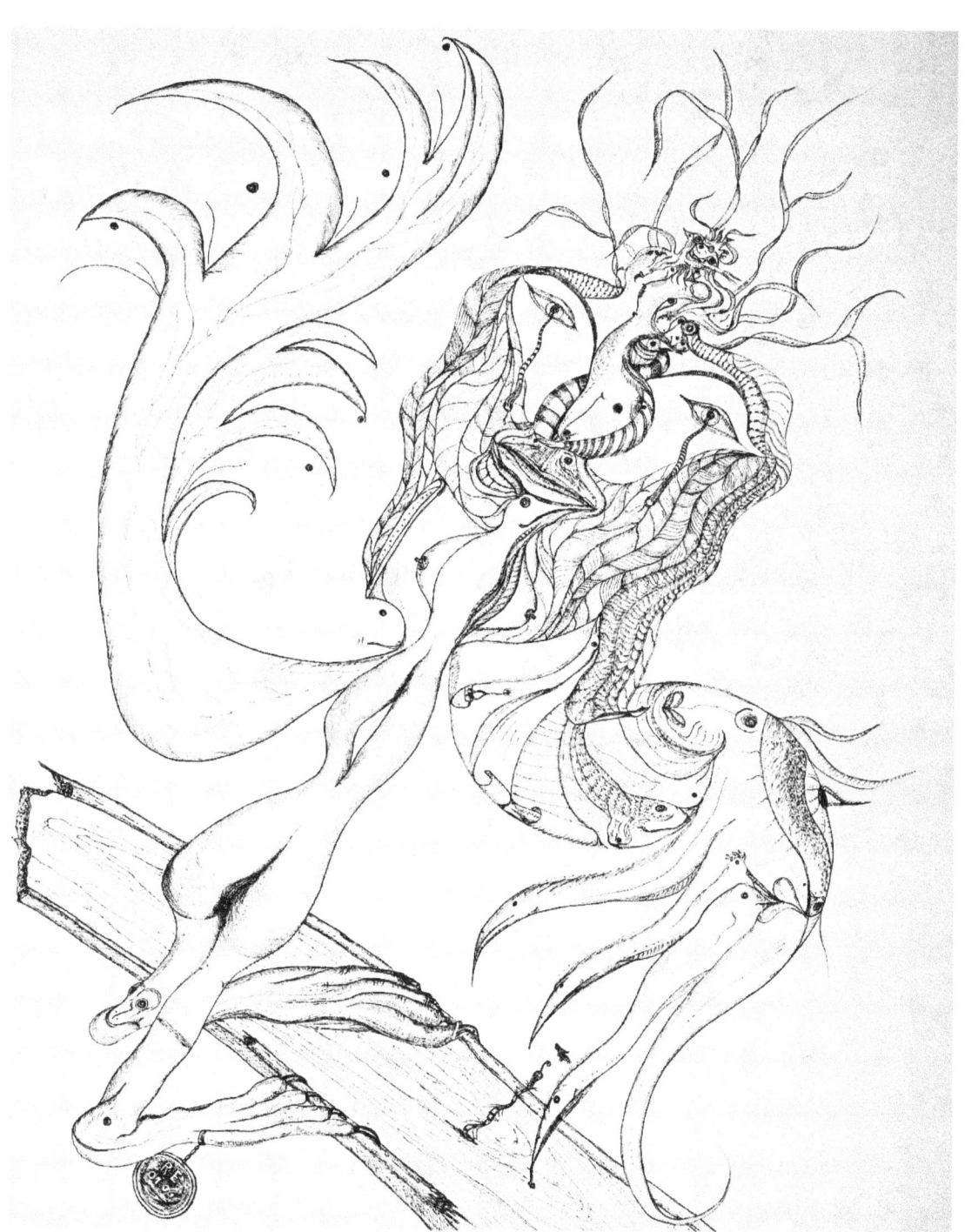

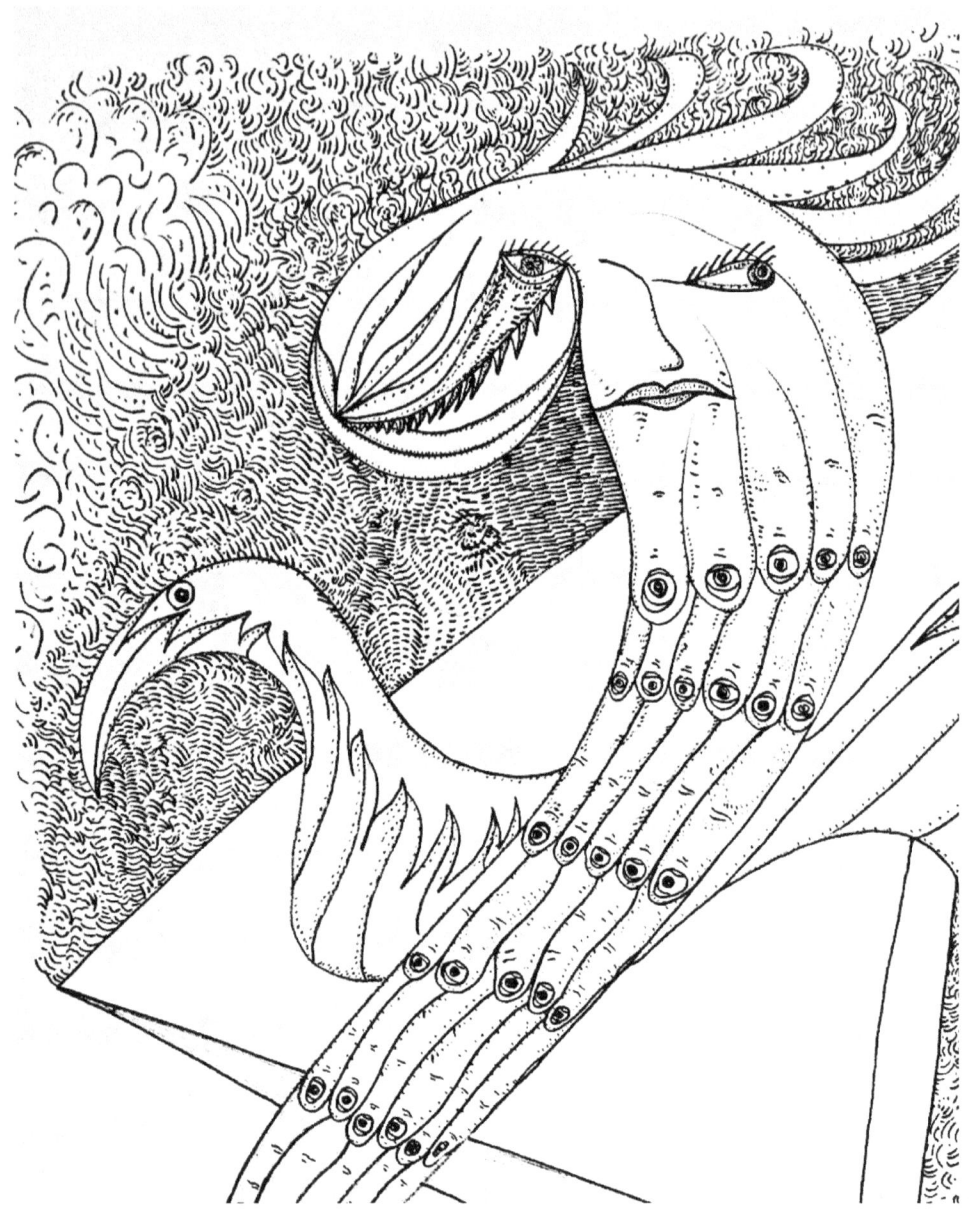

Above: Detail of *Flying Sea Horse*

Opposite: *Flying Sea Horse* (2005) – Ink on paper – 35" x 20"

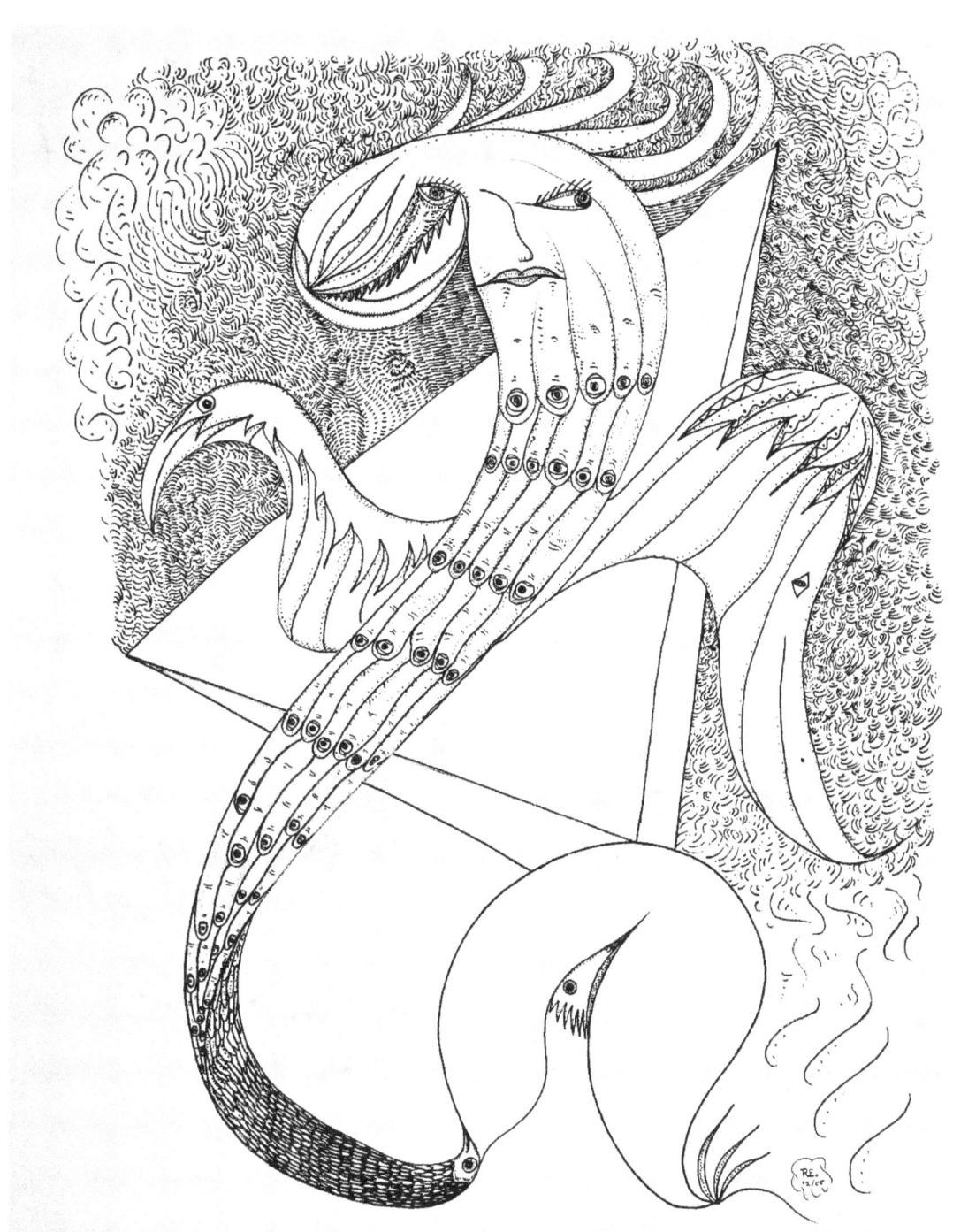

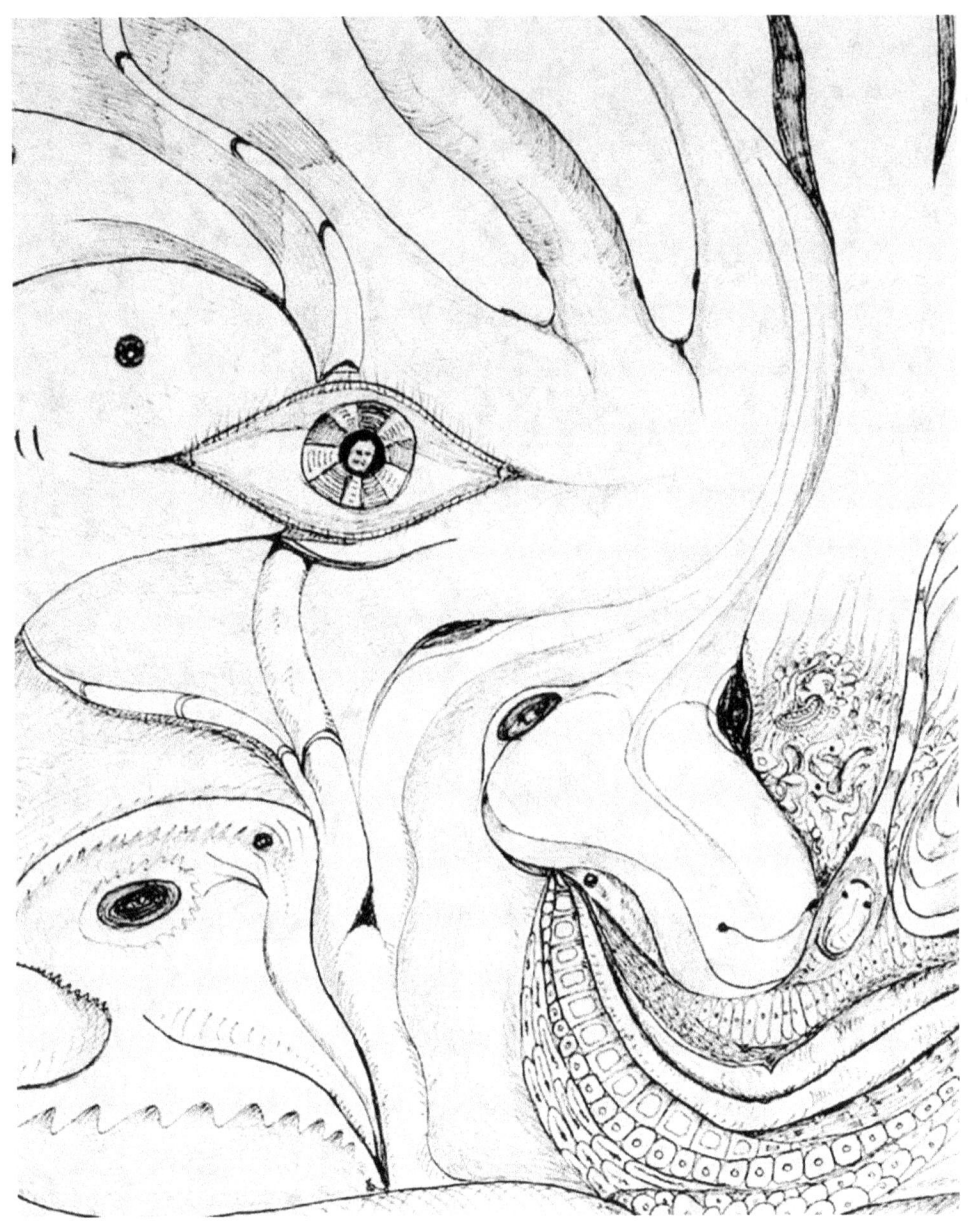

Above: Detail of *Frontal Profiles*

Opposite: *Frontal Profiles* (2005) – Ink on paper – 22"x 30"

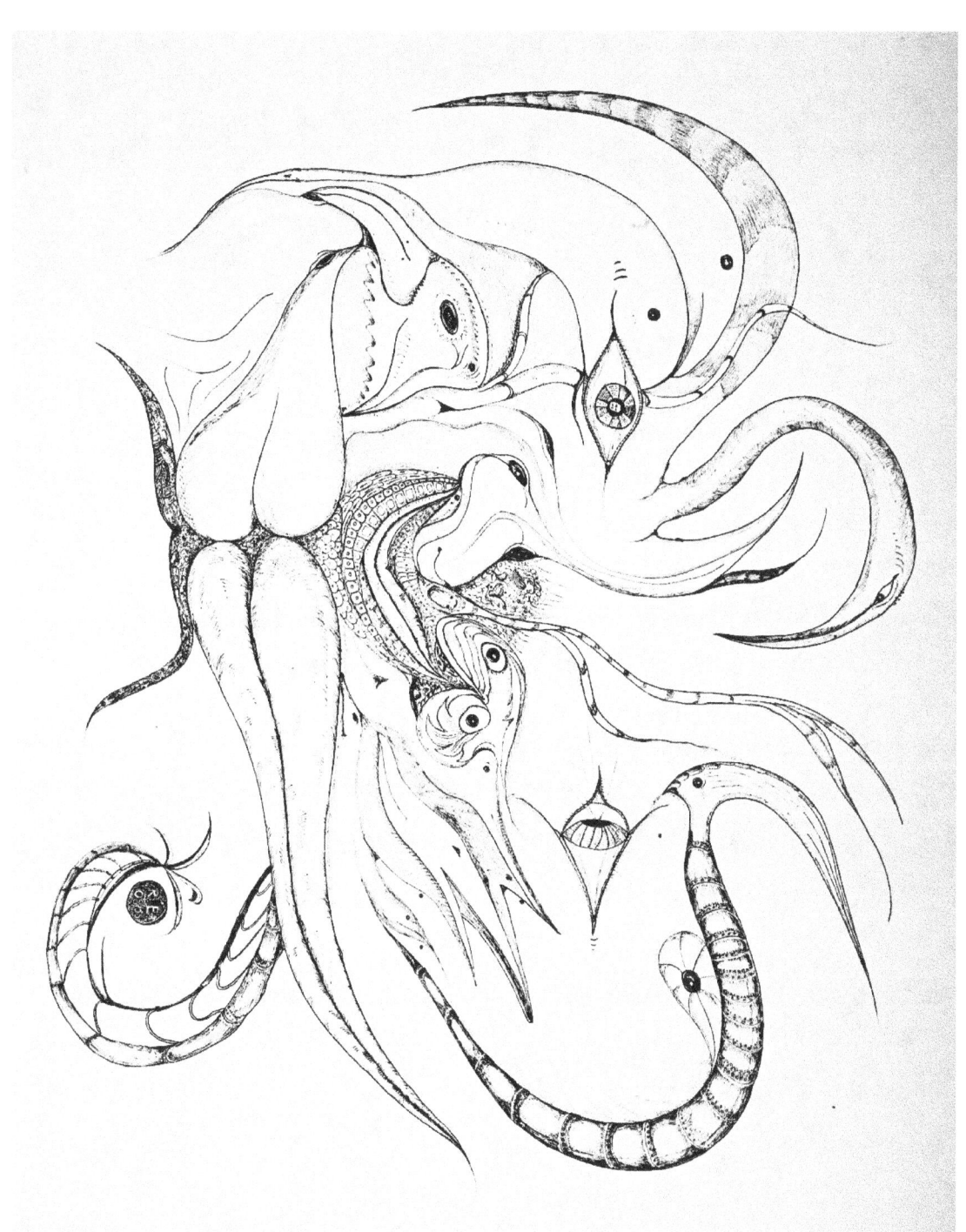

PART III:

THE DADA-TALES

PART III:

THE DADA-TALES

About the Dada-Tales

For many years - day after day - I have been writing about all that happened during my crazy life. I have brought countless events onto paper in long hand writing, as expressed in my childhood tales, in my grown-up stories and in my philosophical essays, always putting it into context and as an insight for future generations who may wonder what the world was like before it became digital.

Many long-forgotten events and emotions spring back to life in a leisure hour when I re-read and enjoy some of these buried (and often forgotten) memories.

A few years ago I found myself sitting at a table with a pen and a clean sheet of paper. I have a weird syndrome that -whenever that is the case- I feel compelled to fill the blanks. That particular time, however, instead of drawing my usual *Weirdoes*, I wrote a series of words just as they came to mind and then continued writing without interruption, until the entire page was covered with text. It was the beginning of my *Dada-Tales*, which are somehow the written equivalent of my pictorial Dada-Drawings.

In *Les Champs Magnétiques* (The Magnetic Fields – 1920), André Breton and Philippe Soupault came up with the principle of what they called *Automatic Writing*. It is a process of writing text that does not come from the conscious thought process of the writer who is unaware of what will be written, but is instead created at the spur of the moment.

I must confess that I find it too silly (and easy) to write entirely nonsensical stories by just lining up words and sentences that make no sense. The world has dramatically evolved in the past century, which makes it difficult for me to read (and impossible to write) nonsensical text. My Dada-Tales, as demonstrated hereafter, are only half -or sometimes even less- nonsensical, and always confer an illusion, in a sort of literary *trompe-l'oeil* manner, of some halfway intelligent information.

Here is how it works: First, I write down the exact time, date and location of where I happen to be. Then I begin writing and never allow myself to stop until the page is entirely filled, often in one single sentence. In that manner I write *from my guts* and on the spur of the moment, without ever thinking more than just two or three words ahead, nor permitting myself to stop until my page is entirely filled. By keeping a scrupulous time record, I always attempt to achieve a strict minimum involvement of the brain, so my rational thoughts won't interfere with my *automatic writing*.

The resulting *Dada-Tales* are a unique blend of thoughts that mingle the news of the day, my surrounding environment and some (often strangely) related ideas thereof. At the end of each page filled with a Dada-Tale I go back to the top and write down a title that fits the story.

I wrote my first Dada-Tale on August 4, 2008, and called it *Pedicure,* which took me just twelve minutes to write. The result of my first Dada-Tale was so encouraging and well received by some of my friends that I decided to keep on going and writing many more stories of a similar nature. I got into problems with Angelika, though, my sweet and tender wife of forty years. She pretended to notice certain strange alterations in my psyche; but she couldn't stop me, since artists can never be stopped from what they have to do…

English Dada-Tales

Pedicure

(First Dada-Tale)

Hand written by Rudy Ernst without interruption

On August 4, 2008

In New York City, Top of the One on the 44th Floor

From 7:20 to 7:32 PM

…And as I write this tail, the sky above me is wiggling the toe of my sweet and tender wife in the wind that carries the airplane and the automobiles upon the setting sun in Japanese culture, far away from the upcoming Olympic Games, a fly sitting on my knee, just below where they cut the skin to make the graft onto my arm 43 years ago, upon which I am writing here with a point five millimeter pen that covers this white page, slowly, line after line, just above the underlying art book that rests on my tummy, which is covered by my blue tee shirt, and below my bathing suit that is patiently waiting for the swimming pool to become empty of those elderly ladies who betray the tranquility of the blue water in the sun, which is by now almost ready to set, while the wind is picking up to the point that I have to hold my book and pen firmly in my hands, so they are not being carried away into the noise of yet another airplane above me, while the clouds in their sheep-like appearance definitely show all the signs that the wind is blowing from the south, while –to the contrary- it whirls around in circles here on the 44th floor of this Manhattan building, with Angelika's neatly pedicured red toe nails swinging slightly in the wind, and the sirens of a by-passing ambulance car down at the Lincoln Center reminding the untouched mind that all is not as well in the world as my 67 billion cell colony count that enjoys being still alive, even though it is not easy to hold the darn thing together … just imagine!

Just imagine how cool it would be if all the living things in the Universe were singing the song of IMAGINE, and all the Quebec buses were not crowding the entrance to the Strawberry Fields to the point that the yellow and the white flowers there are praying every night to the moon that the next day at sunrise the tourist nightmare would end and all the losers of the world would stay home. But wait, where would all the money come from if all the losers of the world would suddenly stay home? And would all the losers of the world stay in bed and produce new losers? Is that the explanation why we are soon going to be seven billion people on this planet?

All those Happy Trees

While it is difficult on a day that is gearing up to become another Black Friday, like a repetition of 1929, I must force myself to think of the moon and the stars and the sun, and all the little birds that are getting ready to face the winter here in Central Park, where the the theme of central is every bit as central as those birds still singing and the rocks still waiting to become animated in ways never seen by any human beings that have only been around for about five million years, as compared to those rocks who have been inanimate for about one billion years or so (give and take a few billions), but not at all like the economy, which is now in the trillions and therefore compares very favorably to those rocks in Central Park, where the birds and the squirrels are still meeting on a daily basis and drinking tea together (or is it beer, or even champagne?), which shows you how irrelevant - in the mind of those flowers that surround the rocks - the idea of a crashing economy really is, compared to the crispy, lovely sun that is now rising over the discoloring leaves of the trees just above them, and more than happy (I mean the trees) that they have not been attacked by those mean bugs that took a lot of them down those past few years, knowing full well (I mean the bugs) that even though they are hiding these days, they will still be around in about five hundred million years, of which I can say that if they were not years, but rather dollars, I would feel very good to have them in my pocket, although I would be at a real loss about figuring out how to invest this money on a black Friday, which reminds me of a very black night with no moon and only some nightingale singing its beautiful melody about fifteen years back in southwest Virginia, when the world was not yet in turmoil, but the old rocks here in Central Park still quietly smiling at all the crazy follies of all the happy little animals all around them ...

All Those Happy Trees
Dada-Tale
Hand written without interruption
On Friday, October 24, 2008
In New York City – at Central Park West –
From 8:41 to 8:59 AM

…While it is difficult on a day that is gearing up to become another Black Friday, like a repetition of 1929, I must force myself to think of the moon and the stars and the sun, and all the little birds that are ready to face the winter here in Central Park, where the theme of central is everything as central as the birds still singing and the rocks still waiting are, to become animated in ways never seen by any human beings that have only been around for about five million years, as compared to those rocks that have been inanimate for about one billion years or so (give and take a few billions), but not at all like the economy, which is now in the trillions and therefore compares very favorably to those rocks in Central Park, where the birds and the squirrels are still meeting on a daily basis and drinking tea together (or is it beer, or even champagne?), which shows you how irrelevant -in the mind of those flowers that surround the rocks- the idea of a crashing economy really is, compared to the crispy, lovely sun that is now rising over the discoloring leaves of the trees just above them, and more than happy (I mean the trees) that this year they have not been attacked by those mean and nasty bugs that took a lot of them down those past few years, knowing full well (I mean the bugs) that even though they are hiding these days, they will still be around in about five hundred million years, of which I can say that if they were not years, but rather dollars, I would feel very good to have them in my pocket, although I would be at a real loss about figuring out how to invest this money on a Black Friday, which reminds me of a very black night with no moon and only some nightingale singing its beautiful melody about fifteen years back in southwest Virginia, when the world was not yet in turmoil, but the old rocks here in Central Park still quietly smiling at all the crazy follies of all the happy little animals all around them…"

A Political Statement
Dada-Tale
Hand written without interruption
On October 10, 2008, from 3:58 – 4:25 PM
At Lake Pemaquid's Duck Puddle Camp Ground

Style over Substance. Isn't that what life is all about? Who would ever bother about facts when you can have beautiful talk? How blessed are we as a nation to have all those great lawyers in Washington who represent us with their eloquent speeches! I find it so saddening that their approval rate is a mere nine percent, when they use the very best of Shakespeare's vocabulary in such random ways that the sheer delight of listening to what they appear to be saying between the lines of their magnificent vocalizations is so often misrepresented, since it is the empty space after all that fills the world around us, just as the probability of a proton being shot through the center of our planet all the way to Australia and hitting any nuclear particle on its eight thousand mile journey is infinitely small. Yes, I tell you: it is the nothingness that counts, the space between the lines, the emptiness of the words! Any affirmation to the contrary is pure propaganda, even though propaganda can be very smooth and charming and elevate us to this wonderful sense of beauty, comfort and security, which we just lost during the past nineteen sessions of the US stock market, when eight point three trillion dollars were lost in this country. But who cares about zillions when you can admire the beauty of a loss, which points to that Zen Buddhist notion of emptiness with its infinite calm that suddenly overcomes you when you look at it from that very different angle, although angles have something sharp and unpleasant about them, which we have to gracefully overlook; but overlooking is the thing to do, since it points our sight far out towards the horizon, the sunset, the stars and the serene notion of eternity, which we always have a tendency to overlook when we follow the false priorities of putting substance over style and beauty…

A Fascinating Experiment
Dada-Tale
Hand written without interruption
On October 11, 2008
At Lake Pemaquid's Duck Puddle Camp Ground
From 7:18 – 7:33 PM

If you have the reoccurring urge to prove to yourself that there is a God, you can do a simple experiment that will help you along the way: take a dry piece of pine wood and hang it on a thin thread into mid-air, making sure that the wind-chill factor does not exceed three percent on the Richter Scale. Now, if the wood tilts to the left, you will have to hammer a small nail onto the right hand side of that piece, so that it will now be in a state of perfect mental equilibrium; if –on the other hand- your piece of wood has a tendency of moving to the right, go drink a glass of Chardonnay wine and observe it again through the reverse end of the right side of your binoculars. Whatever the result of your amazing experiment may be: You have just proven to yourself your very own point. And what is even more staggering, no matter how many times you repeat this test, the result will always come out to be exactly the same. With the one exception, of course, which is that the more you become involved in your own repetitiveness, the more your wine will get you drunk and ever more happy. Which is further proof that you should never have doubted your own beliefs in the first place, since spontaneity is the mother of all virtues, the best of which is always to reach out to your bottle when in doubt, so you can have peace of mind and of the body in order to avoid dirty tricks that are often not irreversible, such as any clown on a high rope will tell you (if he is still alive) after having performed his scary walk for a number of times. Yes, indeed, it is every bit as difficult to be a believer as it is to be a non-believer. Otherwise, there wouldn't be any evolutionary theory…

Knowledge

Dada-Tale - Hand written without interruption
On October 11, 2008, from 1:54 – 2:10 PM
At Lake Pemaquid's Duck Puddle Camp Ground

Just like a good philosopher knows nothing about philosophy and a good teacher knows nothing about teaching, or even like a good lawyer knows nothing about painting, and a good Alfa Male knows nothing about sex:, all of which defeat entirely the purpose of what they are supposed to do, and all being of course independent proof why a banker knows nothing about banking and so many other good things in life, and why the bottomless bottom (of the stock market) is now falling out from underneath all of us. How refreshing, on the other hand, is the knowledge that we are all protected under the Constitution of the United States as one Nation under God, and that all the great politicians in Washington guarantee each one of us with their unconditional commitment that the sun is indeed rising every morning, even though we don't see it during rainy days; and how heartwarming is this unwavering knowledge of being protected every single day (and sometimes even at night) by those elegant black limos carrying these courageous men who bring us all the good news under the vast skies above us, like the Messiah we have all been waiting for! And if we push ourselves into the freezing waters of the true believers, we can all see the glorious days of happiness, riches and good sex right in front of our sinful eyes that have been blindfolded for so long, to finally applaud the emergence of a better tomorrow for our bank accounts and for the polar bears who are so worried about the melting ice that used to form their blanket for a sleepover into happier days, and also for the black panther, whose ivory teeth are recently so much in demand by our merciless society, as ivory has become even a substitute for the dwindling prices of oil and aluminum, not to speak about those juicy Mc. Donald's Big Mac burgers…

Love and Care

Dada-Tale

Hand written without interruption

On Saturday October 11, 2008

At Lake Pemaquid's Duck Puddle Camp Ground

From 9:05 – 9:17 PM

Are you a loving, caring person? Do you stand up for other people who are being abused by the system? Do you enjoy the beauty of a sunset? Is the colorful wing of a butterfly more important to you than the next thousand dollars in your bank account? If and when your answer is a non-equivocal "yes!" to all the above questions, then there is no doubt in my mind of a professional consultant that you have all the most precious qualities needed to become a lawyer! And when I say lawyer, I mean one of those valued professionals who thrive to make this society a Heaven on Earth for all of us animal lovers who are concerned that the animal within us still is so very much preponderant. In your heart of hearts you are one of the best and you deserve to be elected to your local community boards, to the states legislature and even the Congress in Washington, because you know how to stand up for the rights of the swallows who tend to come back ever later from the warm weather in the South, since the flies are disappearing due to the pesticides that kill them so very dead and who are therefore substantially diminished in their fundamental rights of being called "pork" in the budgets of the legislators all around the world, while the ignorant silent majority of the people don't even know what is really going on and tend to grossly underestimate the amount of love and dedication that our legal profession is so selflessly committing to this noble cause in order to save them all for the greater good of mankind.

Wisdom

Dada-Tale

Hand written without interruption

On Sunday, October 12, 2008, from 7:55 – 8:14 AM

At Lake Pemaquid's Duck Puddle Camp Ground

The confusion and misunderstanding about such great thinkers as Schlegel, Kierkegaard, Sartre, Hegel, Rousseau, Kant and Karl Marx, and –in a more realistic way- Freud, Adler and Jung, is that if you are misfortunate enough to be blessed with a great memory, your head will be spinning like a gold plated wheel in the crispy morning sun of a lovely October day, following the beauty of a starry night with a full moon that whispers love songs into your ears across the rising fogs of a nearby lake, with all the wisdom and misunderstandings disseminated by political talks, and where the clarity and irrefutable logic of your heart is also filling it with the warmth of this cool morning, just as the great social benefactors are defining the accomplishments of their thoughts by the unparalleled clarity of their language, or –to use a metaphor- just as the song of a bird is defined by the bird itself, or the quiet ferocity of a fish by the shape of its scales, so that the foggy outlook for the glorious future of humanity can equally be defined by the missing dollars in the common man's bank account, as by the uncompromising clarity of my own thoughts in the broader context of an airplane that is disturbing the peace of nature and of my mind, as my beautiful pen is fulfilling its destiny of writing itself out of ink, while my compassion worries about its well-being in the midst of a world so entirely well structured in its chaotic order and self-discipline, and so eloquently praised by our noble scene of political thoughts that it reminds me of the unobstructed logic in this environment of love, beauty and definitely the very best of philosophical thoughts that mankind's greatest minds have prepared us to face our glorious future.

Self-Fertilization

Dada-Tale

Hand written without interruption

On Saturday October 11, 2008

At Lake Pemaquid's Duck Puddle Camp Ground

From 9:05 – 9:17 PM

It is beyond belief why the scientific world appears not to be the least concerned with the fascinating subject matter of self-fertilization, in view of the fact that this amazing natural phenomena certainly presents a unique opportunity to disseminate ourselves and -by doing so- making accessible our uniquely brilliant ego-gene that carries our great qualities to the ever increasing population of our planet earth, thus instilling our own human dignity to a vast number of human beings, without reverting to the often dirty sexual component usually associated with the notion of procreation, and thus ridding ourselves of any presumed sullied intrusion of a sex partner (as is now customary), which would be all the more important, as the environment in which we live these days is already subjected to a generalized pollution of the mind, the overwhelming extent of which appears to be utterly irreversible without a healthy portion of purifying self-fertilization, in spite of all that fast-talk culture that influences almost every aspect of our daily life, to the point that we probably have only a limited likelihood of survival as a specie in a Darwinistic sense, unless we revert to the subject matter of self-fertilization, and thus increase our probability as a race to admire the gorgeous sunsets like the one of this evening for a number of more generations to come…

The Color Gray

Dada-Tale

Hand written without interruption

On Friday, October 24, 2008

In New York City – Central Park West

From 4:40 – 5:05 PM

It is still Friday and that Black Friday curse didn't materialize in such a black way, but turned out to be gray, just as the sun has now disappeared over Central Park and the old rocks have reassumed their gray appearance, and the squirrels and the flowers and the birds also went into hiding, with the sole exception of a few gray-brownish sparrows that are always around where there is hope to get hold of some crumbs to eat, as well as for a small dog on the wrong side of a leash that just pooped (and I spare you the details), while its master is doing what he has to do in light of the fact that the City of New York just increased the fines from one hundred to two hundred fifty dollars to dog owners who don't clean up after their pet, to make up for the upcoming dwindling tax receipts, assuming that if they can fine another seven hundred sloppy dog owners (as they did during the last fiscal year) they can raise close to two hundred thousand dollars, which will keep the good old bureaucracy going, just like they grow the trees and the children and the medical bills for the sublime enjoyment of all the visitors who have come here to Central Park early this year to applaud the thirty thousand marathon runners from about seventy-eight countries around the world, who are bringing their devaluated currencies to the over-filled hotels here in the City, which absorbs them just like a far-distant nebula in outer space absorbs a nice, young, flickering blond star into its black hole, which scientists have for so long wondered about, before they figured out a brand new theory about them, which once again gets them lots of government and private foundation money, so they can continue to make children and feed them, and walk them proudly around here in Central Park, unless this coming Monday is going to be THE Black Monday (which many experts believe), and if that happens they will all have to stay at home and invent new and more exciting theories, so the money doesn't dry up and they can continue to buy sunflower seeds to feed the poor motherless birds outside their window sills, which are under the constant supervision of their domestic cats that have to be kept on a leash

(like the dogs here in Central Park), but for a very different reason: namely not to jump after a feeding bird and –missing it- fall twenty-seven floors all the way down to the asphalt and prove that they are indeed blessed with seven lives, and therefore can repeat that very same maneuver for at least another five times before going to that famous Cat Heaven, where fifty-four virgin cat ladies are already patiently waiting to test their libido under ideal heavenly conditions that would make anybody pale of jealousy, just as there are so many other pale objects here on earth and in the various heavens that accommodate so many people and other creatures who have been as good during their earthly life as I have always been…

Change

Dada-Tale

Hand written without interruption

On Saturday, October 25, 2008

In New York City – In Front of my Computer

From 10:15 – 10:29 AM

Changing socks is like changing moralities: you do it frequently and there are lots of holes in them; I speak of those holes that fill all the void of our existence, which is also full of voids, particularly when it comes to memory, and preferably to selective memory, because we human beings can select so many things (including moralities), and those matters are either precious or not so precious to us, which means that our precious life must be preserved at all cost until we are dead, a state of our bodily presence that comes sooner or later -preferably later-, although it is common knowledge that the early bird catches the worm that was otherwise destined to catch a fish in the otherwise cold water that is so often polluted by the vicious talks of all the vicious people who don't even know about their own soul that will definitely not go to Heaven, of which we all assume that it is upstairs and beyond the clouds, even though we wouldn't need wings like the birds to go up there if we were sure that Heaven were at the place where we assume that Hell is, because it would be very beautiful to walk downstairs, past the wine cellar, into Heaven, where it would be much cooler than up there so close to the sun that otherwise gives us so much comfort during the cold winter days that are about to come, like all the sure things that come and go continuously and create so much boredom, of which we know it is the deadliest plague of mankind in general terms, not considering the fact that changing moralities is a lot of fun, because it is never boring, just as I said before…

Dada-Tale

Hand written without interruption

On October 31, 2008

In New York City – In front of the Dakota House

From 8:51 – 9:05 PM

Since the word goes that children and fools speak the truth, what does that tell you about the truth? Does anybody listen to children and fools? And if so: are they not children or fools themselves? And that is only talking about those who talk and those who listen, which is about ten percent of the population. What about the other ninety percent of the population? Do they not speak the truth, or do they not listen? I mean: where have we come to? Isn't Dadaism the real answer to all the questions that half of the adult population asks the other half of the adult population that understands exactly and precisely nothing more than what they want to hear or understand in the first place, due to the enormous load of misguided education and life experiences, which they carry around as a mental backpack in their binary (action/reaction) preprogrammed mind? --- So, what good would it serve to try and refine our vocabulary to the point of a modern-day Shakespeare, when nobody is remotely capable or willing to understand the essence of what we want to say? Would that not bring a hundred past generations to a big yawn? Would it not be like dripping a single drop of your blood into the oceans of the world and believing that by doing so it would change the chemical composition of their waters into a unique, never before seen or tasted elixir of truth? In the old days the word used to be that so many dogs had pissed at the bottom of the Matterhorn, and yet that majestic mountain was still standing. What does that tell you? Well, it probably explains why the world is so full of dogs, whose ultimate goal is (you know what I mean), while the kids continue to ask all those questions and the adults continue to answer them without really knowing what they are talking about, which brings me to the ultimate conclusion of this Halloween Day: I never really liked Pumpkin Pie.

Questions
Dada-Tale
Hand written without interruption
On Monday, November 1ˢᵗ, 2008
In Leesburg, VA
From 1:47 – 1:59 PM

How come that small children ask so many questions, when the adult world has all the answers so ready-made that you can bank on them like they were carved in stone, even though we all know how comparatively heavy those stones are as opposed to the questions, the most important of which is why tables generally have four legs (like all the primitive animals), while humans walk on two legs and Indian Gurus even on one; the fact being therefore that the number *two* appears to be on a higher level on the evolutionary scale, which is why we should consider making more one-legged tables, meaning also that the one remaining leg would then probably be a lot longer (and longer is of course better), and therefore compare favorably with those wine tastings in Europe, where the bouquet of a wine is also compared to the long legs of a lady, rather than to strawberries like they do here in the United States, which reminds me of the Strawberry Fields right here in Central Park, where you cannot even drink a bottle of wine without the constant danger of being arrested, and considering the fact that arrests evoke the image of a cardiac arrest (I had one) that could really shorten your lifespan to the point that your earthly existence could be over before the age of maturity, which brings me back to the strawberries that also don't taste good before they reach their state of maturity, which –on the other hand- often make us mature people believe that we are superior, while it might be wiser to accept the fact (like Picasso did) that a baby (in its infinite not yet developed wisdom) is a lot smarter with its questions than all those clever adults with their ready-made answers from their TV screens …

Generally Speaking
Dada-Tale
Hand written without interruption
In my (new) car
On Monday, November 10, 2008
In front of the Dakota House in New York City –
From 9:52 – 10:19 AM

Memory is that which you can recall, and while you have already forgotten anything that happened just a few minutes ago, recent scientific research confirms that each time you remember something, you have to re-create the whole event from scratch. What a blessing if we could do the same trick to our stomach, I mean ruminating the best delicacies over and over again, (like a cow, but infinitely better), without the economic imperative of making money all the time to eat foods that are becoming ever more contaminated from Mexican unclean waters, which is most probably responsible for the shorter lifespan of the Mexican population, even though -generally speaking- there appears to be a correlation with those shorter Mexican bodies, which (on the other hand) implies a tremendous advantage not only relating to the economies that are being accomplished by a lesser food intake, but also work when buying textiles for clothing, and this all the more as weather conditions in Mexico are a lot warmer then up north, which is probably why the Mexican billionaire, Carlos Slim Helu, (otherwise not so slim) is reportedly the richest man on this ever warming planet, where the icebergs are now melting and the barber shop business is going downhill in a hurry, because so many politicians are losing their hair over this and cannot get reelected under these precarious circumstances within the ever changing political landscape, even under the aspect that there are not so many landscapers left to take care of the wonderful Japanese and Chinese traditional gardens, where they celebrate those marvelous tea ceremonies that make all coffee drinkers turn pale of jealousy, since the plastic cups from which they have to drink their daily brew are in no way comparable to the beautiful Bordeaux wine glasses that you can find in some of the top high roller restaurants of the world, even though they are also made in China (like so many other things) forcing the Chinese to come up with an economic stimulus package on this very day when the moon is just about exactly three-quarters full, which makes it really exciting to be alive during such amazing times…

Flu Symptoms

Dada-Tale

Hand written without interruption in my car

On Thursday, November 13, 2008

In front of the Dakota House in New York City –

from 8:58 – 9:27 AM

Where does the notion "Sick like a Dog" come from, since I have never seen any dog as sick as I feel today? Or is it simply that dogs cannot write about it, which may well make all the difference in an environment of binary Yes/No information that governs all of our neurological system -in my case much more NO than Yes today- so that in the final analysis a dog may well be most fortunate by not being able to write (or speak, or even bark) about the problem of how lousy it feels on a cold, rainy day like this with these nasty flu symptoms that you fight with antibiotics, anti-histamine and anti-inflammatory medicines to enrich the pharmaceutical companies (even though the flu would be gone in about six days anyway), which -in my case- appears to be highly doubtful, since this thing has already been my loyal companion for eight days, during which time my eighty billion strong cell colony has not been able to chase those ghastly virus invaders out of my otherwise self-protective system, which is really a pain in the neck (really and figuratively speaking), given the fact that the neck is an important part of our body, a statement that would make the shadows of many formerly hanged men readily agree with me, even though one should not talk about nasty things when in such lousy physical conditions as I am in today, but rather look at the bright side of life, which is that many people who don't have the flu must be very happy not to be plagued by it, unaware of the fact that they may not even know what malicious disease may already be creeping up deep inside them, but always happy that their outside appearance still comes across like a healthy looking fruit, though already rotting on the inside, which —of course- holds true not only for fruits, but even more so for the psychological makeup of humanity, which (as I now realize) is such an earth-shaking philosophical thought and statement that it could (and should!) be on the cover of every book on the New York Times bestseller list!

Post Thanksgiving Thoughts
Dada-Tale
Hand written without interruption
In my car
On November 30, 2009
In front of the Dakota House in New York City –
From 10:16 – 10:29 AM

The noise of a hammer onto a piece of metal next to me (where the ever price-increasing heating oil is about to flow into the Dakota House on my right hand side) reverberates into the gray day of this Monday morning, while everybody is still dreaming of their turkey digestion during Thanksgiving weekend, where that stuffing is always so important, to the point that probably next year they will feed the turkey meat to their dogs and cats and just eat the stuffing, which has become an American symbol of gourmet cooking – except for me, because I really don't like that stuffing, and not even the white meat, but much better the dark meat, which is also politically correct at a time and age where being correct means everything, except for its application in grammatical and spelling correctness, where it is even chic to be sloppy to the point that sloppiness has become a status symbol of the ruling class, even though nobody knows anymore who that ruling class is our days, since nobody is ruling anymore, and those who think they are have been in trouble lately, just as the world in general has been alongside that noise of that hammer at that huge oil delivery truck next to me, so that the lovely people who live in the Dakota House, and their lovely little children, will have a warm house when Santa Claus is coming in a few days in the form of a UPS delivery truck that brings them all the fancy, nonsensical stuff, which they have been buying on the Internet, so the precarious economy will be properly stimulated…

Soul Food

Dada-Tale

Hand written without interruption

In my car -- On December 4, 2009

In front of the Dakota House in New York City –

From 12:13 – 12:28 AM

What can the fingernail of your right hand's thumb tell you, as it is firmly pressed against the pen that is writing these lines? Can it tell you anything at all, or is it just there, because it cannot escape its destiny of doing exactly what your brain cell command center is telling it what to do? And does it have any choice, if it hasn't been cleaned in a day or so, since you ate your last shrimp with it and didn't have the courtesy of washing it with soap right thereafter, but rather enjoying the smell of those shrimp in a prolonged fashion? Aren't these thoughts very deep philosophical questions that reach deep into the essence of any human being? Nourishing the thought (for instance) that the said fingernail could be substituted by the abstract notion of your soul that you would leave un-cleaned for several days to enjoy the smell of that unclean soul in a biblical sense? Wouldn't that be a marvelous subject for any preacher of any religion throughout the world, who could thus introduce the idea of smell into all the derivatives of your soul? And, speaking of derivatives, could they branch out to the 662 trillion dollars of derivatives out there that are in no way smelling as good as the thumbnail that has recently peeled those lovely shrimp with that delicious sauce dip that you are now reminded of, every single time you bring your finger close to your face? And by extension: from now on always be reminded that your soul is not as sterile as you were made to believe, but definitely has a smell of its own. And –I might add- a very uplifting one, since you recently rediscovered your Dada-Gene...

THAT LOUSY FLU   Tue, Feb 15, 2011 / 11:52 AM - 12:06
In my car on Central Park West

No siree, we humans don't have no memory for pain,
as I can attest to, since only a few days ago I was
deep in bed with the flu and a horrible cough and
already I can barely remember it, in spite of the
fact that I swore by all that is holy to me (which
is a whole lot) that I would never forget my misery
and be greateful for every minute that my horrible
pain was gone in the future, always being conscient
of the fact that happiness is when we have no pain,
no hunger, no thirst, nor any other envy for anything
in life ___ and now that I am in this perfect
state of happiness I have forgotten what it really
means, instead taking everything for granted and
even getting almost bored by that present state
of happiness that is the absence of all those afore
mentioned problems, and even costs not a single
penny of that money that is getting a little more
worthless every single day of this accelerating
inflationary cycle that kills the middle classes
and the poor, but - thank God - also these seventy
something trillion dollars of unfunded US
debts, which are going to melt away as slowly
as the snow in Central Park here next to me,
with the pond in front of the Boathouse still
solidly frozen, since spring is not here yet, but
the groundhog predicting it to come very soon,
because the ghastly beast couldn't see its own
shadow the other day, as if it really cared about
the happy faces all around that can't wait for this
lousy winter to finally go down in history as one
of the worst, with that lousy flu I just told you about.

That Lousy Flu
Dada-Tale
Hand written without interruption
In my car
On February 15, 2011
On Central Park West in New York City –
From 11:52 AM – 12:06 PM

No siree, we humans don't have no memory for pain, as I can attest, since only a few days ago I was deeply buried in my bed with the flu and a horrible cough, and already I can barely remember it, in spite of the fact that I swore by all that is holy to me (which is a whole lot) that I would never forget my misery and always be grateful in the future for every minute that my horrible pain was gone, always being conscious of the fact that happiness is when we have no pain, no hunger, no thirst, nor any other envy for anything else in life – and now that I am in this perfect state of happiness I have forgotten what it really means, instead taking everything for granted and even getting almost bored with that present state of happiness, which is the absence of all those aforementioned problems, and even costs not a single penny of that money that is getting a little more worthless every single day of this accelerating inflationary cycle that kills the middle classes and the poor, but -thank God- also these seventy something trillion dollars of unfunded US debts, which are going to melt away as slowly as the snow in Central Park here next to me, with the pond in front of the boathouse still solidly frozen, since spring is not here yet, but the groundhog predicting it to come very soon, because the ghastly beast couldn't see its own shadow the other day, as if it really cared about the happy faces all around that can't wait for this lousy winter to finally go down in history as one of the worst, including that lousy flu that I told you about in the first place…

Dyslexia

Dada-Tale

Hand written without interruption

At my Virginia Garage in Rocky Mount

On September 18, 2010

From 9:30 – 9:39 AM

Dyslexia is when the beginning of the end is in the middle part of your left shoe that has already been worn out through so many worn out stories that always come to mind in the middle of the night, when the sun stands at the zenith of its daily obscurity at the opposite side of our green planet, which has become so dangerous, because the bed bugs are taking over from the missing spiders that have abandoned their fishing net in the Gulf of Mexico, where the oil spills murmur a beautiful serenade of ointment, so the violins don't scratch anymore under the skilled hands of the young music lovers who play uninterruptedly the same piece on their green pianos, so the planet earth remains pure of dyslexia, which tends to contaminate the human dirty minds of ever occurring news at the top end of every single hour, all days and evenings long and short, always mindful of the fact, that facts have to be factual to be considered essential for the survival of the human race, which otherwise tends to be lost in the sea of time, due to that ever-present instinct of dyslexia…

Happy New Year!

Dada-Tale

Hand written without interruption

At the Smith Mountain Lake in Virginia

On Tuesday, January 5, 2010

From 4:42 – 4:58 PM

A New Year --- Happy New Year! How many of those did I have during my 72 years of age? I should be a very happy person by now, since 72 times 100 Happy New Year's cards is 7,200 times happiness for an entire lifetime! That's a lot, and it also explains why I am such a happy person, which is the general perception of me; and since perception in life is everything, it doesn't matter what the underlying realities are, for as long as perceived perceptions keeps the perceptions being perfected in this most perfectly perceived perfect world of all possibly perceived worlds of -dare I say it? – *Nothingness*, which is also known as zero --- but as we all know, zero is as curious a number as infinity, because it could either really be zero in both cases, or everything at the end, in the beginning and in the middle, just as you please to look upon it, and at various hours of the day and of the night, which means it is highly dependent on the position not only of the sun, but also of the moon, of which we know that there were two (!!) Blue Moons just this past month of December, I should say two full moons, which is really staggering, considering the fact that extremely rare things happen only once in a blue moon, and now they happen even twice in a period of only 29 days, which means that you can say almost anything and get away with it if it sounds halfway scientific, such as global warming, which is freezing up the lake in front of my window and making the poor little birds eat like crazy from my feeder, without even realizing that without global warming they would all be dead, and the notion of a Happy New Year would then not apply to them…

For the Birds

Dada-Tale

Hand written without interruption

At the Smith Mountain Lake in Virginia

On Tuesday, January 5, 2010

From 6:35 – 6:47 PM

Why should I agree with the age-old saying "It is for the birds," when the little birdies in front of me, here, next to my Virginia studio, are so very happy about life when I feed them, and are rubbing off some of those happy feelings onto my own (gray) soul that has nourished so many varied feelings from utterly dark to finding so much colorful light in my work of Sculptomania, which is currently filling my spring days here in Virginia, where Angelika cooks at least two fabulous meals every day, here in the middle of the woods and at that huge lake next to us, where the fish are not biting yet, because the water is still too cold for them --- I was almost writing too wet, since it is raining today, one of those lovely spring rains that make the trees bloom and the noses run, since the pollen count is very high, in spite of what people sometimes think, when nature is not all green yet to make the human mind feel calm about nature's ever revolving seasons of love, torture and freezing cold --- which reminds me that just three weeks ago I resumed skiing after 25 years, and it felt great (after a wobbly beginning), and I decided that I can still do it, like so many other things I am still doing, including -come to think of it- feeding the birdies...

A Touch of Christmas in the Air
Dada-Tale
Hand written without interruption
At the Smith Mountain Lake in Virginia
On Sunday, December 27, 2009
From 3:40 - 3:54 PM

The melting snow is crackling all around me, as I sit here in southwest Virginia, enjoying the last sunrays upon my wrinkling face, which is the exterior sign of my inner beard that keeps growing, invisible to the outside world, which would be better off to be *outside-in* instead of *inside-out*, as the lobster tails in their butter-flied state are finding out the hard way in Angelika's broiler that is about to spit out the last of our wonderful Christmas meals, just as the sun is setting behind the leafless trees on the southern horizon, which evokes so many distant memories, that I would want to go there in spite of my pen that remains stubbornly on my white sheet in front of me, with the background music of many happy birds and a woodpecker right behind me, eating their last meal (before the sun sets) from my birdseed feeder that makes them so happy and thankful for this Christmas season, even though they probably cannot relate to the Gospel, as everybody around here can, and as they demonstrate it with so many lovely lighted objects and trees all around in this otherwise deserted land, where the foxes and the rabbits bid good night to each other, as soon as the sun sets with a slight upcoming breeze from the South, where all the other birdies have already disappeared, while awaiting another spring season, which I can already feel deep in my bone marrow, which is a fine delicacy if it comes from a beef bone and is usually served with salt and toast, and not to forget a glass of Champagne to remind you that I am really getting hungry while writing down these lines about so many delicacies that already make all my juices flow as a prelude to a wonderful dinner.

How come the iceberg salad in front of me - a whole head of it - costs no more than $1.20? Should the age where all those icebergs are melting not reflect upon the price of the iceberg salads? In other words: when there is scarcity of polar bears, as we all know, should there not be a parallel lack of iceberg salads that drive up their price, according to the most basic principles of economic price theories? Or is it simply that there are fewer icebears that eat iceberg salad these days? What profound and important questions those are in the grand scheme of things, where that huge iceberg of almost the size of Rhode Island is now threatening the naval trafic on the west side of Australia and may well be landing there very soon, so that the kangaroos there are going to 'hop over' to eat all that wonderful iceberg salad and become polar kangaroos that will slowly take over and threaten even more the living space of the polar bears, or - even better - have sex with one another, which would create a new race of polar bear kangaroos that could stun the scientific community as a truly unique phenomenon in the chain of evolution. However, the nasty consequence may well be that a little polar bear-kangaroo baby may discover from the pocket of his mother that iceberg salad is something really good and jump out to eat it right there, even though it doesn't have olive oil and balsamic vinager to enhance the taste like I do, but that may just be a question of time, since the Italian olive oil and balsamic vinager industries are really good in their global marketing strategies, which could so dramatically increase the price of an iceberg latuce that, next time we go to Walmart's, we may find that we have to pay $12 for that same delicacy...

Icebergs

Dada-Tale

Hand written without interruption

At the Smith Mountain Lake in Virginia

On Tuesday, January 5, 2010

From 6:54 – 7:11 PM

How come the iceberg salad in front of me -a whole head of it- costs no more than $1.20? Should the age where all those icebergs are melting not reflect upon the price of the iceberg salad? In other words: when there is scarcity of polar bears, as we all know, should there not be a parallel lack of iceberg salads that drive up their price, according to the most basic principle of economic price theories? Or is it simply that there are fewer ice bears that eat iceberg salad these days? What profound and important questions those are in the grand scheme of things, where that huge iceberg of almost the size of Rhode-Island is now threatening the naval traffic of the West Side of Australia and may well be landing there very soon, so that the kangaroos are going to hop over to eat all that delicious iceberg salad and become polar kangaroos that will slowly take over and threaten even more the living space of the polar bears, or -even better- have sex with one another, which would then create a new race of polar bear-kangaroos that would stun the scientific community as a truly unique phenomenon in the chain of evolution. However, the nasty consequence may well be that a small polar bear-kangaroo baby may discover from the pouch of its mother that iceberg salad is something really good and jump out to eat it right there and then, even though it doesn't have olive oil and balsamic vinegar to enhance the taste like I do, but that may just be a question of time, since the Italian olive oil and balsamic vinegar industries are really good in their global marketing strategies, which could so dramatically increase the price of an iceberg lettuce that, next time we go to Wal-Mart, we may find that we have to pay $12 for that same delicacy…

Judgment Day

Dada-Tale

Hand written without interruption

In Leesburg, Virginia

On November 9, 2008

From 3:34 - 3:50 AM

Whatever the importance of a very important thought may be, as compared to a single crack in the wood of my underlying table, it does not reach as far as my pen may reach with respect to the out-flowing ink on the bottom side rather than on the top, which would (of course) make a bit of a mess and not leave a trace of my important thoughts on this piece of paper that looked so innocently white before I started to sully it with my all important thoughts, which might otherwise have been lost to that fabulous humanity, which changes one hundred percent about every seventy years or so, but still thinks collectively that its immortal thoughts will survive even Judgment Day, that nebulous notion that may never even come under the circumstances of such diverse philosophical thoughts that frighten even the dumbest of all college students who learn just about nothing that will serve them in real life, other than how to distinguish one beer from another empty bottle, which they have been taught to dispose of in very environmentally friendly ways, so it can be recycled for the next idiot who may not even be able to draw a distinction between two almost similar beers, and may still be drinking more, so he can get to the bottom of that bottle, where he thinks that the *real* truth is buried under the dire circumstances of an ever changing environment that remains every bit the same for as long as there are ants to clean up the mess after one busload has gone and the next bus is about to arrive to let those hordes of people out who are all excited about the importance of those geniuses of past generations, as compared to their own miserable existence.

(D)Education

Dada-Tale

Hand written without interruption

In Leesburg, Virginia

On November 2, 2008

From 12:24 - 12:48 PM

I went to school for twenty-one years, then I was an economist for eighteen years, and now I have been an artist for over twenty-five years; and what became of me? A Dada-Tale writer who bypasses the screwed-up brain and writes from the guts, just as the Dadaists in Zurich did, exactly ninety years ago, even though when re-reading my Dada-Tales it seems to me there is a bit more flesh around the bone of my writings than there was in the case of those Zurich guys between the two Big Wars. Whether that's good or bad, I don't know, it might just be different and my stuff appears to make a bit more sense, even though it doesn't, and is not even supposed to, because what comes from the stomach does make sense only when you compare it to what and when you ate the last time, and even the way you have been in a vertical and horizontal position when you started to digest, unlike the brain food that gets mixed up in your gray cells and comes out as more or less pre-selected garbage, according to your mouth piece, which polishes up that final output considerably if you are one of those highly paid lawyers, or any other of the highly regarded professionals that make it all the way to the top of the corporate or the political ladder, of which we know that they are dangerous, because all of these ladders are of a very bad quality of wood that makes them crumble sooner or later, and then they fall down on the concrete floor below, and the expensive varnish is all gone, and the reality is all spreading out on the floor in all its disgusting realities (since realities are always on the disgusting side.)

A Botanical Hind

Whatever a beautiful red rose may be thinking all alone
in the middle of a dark night is relatively unimportant
for the rest of the botanical environment on the opposite
side of the globe, since the turtles who eat the grass over
there can withdraw their neck from the outside in such a
fraction of a second that playing turtle has become
one of the favorite passtimes of many people who
cannot stand the limelight of their fifteen minutes
of fame, as compared to the masses who are still
waiting for their own fifteen minutes, which usually
don't come during their lifetime, so they have to be
satisfied with applauding those empty-headed
celebrities that look almost as good as my beautiful
red rose in the middle of this night, which is
so dark that you don't even need a very sharp
knife to cut its darkness into two uneven halves,
since it would not be very original if you tried
to slice it into two very similar pieces, particularly
not if you consider that tomorrow (or the day after
tomorrow) there may well be a glimpse of a moon
out there, whose light is usually so cold that it
may well wake up some dead people in the cemetary
who never had their fifteen minutes of fame, since
they used to belong to those masses who are never a
minute late when they go to work in the morning,
because if they were, they could be fired on the spot,
which is not a very spotless outlook on life under
the circumstances of a terrible economy, which is
shrinking even without them being fired to accomo-
date the cash-flow of those giant corporations that
need the money so urgently to pay billions of dollars
to their geniuses of top managers on their way out.

A Botanical Mind

Dada-Tale

Hand written without interruption

In Leesburg, Northern Virginia

On November 9, 2008

From 3:08 - 3:24 AM

Whatever a beautiful red rose may be thinking all alone in the middle of a dark night is relatively unimportant for the rest of the botanical environment on the opposite side of the globe, since the turtles who eat the grass over there can withdraw their neck from the outside world in such a fraction of a second that playing turtle has become one of the favorite pastimes of many people who cannot stand the limelight of their fifteen minutes of fame, as compared to the masses who are still waiting for their own fifteen minutes, which usually don't come during their lifetime, so they have to be satisfied with applauding those empty-headed celebrities that look almost as good as my beautiful red rose in the middle of this night, which is so dark that you don't even need a very sharp knife to cut its darkness into two uneven halves, since it would not be very original if you tried to slice it into two very similar pieces, particularly not if you consider that tomorrow (or the day after tomorrow) there may well be a glimpse on a moon out there, the light of which is usually so cold that it may even wake up some dead people in the cemetery who never had their fifteen minutes of fame, since they used to belong to those masses who are never a minute late when they go to work in the morning, because if they were, they could be fired on the spot, which is not a very spotless outlook on life under the circumstances of this terrible economy, which is shrinking even without them being fired to accommodate the cash-flow of those giant corporations that need the money so urgently to pay billions of dollars to their geniuses of top managers on their way out.

The Camel's Back

Life goes on - as they say - until that last straw breaks the camel's back; but did you realize? They talk about one single camel, meaning that for all the other zillions of camels that populate our planet life still goes on — not to talk about all the other animals and people, and, yes —even bacteria — which take it yet to another level! So, what sense does it make to talk of a single camel whose back just broke, because some idiot loaded another single straw on its poor, unnaturally curved back? That will teach them to breed other camels so poorly engineered that a single straw will break their back. And — while talking about poor engineering, why is it that human beings don't have six legs and two pairs of wings, which would make the idea of survival of the fittest so much more probable in an environment where everybody is trying to break a leg, so they can take over to become the queen bee that you always wanted to be? And — speaking about queen bee — why was nobody ever referred to a leader as the "King-Bee"? How much more macho would that image be in the cut-throat environment that we live in? I can only imagine to be a "King Bee" instead of a short-lived drone of nothingness that nobody will ever remember, except for that one-time sexual act of creating a new string of bees, which has nothing to do with string-beans that are much less exposed to sudden death, unless they get harvested, and snipped, and peeled to please our green-peas (sorry - I was going to say "Green Peace" Society, which is so incredibly dedicated to the idea that the life of every single species goes on forever, even though it is common knowledge that every day there are at least one thousand and fifty-seven species that come to life, while (on the other hand) one thousand and sixty-one species disappear on a daily basis, taking into account (however) that the full moon plays a significant role in the balance of power of all powerless creatures . . .

The Camel's Back

Dada-Tale

Hand written without interruption

In Leesburg, Virginia

On Saturday, November 8, 2008 -- From 2:11 - 2:31 PM

Life goes on -as they say- until that last straw breaks the camel's back; but did you realize? They always talk about one single camel, meaning that for all the other zillions of camels that populate our planet, life still goes on – not to talk about all the other animals and people, and, yes – even bacteria -- which take it yet to another level! So, what sense does it make to talk of a single camel whose back just broke, because some idiot loaded another straw on its poor, unnaturally curved back? That will teach them to continue breeding other camels so poorly engineered that a single straw will break their back. And -while talking about poor engineering- why is it human beings don't have six legs and two pairs of wings, which would make the idea of survival of the fittest so much more probable in an environment where everybody is trying to break someone's leg, in order to take over to become the queen bee that you always wanted to be? And -speaking of queen bee- why has nobody ever referred to a leader as the "King-Bee?" How much more macho would that image be in the cutthroat environment that we live in? I can only imagine to be a "King-Bee" instead of a short lived drone of nothingness that nobody will ever remember, except for that onetime sexual act of creating a new string of bees, which has nothing to do with string beans that are much less exposed to sudden death when they get harvested and shipped, and peeled to please our green-peas (sorry, I was going to say "Green Peace" movement), which is incredibly dedicated to the idea that the life of every single species is going on forever, even though it is common knowledge that every day there are at least one thousand and eighty-seven new species that come to life, while (on the other hand) one thousand and sixty-one species disappear on a daily basis, taking into account (however) that the full moon plays a significant role in the balance of power of all powerless creatures…

Methodologies

Dada-Tale

Hand written without interruption

In Leesburg, Virginia

On November 2, 2008

From 10:17 - 10:33 PM

On the other side of the other hand – which is another way of saying "On the reverse side of the reverse side of a medal" – it has been said that one can barely deduct that the deductive method in methodology is always deductible from a sum of the whole entity, which is often not as entirely whole as it may appear to the uninitiated (even clever and instructed) mind of an average person out there in limbo and on the mercy of the ever changing winds of wars that are much rougher than people may assume in their casual houses while sitting in front of their artificial fireplaces, which are every bit as comfortable as the real ones, because the fumes of the burning wood is not very healthy for your body, and by extension for your mindless mind that is often so mindful of getting the mind full of new ideas, which are always going in circles, like a merry-go-round, and therefore only leave you with the illusion of being really inventive, or discover new findings that might change the course of humanity by applying the before-mentioned inductive, or -better- deductive, method of scientific discoveries, which are but one very limited aspect of our egomanialistic existence in this universe of infinitisms of the mind and anti-matters that connect each other in such unforeseen ways, that the result is often amazingly the very same as if we had not started the entire discovery process at all, instead of rather going back to the cavemen society that also lived in (mental and real) caves and had fire places in front of them to illuminate their ideas, so they would involve to the point where they could build an atomic bomb (thirty thousand years later) and go to a McDonalds restaurant to enjoy an ice cold Diet Coke…

A Self-Reminder
Dada-Tale
Hand written without interruption
On Friday, December 1st, 2008
In southwest Virginia
From 8:50 – 9:09 AM

I am so sick and tired of being sick and tired that I have to sit down, take up my pen and bring onto paper the fathomless feeling of desperation with my old body and the negative thoughts that have overcome me over the past four weeks, since I got that merciless flu. Slowly, my ten (or so) sinus cavities were filled with pus, which then descended into my lungs and provoked a downspin of ungodly proportions. First, I took an Ibuprofen as an anti-inflammatory idea, then some Benadryl to dry up my running mucus, and finally some generic penicillin for a week. That helped for a few days, but then I got infected again and it was all downhill from that point on. And today, finally, I jumped over my own shadow and went to see an otorhinolaryngology doctor who put on a very severe look behind his thick eye glasses when he discovered all that pus in my throat… Anyway, I am not writing down all that miserable (almost suicidal) condition to complain, but rather as a self reminder about those terrible sick days once my health will be restored. To be telling myself (if I ever get my hand again on this sheet of paper) how very grateful I should be in good times when nothing is aching and my outlook on life is once again positive. Become conscious of all those happy times and enjoy every minute rather than taking good health for granted and lose myself in meaningless daily routines with all their petty sideshow problems that mask the reality of how well things really are.

Dada-Tales in Other Languages

Tree Frogs

Dada-Tale

Hand written without interruption

On October 7, 2008

In my car on Central Park West

From 11:35 to 11:55 AM

(Translated from German)

The question arises whether the questioner is really up to the level of the question he is asking, or even whether the questioned person realizes the profoundness of that certain question before coming to answer the particular theme raised by that specific question, just as any human being is not just stepping forward while he or she is walking in his or her shoes (or for that reason in any other footwear he or she might be wearing), but to be able to step forward in that very same -almost unaltered- manner through life, and specifically through a myriad of intellectual problems like walking through the thorny path of a rose garden, while those intellectual levels should strictly be separated from their physical appearance, in the very same manner as one cannot simply confuse a tree-frog with a ghastly brown toad, (although they both catch flies for a living) since that very tree-frog is not equipped with those wicked poisonous glands that leave you with some nasty nettle-rashes as a legacy, although this legacy is unlike the other legacies with which any last will executor may be faced, since those executors are not always entirely honest (as we would all like them to be), while -on the other hand- one cannot entirely dismiss the fact that most executors are usually lawyers of whom we all know that they have not all be spoon-fed with matters of the law, but -while scooping up their soup with that same spoon-often realize that the soup tastes too salty, while it is common knowledge that salt is not doctor recommended for people with high blood pressure, since their heart could easily be adversely affected and thus endanger all those wonderful books that were written across the ages about matters of the heart and love, whereupon a big misfortune may never be able to be reversed, and since such matters of the heart may well be every bit as good as a spoon full of bee honey in an environment where bees become even further extinct by the pollution of our precious planet, where so many pseudo-scientists are so intimately tied to it that one would start right at the beginning where the question arises whether... (continue to read, back at the beginning).

~~Laubfrösche~~   im Auto am CPW v. 11:35 - 11:55 am

Oft stellt sich die Frage, ob der Fragesteller der Frage selbst gewachsen sei, oder ob der Befragte sich überhaupt Rechenschaft über die Tiefschürfigkeit ~~je d'hooba~~ einer bestimmten Frage gegeben hat, bevor er ~~zur~~ zur Beantwortung des ihm durch die Frage gestellten Themas schreitet, so wie der Mensch ja überhaupt nicht nur in seinen Schuhen (oder anderen Fuss-Bekleidungen) schreitet, sondern auch in derselben, beinahe unveränderten, Art durch das Leben ganz allgemein, und im speziellen durch die geistigen Probleme wie durch einen dornigen Rosengarten zu schreiten imstande ist, obschon man die geistige Ebene eigentlich strikte von der rein physischen Präsenz klarstens auseinander halten sollte, grad so wie ein Laubfrosch auch nicht einfach mit einer garstigen Kröte zu verwechseln ist, denn obschon sie beide Fliegen fressen, so hat doch der Laubfrosch keine bösen Drüsen, die einem beim ~~beim~~ Anfassen ein Nesselfieber-artiges Geschwulst hinterlassen, dessen Hinter-Lassenschaft nicht für Testamentsvollstrecker bestimmt ist ~~sind~~, denn die Testamentsvollstrecker sind ja auch nicht immer so ehrlich, wie man sie gern haben möchte, ~~deute~~ und andererseits darf man kaum vergessen, dass die Testamentsvollstrecker normalerweise Juristen sind, die auch nicht immer das Gesetz mit Löffeln gegessen haben, weil ihnen die Suppe oft entweder zu heiss, oder aber manchmal auch versalzen vorkommt, und Salz ist ja bekanntlich für Leute mit hohem Blutdruck nicht sehr bekömmlich, denn es ist schädlich fürs Herz, von dem es ja so unendlich viele Liebeslieder gibt, dass es schade um jene ganze Literatur wäre, wenn dort ein Unglück passierte, das nicht wieder gut zu machen wäre, denn das wäre dann etwa nicht so gut wie ein Löffel von allerfeinstem Bienenhonig in einem Umfeld, wo die Bienen immer mehr ~~ausgerottet~~ werden durch die Verschmutzung unseres Planeten ~~und~~ die Pseudo-Wissenschaftler, die damit verbunden sind, und von denen man sagen kann: ... (siehe zurück zum Anfang)

Visions

Dada-Tale -- Hand written without interruption
On October 27, 2008 – from 7:46 – 8:02 PM
In New York City (Translated from German)

I wouldn't know where to begin, if my shoelaces were not fitting me as tightly as the bowtie that I have not been wearing for so many years, even though my perfect vision suffered a bit of an adjustment, insofar as I am now wearing eyeglasses for the better understanding of the world, which is about to go entirely berserk to the best of anybody's prediction, even though the majority of the folks out there think that everything is just fine and things will get a lot better, while ignoring the fact that – according to a famous German proverb- better is often the enemy of good, particularly when it comes to sweets shortly after eating your cheese at the end of a great meal, since those sweets threaten to harm your digestive system, just as during the past few centuries so many people have been harmed after being exposed to the wrong cabbage heads, and since those heads puff your system up like the frog in the fable and can do an enormous amount of harm to lots of people, without anybody being able to do the least about it, just as nobody can do anything about the fact that the sun rises every single morning once again and nobody can even prevent it from setting in the West, although it appears that the westerly horizon is getting increasingly clouded, which directly disputes the old saying that a red sunset promises a lovely upcoming morning, which shows you once again how deceptive some predictions can be, particularly when emanating from very expensive computer systems that have no right under any current law to be ever wrong, but which is also proof of how very fragile our entire legal system upon which we base all our trust really is ...

Stiff

Dada-Tale

Hand written without interruption

On August 8, 2008 -- From 10:18 to 10:32 AM

In my car on Central Park West

(Translated from German)

…and as I am waiting in my car under a partial sun, with the air condition blowing mercilessly at the scars of my broken knee, and as the noise of my running motor gets overpowered by a pneumatic hammer of a nearby street worker, I think of the little birdies in the woods, how they sing and play with their offspring babies, just as the babies in the strollers here all around me are proliferating ever more, and the women are beginning to wear skirts again all over New York; and like the Irish back pipers who also don't carry underwear under their skirts, while the fact remains that I don't like back pipe playing quite as much as lemon ice cream, even though I refrain from eating any of it, so my fingers don't get stiff from the cold and I can continue to write about stiff body parts, which get the stiffest once we are dead, although (hopefully) there is still a long way until that happens, a road every bit as long as the Russian tanks that have been driving all the way from Moscow to Georgia, while here in Central Park the trees are getting greener by the day, even though the Park Conservancy is begging for money again, so the famous elm trees won't get eaten up by those bark-beetles that will survive our Last Judgment Day by millions of years, since they can eat all the interior of our Planet Earth, which is filled and governed by hydro-carbons, just as Marie-Antoinette also governed those French cake-eaters before the 1789 Revolution, and as the streets of New York are governed by a lot of police cars that slapped me with a ticket just yesterday for a full one hundred and sixty-five dollars, whereupon I pronounced a biblical curse upon them, which will harm them a lot more than the benefit of those few dollars.

WATERLOO

Je vous dis qu'il ne suffit pas que le soleil brille — non,
il faut que la vache puisse se nourrir pour donner le
lait quotidien qui nous assure la survie de la planète verte.
Et ils ont dit que le monde entier aurait pu périr sous
la chaleur de la pluie qui est tellement mouillée que les
chiens ont peur de s'y baigner, bien que leur peau soit
un peu déchirée de la bagarre constante qui règne sur
le continent où Napoléon aurait presque gagné la
bataille de Waterloo, si cet idiot de Général Nelson
n'avait pas souffert de constipation proverbiale au
coin de la forêt vierge d'où il sortait de temps à
autre pour s'amuser avec les pucelles d'antan. Oui,
je ne plaisante pas, c'est le ton qui fait la musique
dont les orgues de barbarie ne forment qu'un aspect
dérisoirement incohérent, pour ne pas dire en
vain de la société universelle qui est en train
d'envahir la planète qui souffre tellement des
chants magnifiques de ces oiseaux cachés dans les
coins de la cathédrale magnifique avec les ornements

un peu désabusés par les centenaires de la poussière
grise qui couvre les abîmes des âmes perdues sans
créer en Dieu ou craindre le diable qui pourtant
réside dans tous les détails, comme il est bien
reconnu par les grands maîtres chanteurs que c'est le
ton qui fait la musique, à moins qu'il soit mangé
dans une assiette à sardines qui est notablement fort
sain pour l'ossature vieillissante d'un homme autrement
tout-à-fait en vigueur, notamment en ce qui concerne
la passion pour l'amour physique dont il est souvent
préférable de ne pas parler, par crainte de faire croire
le monde que parler est infiniment plus simple que
l'action concrète. Je pense que vous pigez ce que
je veux dire avec la conviction d'un sage qui a
prouvé d'être infiniment dérisoire maintes fois
dans le cours de sa vie autrement plutôt folle, si
on la mesure avec un thermomètre un peu cassé au
bon endroit ...

New York, le 23 septembre 2000/8:47 - 9:07 /   Rudy Ernst

Waterloo

Dada-Tale

Hand written by Rudy Ernst without interruption

On Friday, September 23, 2008

In New York City – at Central Park West –

from 8:47 to 9:07 AM

(Translated from French)

And I am telling you: It is not good enough for the sun to be shining – oh no! It is necessary that the cows be able to eat grass, so they can give you your daily milk that guarantees the survival of our green planet. It has been said that our entire world could have perished under the heat of the constant rains that are so wet that every dog is afraid to take a bath therein, even though their skin has been badly torn by the never ending fights that have been ravaging the Continent where the emperor Napoleon had almost been victorious at the battle of Waterloo, had this idiot of General Nelson not suffered of his acute and proverbial constipation at the corner of the woods from where he emerged from time to time to amuse himself with all those virgins around him at the time. Yes, I am not joking: it is the sound that produces the music, of which the French *Orgue de Barbarie* represents but an infinitely incoherent aspect, not to speak in a pointless way about our universal society, which is currently invading our planet, and which is also suffering so desperately from the beautiful songs of all those hidden birds singing in the multi-colored cathedrals with all those ornaments that were dilapidated by the abuse of the centuries of gray dust covering the abyss of the lost souls, not believing in any God or even fearing the Devil that is always hidden in the detail (as we all know), since all grandmasters of blackmail also recognize full well that it is indeed the sound that produces the music, unless it may have been previously eaten up from a full plate of sardines, since it is well known that they are very healthy for the bones of any aging person (otherwise in excellent health), particularly in connection with physical love making, mostly not mentioned out of fear that the world might believe that talk is infinitely more easy than concrete action. I think that by now you understand what I am trying to tell you with the conviction of a Buddha-like sage, who has proven many times before and during the course of his life that it is entirely irrelevant or even foolish if measured with a thermometer somehow a bit broken just at that exact specific point…

Form Over Substance

Dada-Tale - Hand written without interruption
On October 17, 2008, from 8:12 – 8:13 PM
(Translated from the original German)

The well-known fact that form is considerably more important than substance is not solely recognized by the alphabetical priority of the two words, but is also established historically for over two thousand years, when the great orator Demostenes filled his mouth with pebbles to chase away his stuttering, in order to enter the sublime form of his unverifiable speeches into the annals of world history, which (once again) is irrefutable proof of the fact that the spoken word is infinitely superior to the underlying (usually irrelevant) substance of the written word, just as the Holy Bible also states that in the Beginning there was the Word and not the substance, which came to be much later and out of the chaos of the Universe, to bring to the first man Adam an apple and a snake in a disgraceful way, of which we are all aware into what chaos they have recently been plunging our world, where even the Word on Sunday is leaving us with such meager meaning, while the substance of all the perpetrated trivialities (through the message of their anti-intelligence) is being pushed ever more into the foreground, to the ecstatic joy of all the illiterate masses, who have been framing this absurd development with a hammer and a nail against a wall, of which it is well known how structurally fragile its crumbling structure really is, right from the beginning of this critical time period of our cultural decline and disintegration of the underlying so-called preservation of the Substance in our economy, in which even gold is losing its value every single day, while trying to establish and to justify once again the thesis of the sublime supremacy of the Word over what is commonly referred to as Substance, an evolution that has been taking place gradually across so many of our preceding generations.

Wenn der Schatten meines Daumens sich mit dem
Sonnenlicht unter meinem Schuh vereint, so sind die fallenden
Eichenblätter von mir auf der Strasse auch nur noch ein Schatten
ihrer selbstsicheren Vergangenheit, die ja auch immer in die
Zukunft weist, vor allem wenn die Börsen rund um die Welt
so verrückt spielen wie zwei Hunde vor mir, die auch verrückt
spielen am Eingang zu den Strawberry Fields, wo die Herbstsonne
sich in meinem Gehirn widerspiegelt und ihre Strahlen
durch mein Nerven-System in die Feder fliessen lässt, die
ja letztlich auch nur ein Instrument in den Händen einer
höheren Macht beinhaltet, ohne dass die Weltgeschichte
ganz bös im Eimer wäre, denn es ist ja klar, dass
Einer nicht nur zum Wasser halten da sind, denn sie
reimen ja auf "Reiner", d.h. sie sind auch zu etwas
höherem geboren wie wir alle, die hochwohlgeboren etwas
auf unsere Herkunft geben, obschon die Herkunft sein
theoretisch kann ins Gewicht fällt im Zusammenhang mit
dem Ziel, dem wir alle zueilen, welches ja nicht etwa
der Tod oder das ewige Leben, sondern vielmehr das
ganze Klimbarium und drum und dran unserer
Existenz betrifft, obschon die Dame dicht neben mir
ein so unerhört dummes Zeugs in ihr Handy hinein
schwafelt, dass sogar dem Hund vor ihr die Ohren
zu Berge stehen. Tja und nun ist besagte Dame schon
in ein neues, so unglaubliches "Jesus Christ!" Gespräch
verwickelt, dass ihrem Broker noch die Magenschleimhäute
verfärben, denn dem Thermostat in ihrem Apartment
hat es ja scheinbar auch schon angehängt im Umfeld
dieses Chaos von unzusammenhängenden Dummheiten,
obschon ja die Dummen eher in den Himmel kommen
als die Reichen, die ja alle per Definition schlecht sind,
während die Dummen immer gut sind, wie es auch
in der Bibel (ich meine im Neuen Testament) zu lesen
steht. In diesem Sinne fliesst das Lebenslichtlein weiter
im Tramp der alten Schuhe, die ich trage, und die
wohl bald einmal ausgewechselt werden müssen, so
wie die Hosen und die Hemden auch auszuwechseln
sind, falls man solche überhaupt noch zu tragen im
Stand sein könnte...

Existence

Dada-Tale

Hand written without interruption

On Monday, October 6, 2008

In New York City – at Central Park West –

From 12:22 to 12:41PM

(Translated from German)

As the shadow of my thumb joins the sunlight under my shoe, and as the falling oak leaves in front of me on the street are but a shadow of their glorious past, which (as we all know) always points to the future, and particularly on a day when the stock markets all around the world play as crazy as the two dogs just in front of me, just here at the entrance to the Strawberry Fields, where the autumn sun reflects itself from my brain and flows through the complex nervous system into my writer's pen, which ultimately is also held in the hands of a much higher authority, without which the history of the world would be badly in the tank, and since it is clear that tanks are not only meant to contain water or gasoline, but also rimes with *banks*, which is what this stock market debacle today is all about, and since it elevates my story to a much higher level of a creature being born for a higher cause, even though the fact of being born for a higher cause barely carries any weight when compared to a perceived finish line towards which we are all rushing, and which has nothing to do with death or eternal life, but rather with the whole shebang of our earthly existence, although the lady right next to me is babbling such an unbelievable nonsense into her cell phone that even the dog right in front of her is raising his long ears out of frustration. Oh yes, and said dame is now involved in a new "Oh Jesus Christ" conversation with her broker, so that I can literally see that man's stomach mucus dry up in a hurry, while apparently even the thermostat in her apartment quit on her last night in the general environment of this generalized chaos of incoherent stupidities; although the dumb people can easier go to Heaven than the smart ones, let alone the rich who are all bad by definition, while all the dumb ones are always good, as it is also written in the Bible (I mean in the Gospel). And in this particular sense the electric bulb of our life continues to glow in the same way as my warn-out shoes, which might have to be replaced soon, just as the shirts and pence we are wearing, even though it is highly questionable how much longer we shall still be wearing any of them…

PART IV:

SMALL DADA-DRAWINGS

PART IV:

SMALL

DADA-DRAWINGS

A Lifelong Obsession

Once again, the child -in its infinite wisdom- has it right, since in the mind of the silent majority of the museum goers *Doodling ain't art*. Rather, as they pretend in the medical field, doodling is known as *Art Therapy*, which is generally recognized as a *Vital Healing Tool*. The U.S. College Search website lists over 4,000 colleges and universities offering courses and degrees in *Art Therapy*. How about that?

But if *good art* is the expression of the essence of any given artist (which is my belief), then these small Dada-Drawings somehow crystallize the essence of who we are. Why would I need to explain, or come up with, a host of psychoanalytical explanations rather than doing simple images of Dada-Drawings to express myself?

I have done what I now call my Dada-Drawings for well over forty years. Looking at them today, I see indeed a consistency that transcends the spur of the moment and opens a small window into the essence of who I am. The following Dada-Drawings include some samples of a period when my artist name was *Othmar*.

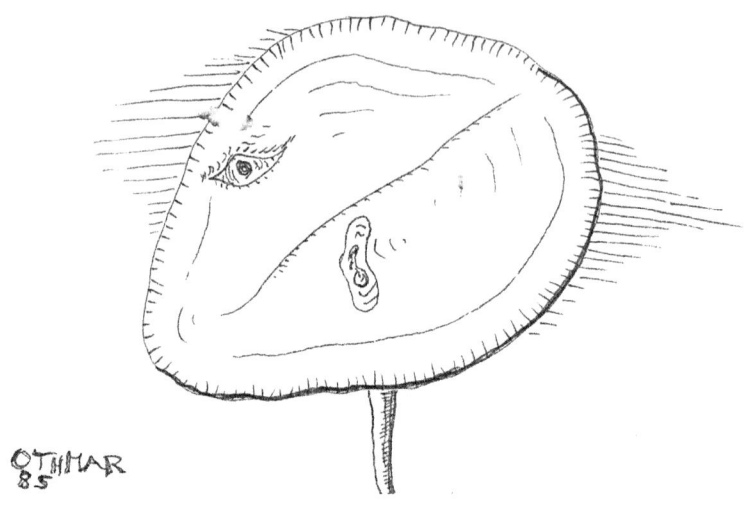

Awakening (1985) - Ink on paper - 4"x 6"

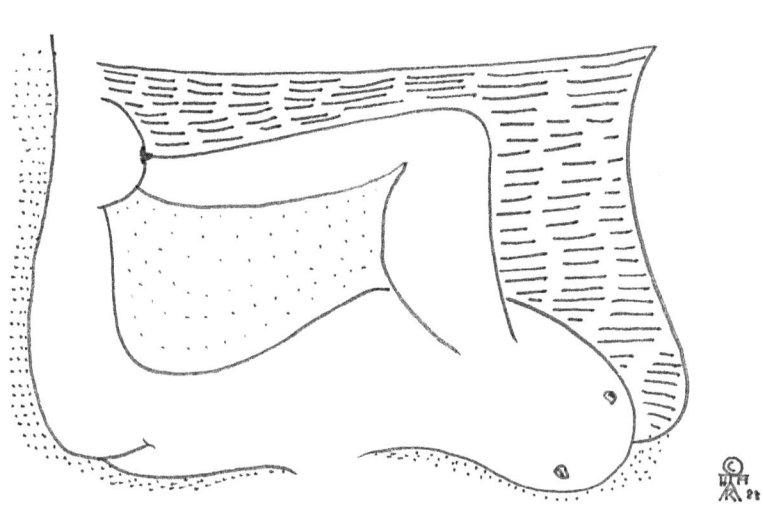

On the Beach (1988) - Ink on paper - 4"x 6"

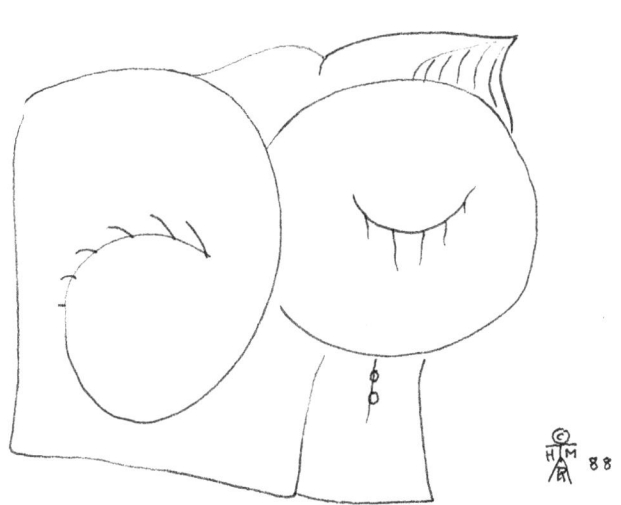

Peaceful Togetherness (1988) – Ink on paper – 4"x 6"

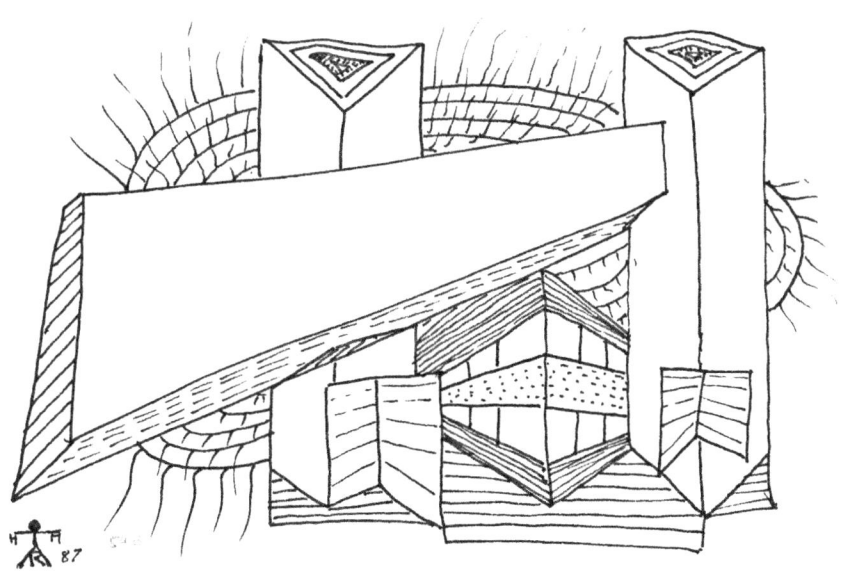

Sketch for New Dada Headquarters (1987) - Ink on paper - 4"x 6"

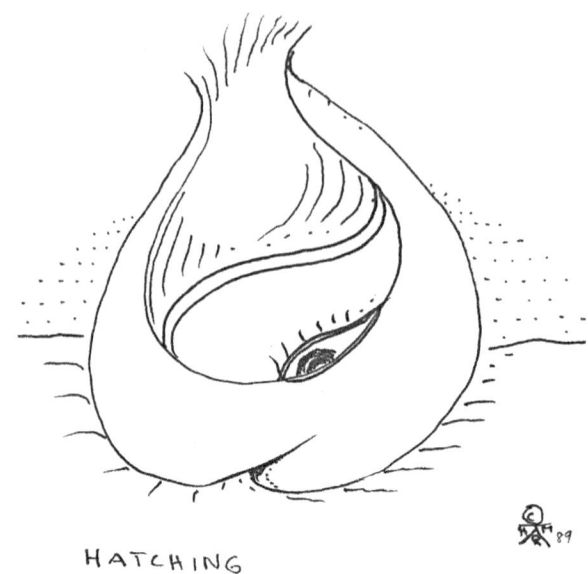

HATCHING

Hatching (1989) - Ink on paper - 4"x 4"

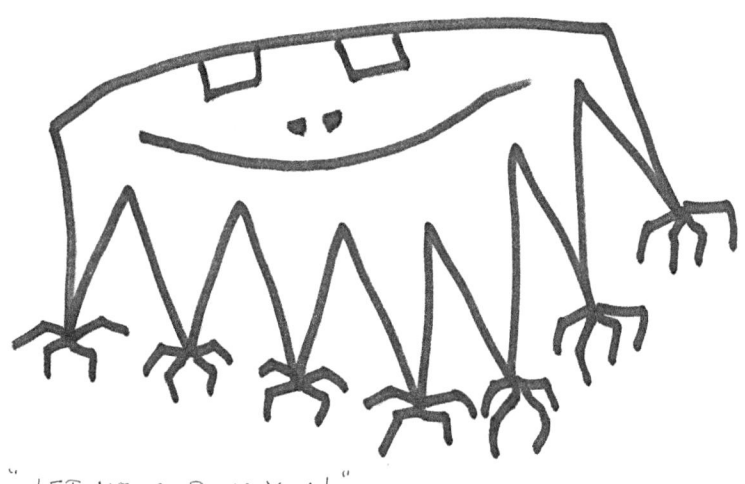

" LET ME CARESS YOU ! "

Let Me Caress You! (1989) - Ink on paper - 4"x 6"

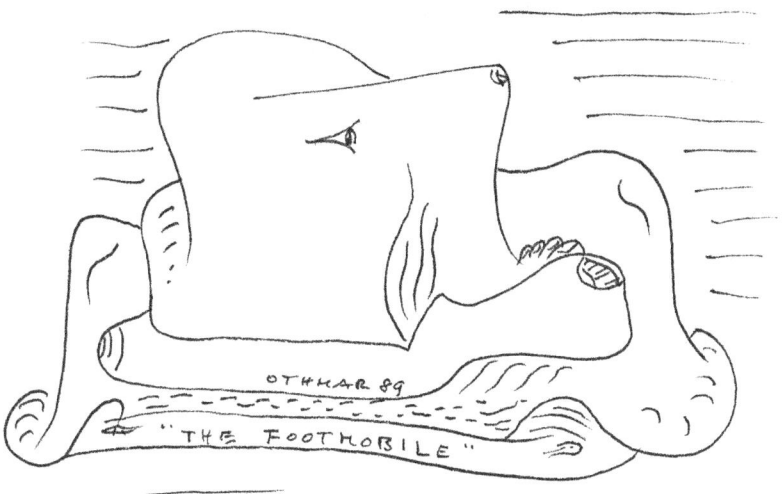

The Footmobile (1989) - Ink on paper - 4"x6"

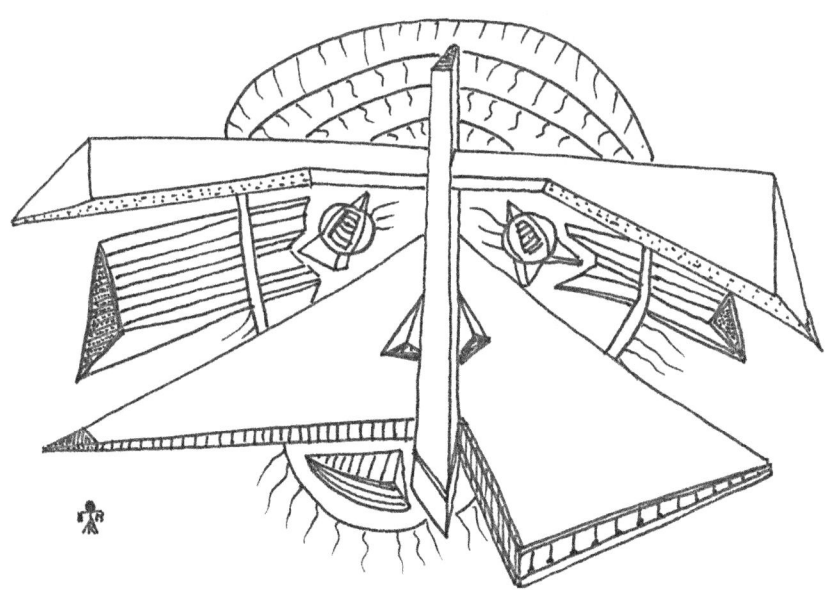

Golgotha (1988) - Ink on paper - 4"x6"

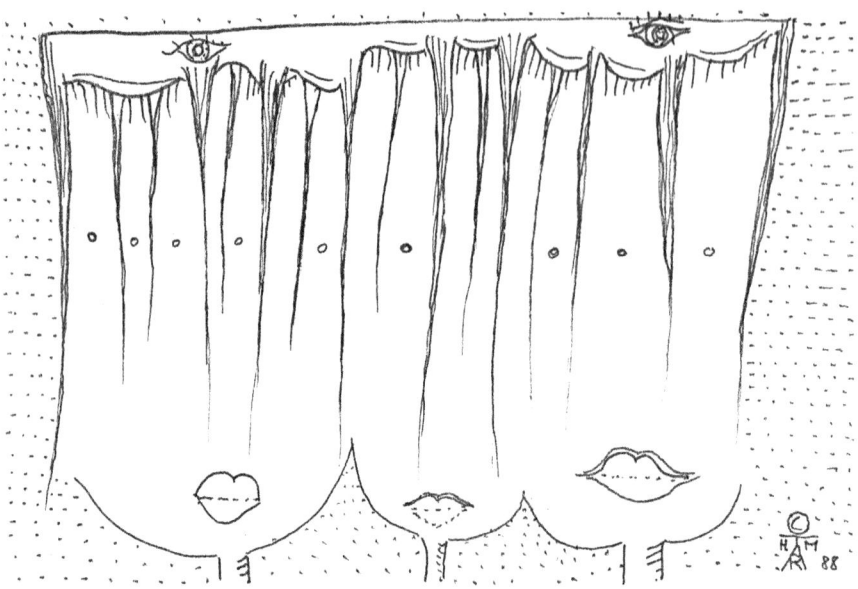

Young Ladies (1988) - Ink on paper - 4"x6"

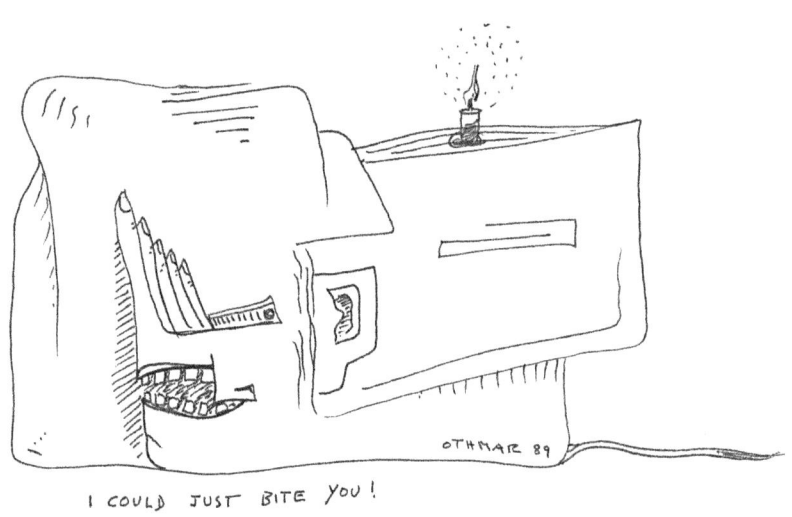

I Could Just Bite You (1989) - Ink on paper - 4"x 6"

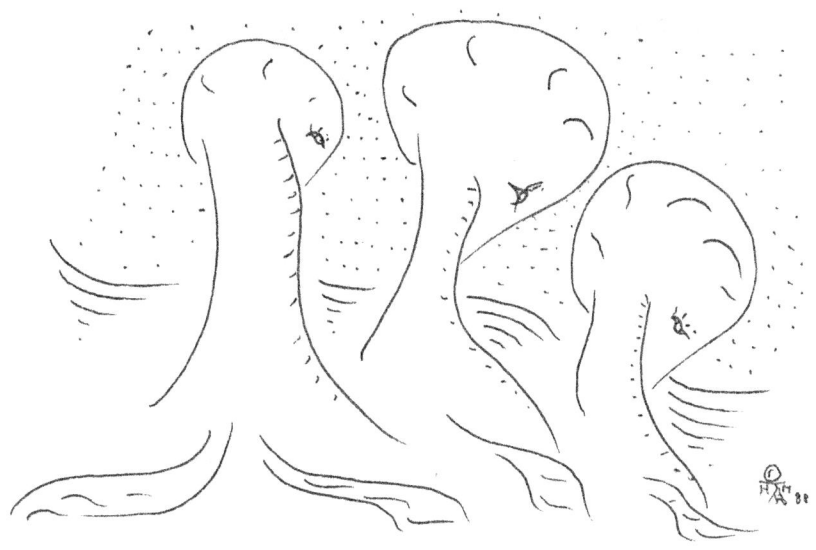

Teen Age Mushrooms (1988) - Ink on paper - 4"x6"

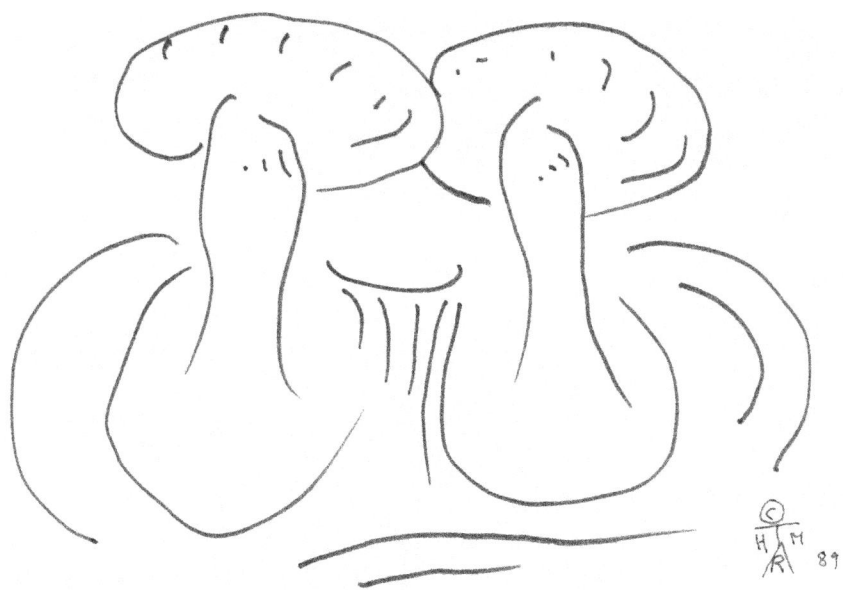

A Taste of Spring in the Air (1989) - Ink on paper - 4"x 6"

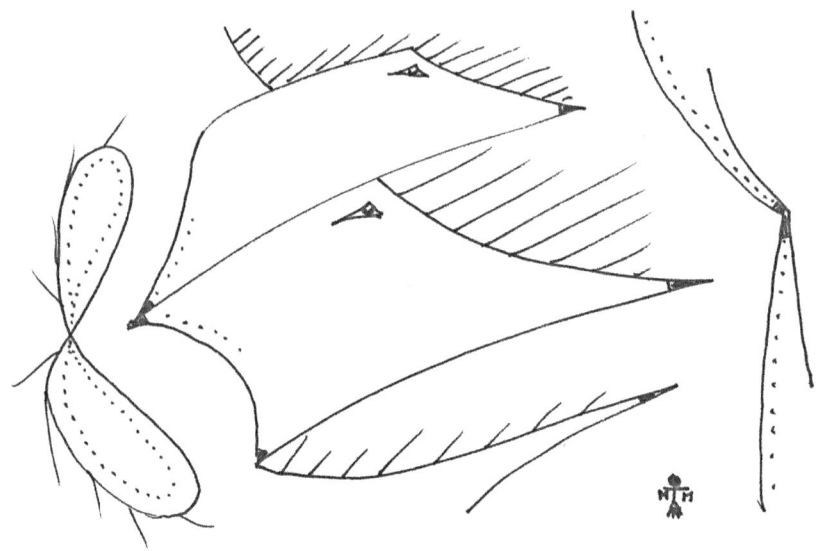

Greyhound Breeze (1988) – Ink on paper – 4"x 6"

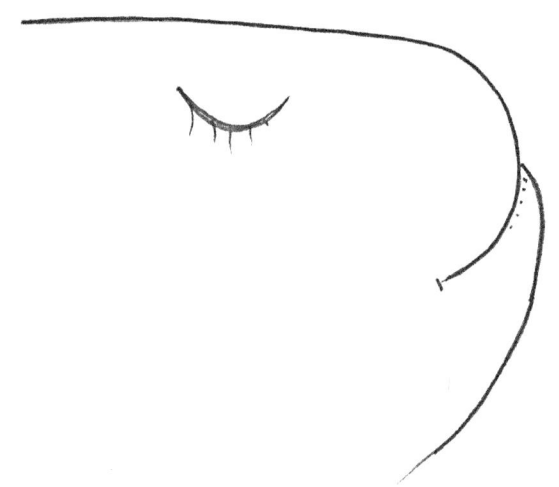

Nude Beach Impression (1988) – Ink on paper – 4"x 6"

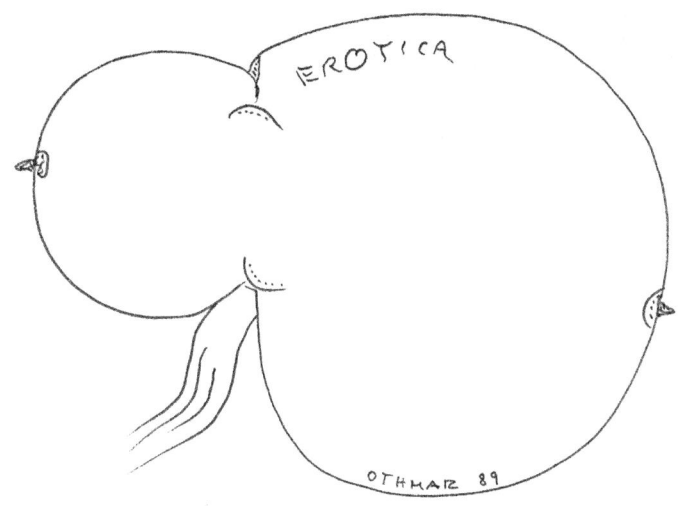

Erotica I (1989) - Ink on paper - 4"x6"

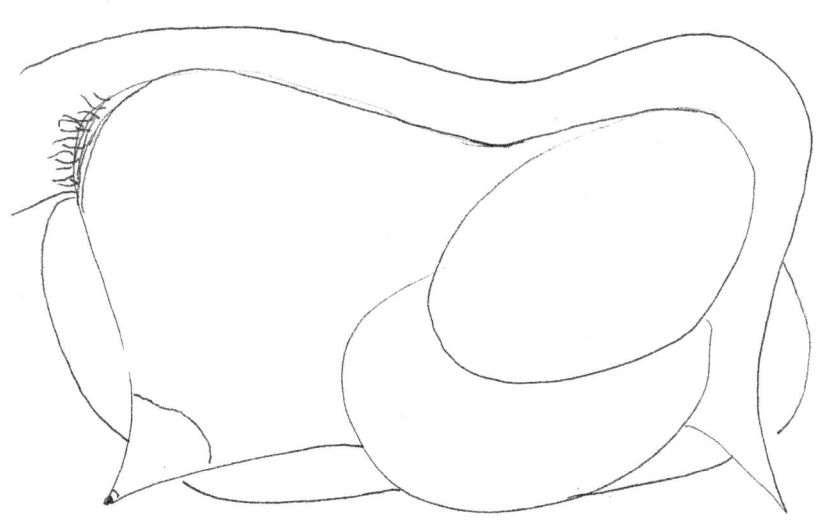

Erotica II (1989) - Ink on paper - 4"x 6"

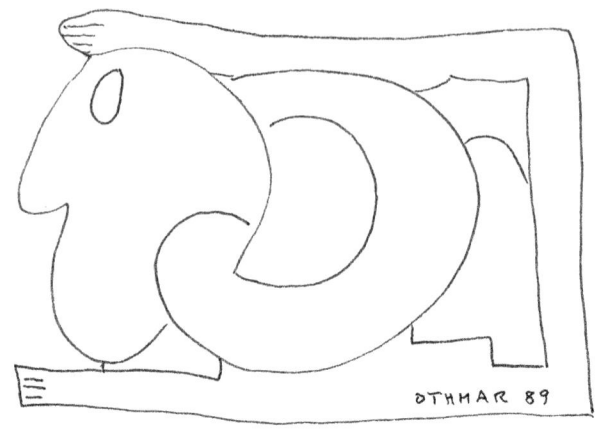

Diogenes Looking out for an Honest Man (1989)
Ink on paper - 4"x 6"

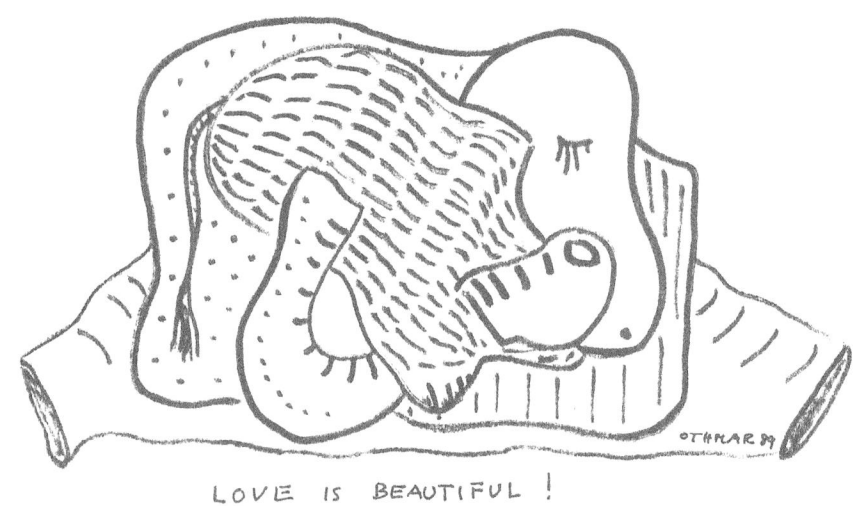

LOVE IS BEAUTIFUL !

Love is Beautiful (1989) - Ink on paper - 4"x6"

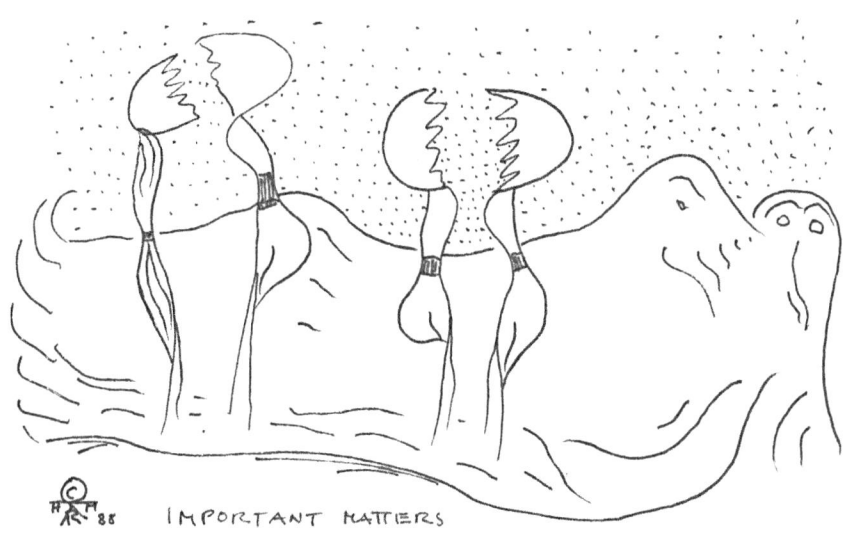

Important Matters (1989) - Ink on paper - 4"x 6"

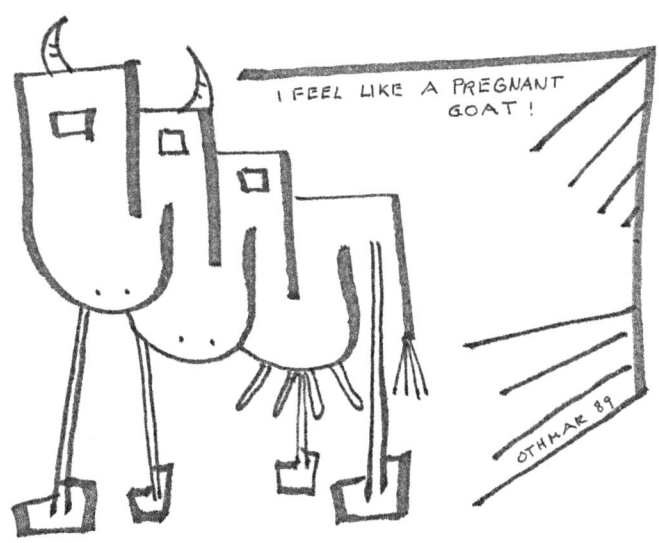

I Feel Like a Pregnant Goat! (1989) - Ink on paper - 4"x 6"

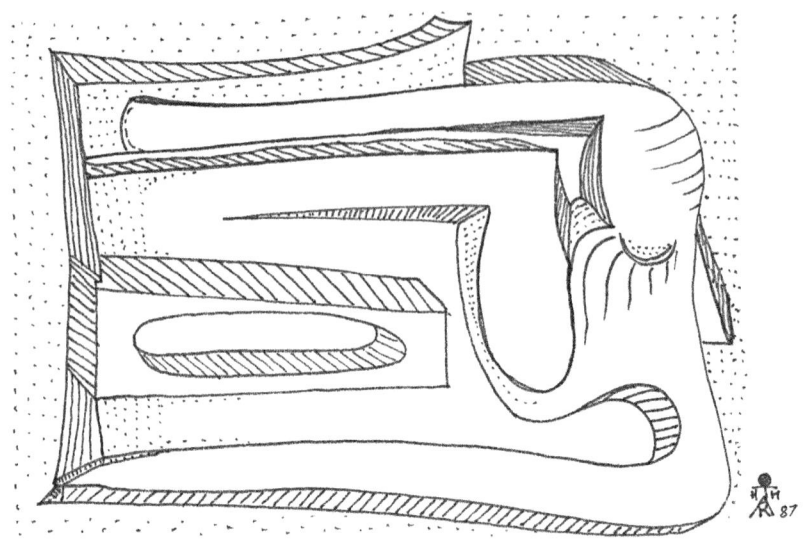

Happy Mummy (1987) – Ink on paper – 4"x 6"

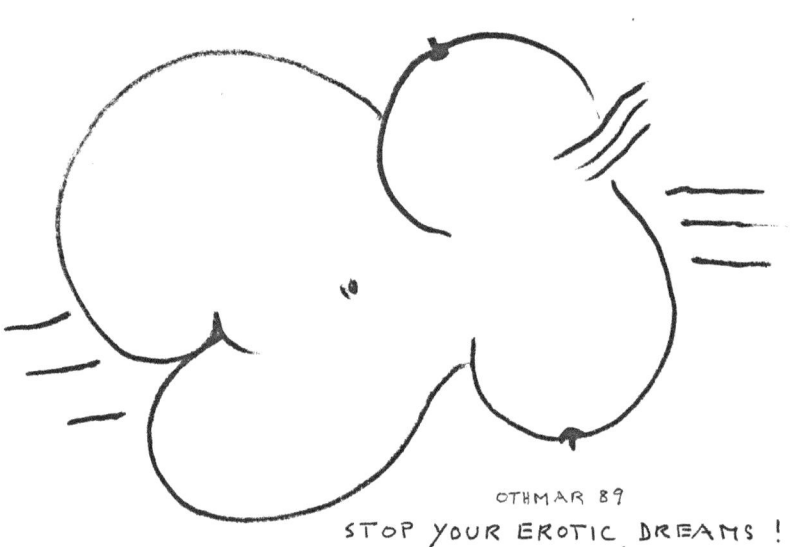

Stop Your Erotic Dreams! (1989) – Ink on paper – 4"x 6"

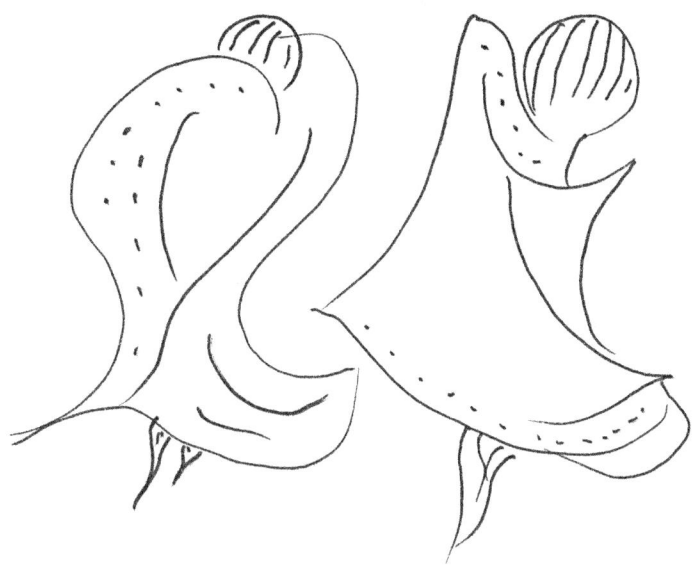

Ladies in the Snow (1987) - Ink on paper - 4"x 6"

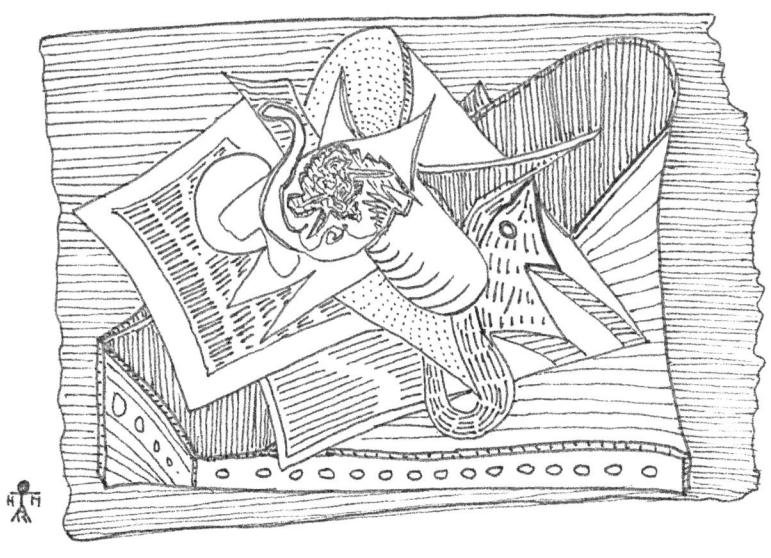

Happy Birthday! (1987) - Ink on paper - 4"x 6"

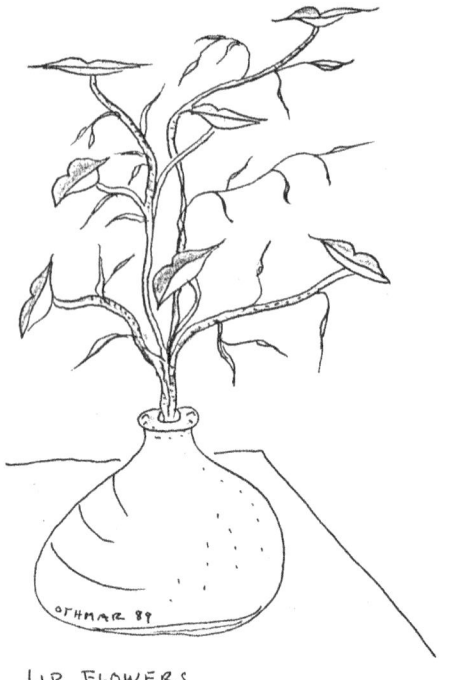

LIP FLOWERS

Lip Flowers (1988)
Ink on Paper - 6"x 4"
(Reduced Size)

The Explorobile (1989)
Ink on Paper - 6"x 4"
(Reduced Size)

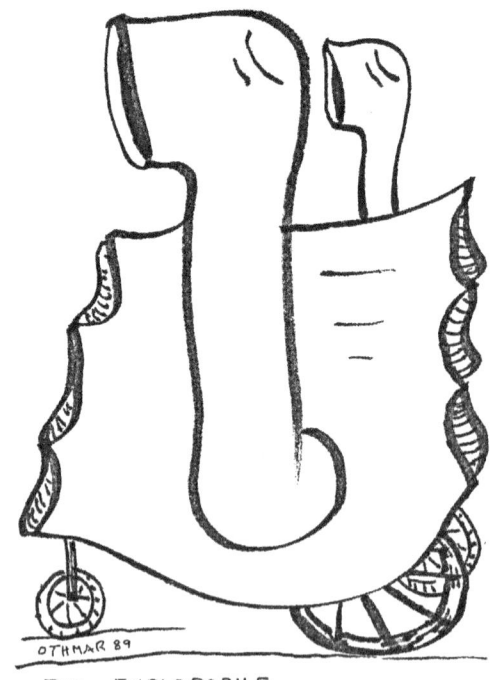

THE EXPLOROBILE

Australian Finger Toe Tree (1989)
Ink on Paper - 6"x 4"
(Reduced Size)

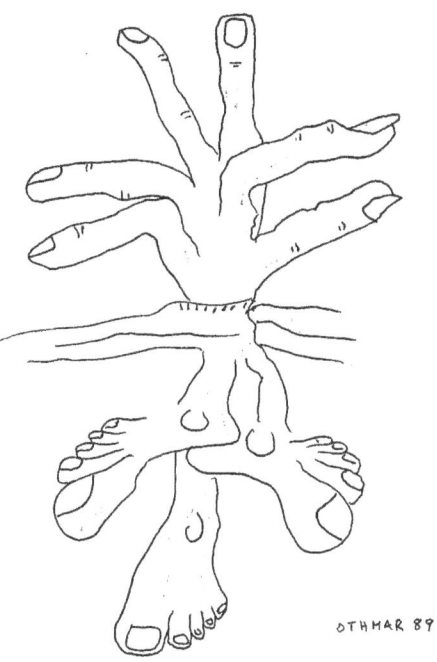

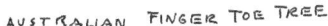

Halloween II (1989)
Ink on Paper - 6"x 4"
(Reduced Size)

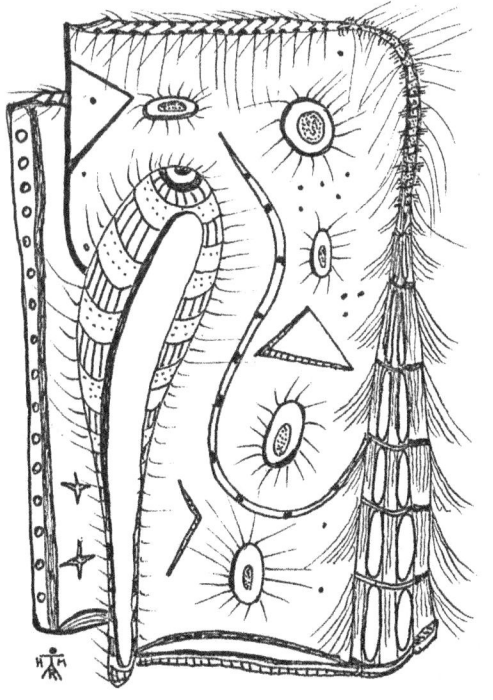

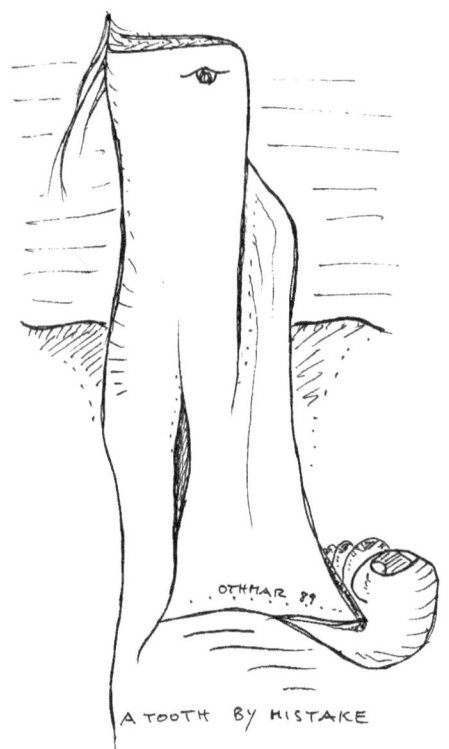

A Tooth By Mistake (1989)
Ink on Paper - 6"x 4"
(Reduced Size)

Squirrel & Co. (1989)
Ink on Paper - 6"x 4"
(Reduced Size)

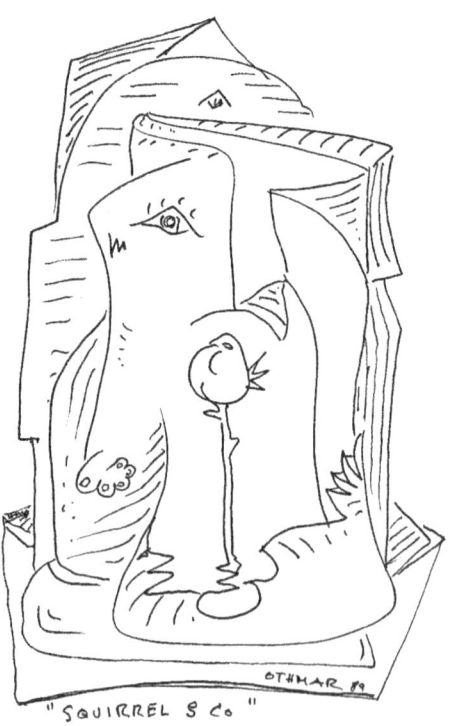

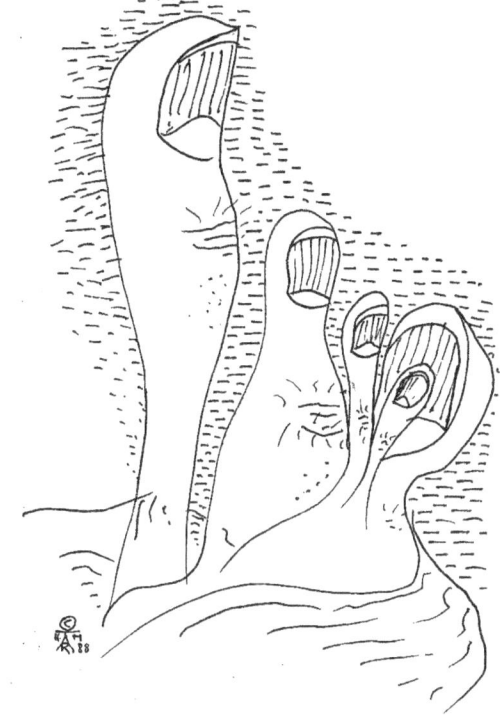

Finger Mountains at Sunrise (1989)
Ink on Paper - 6"x 4"
(Reduced Size)

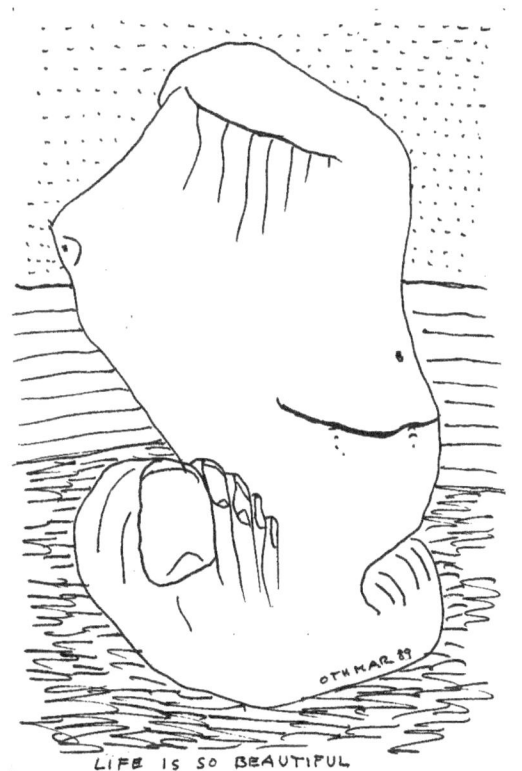

Life is so Beautiful (1989)
Ink on Paper - 6"x 4"
(Reduced Size)

LIFE IS SO BEAUTIFUL

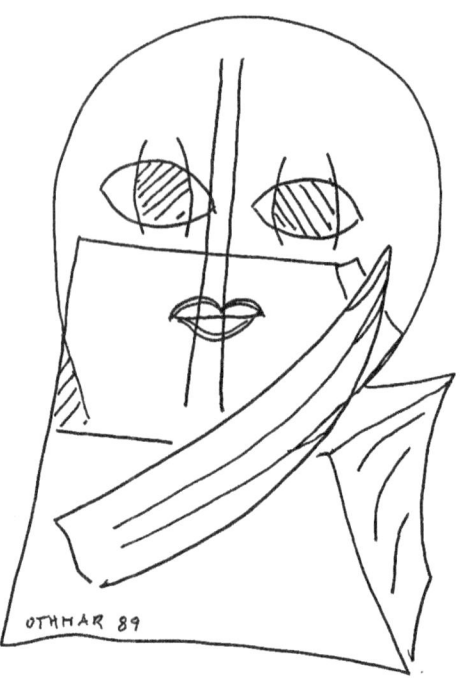

Mlle. Pogany (1989)
Ink on Paper - 6"x 4"
(Reduced Size)

A Big Hurdle (1989)
Ink on Paper - 6"x 4"
(Reduced Size)

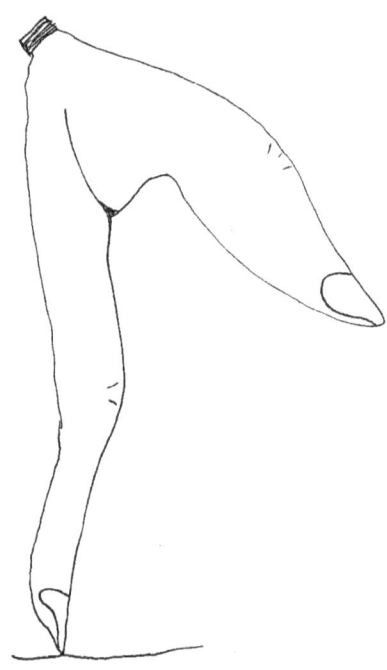

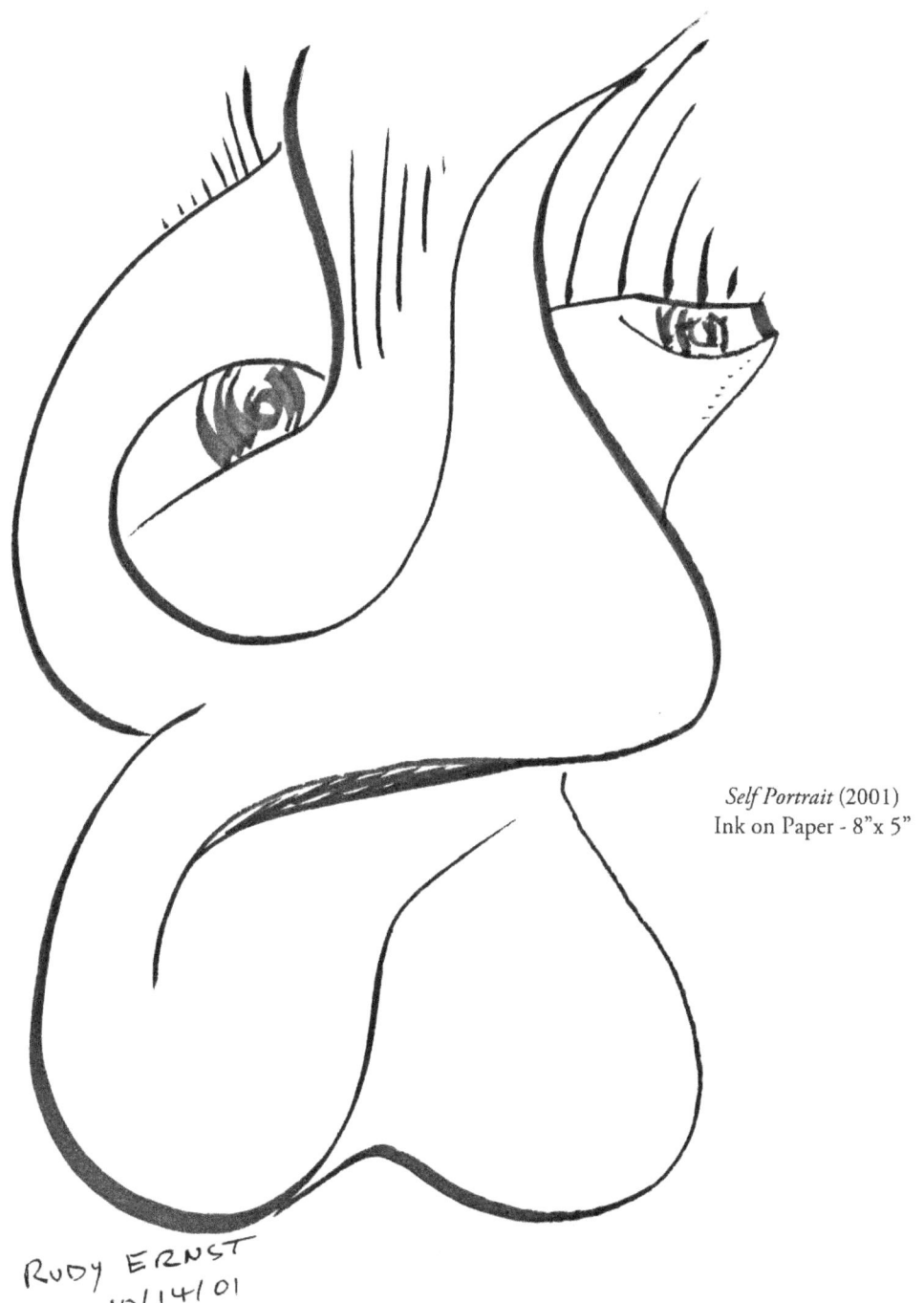

Self Portrait (2001)
Ink on Paper - 8"x 5"

RUDY ERNST
10/14/01

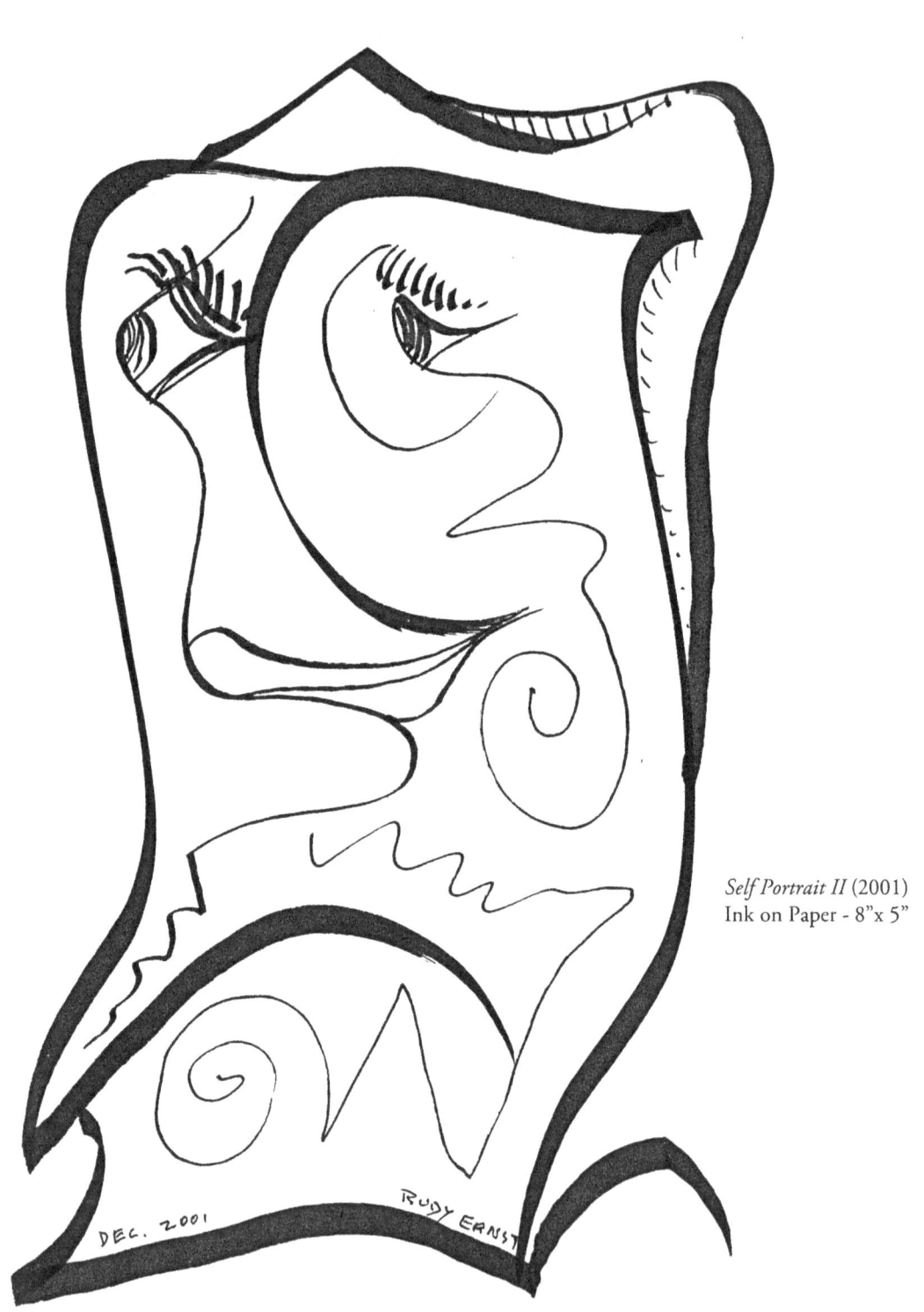

Self Portrait II (2001)
Ink on Paper - 8"x 5"

DEC. 2001   RUDY ERNST

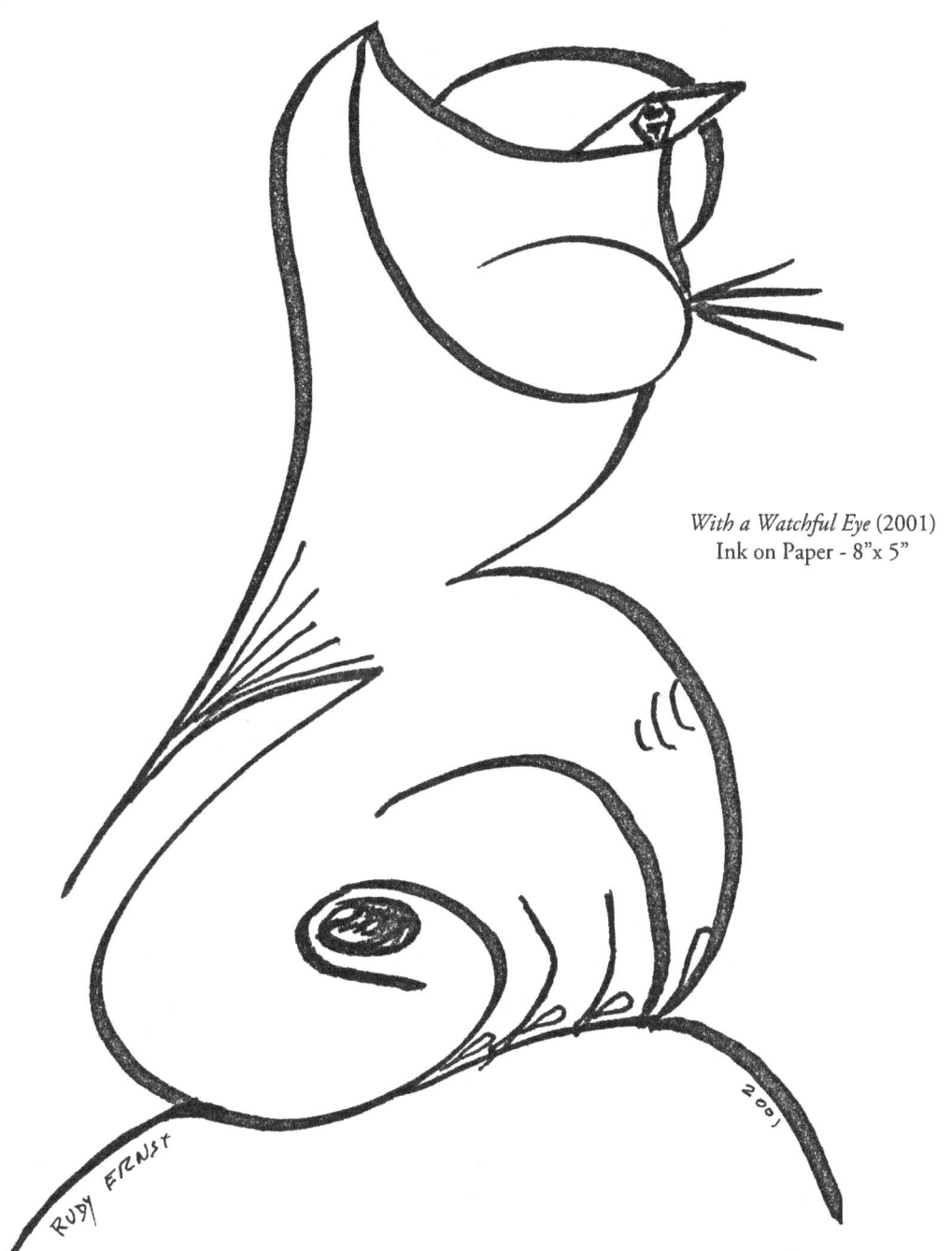

With a Watchful Eye (2001)
Ink on Paper - 8"x 5"

RUDY ERNST

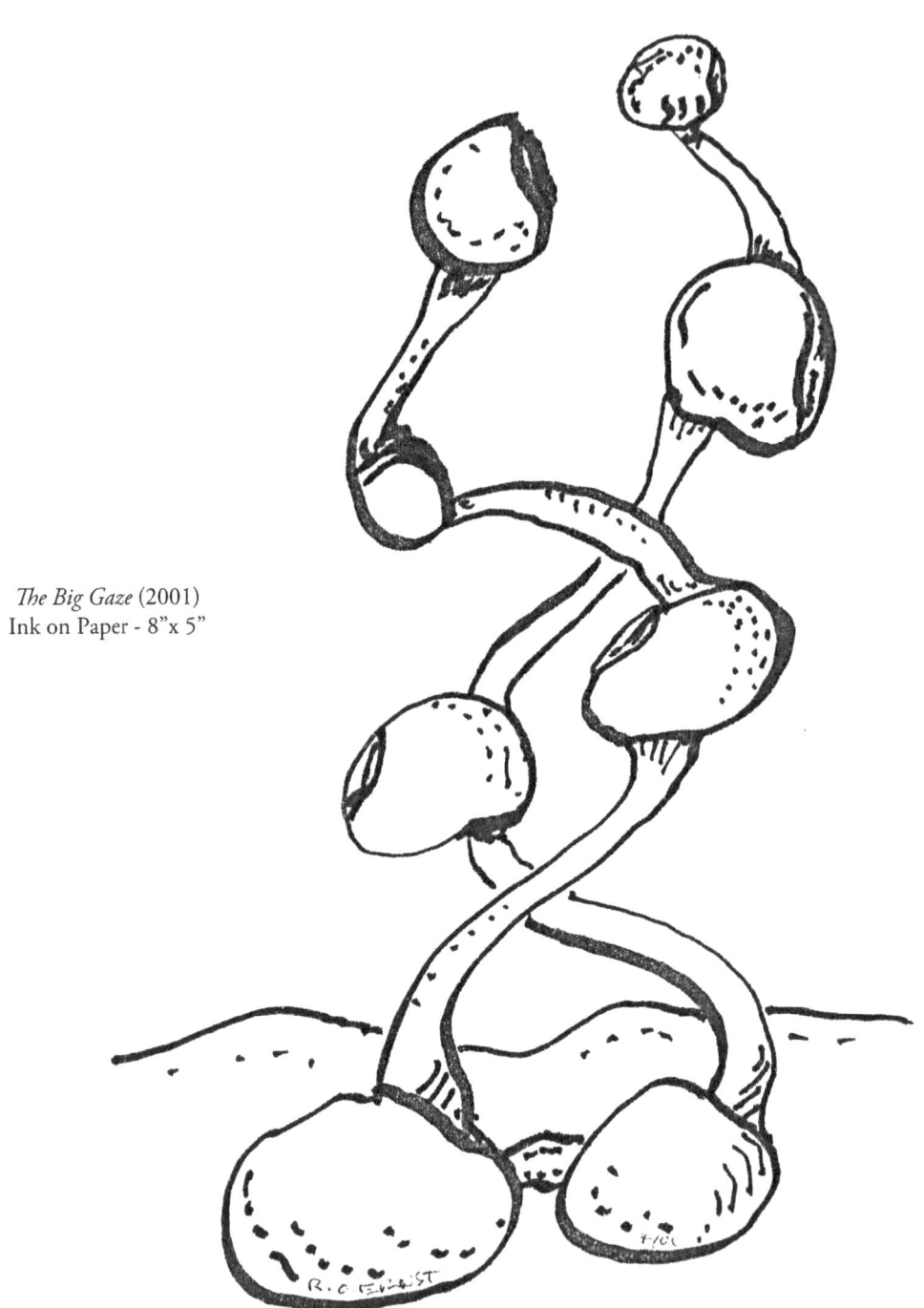

The Big Gaze (2001)
Ink on Paper - 8"x 5"

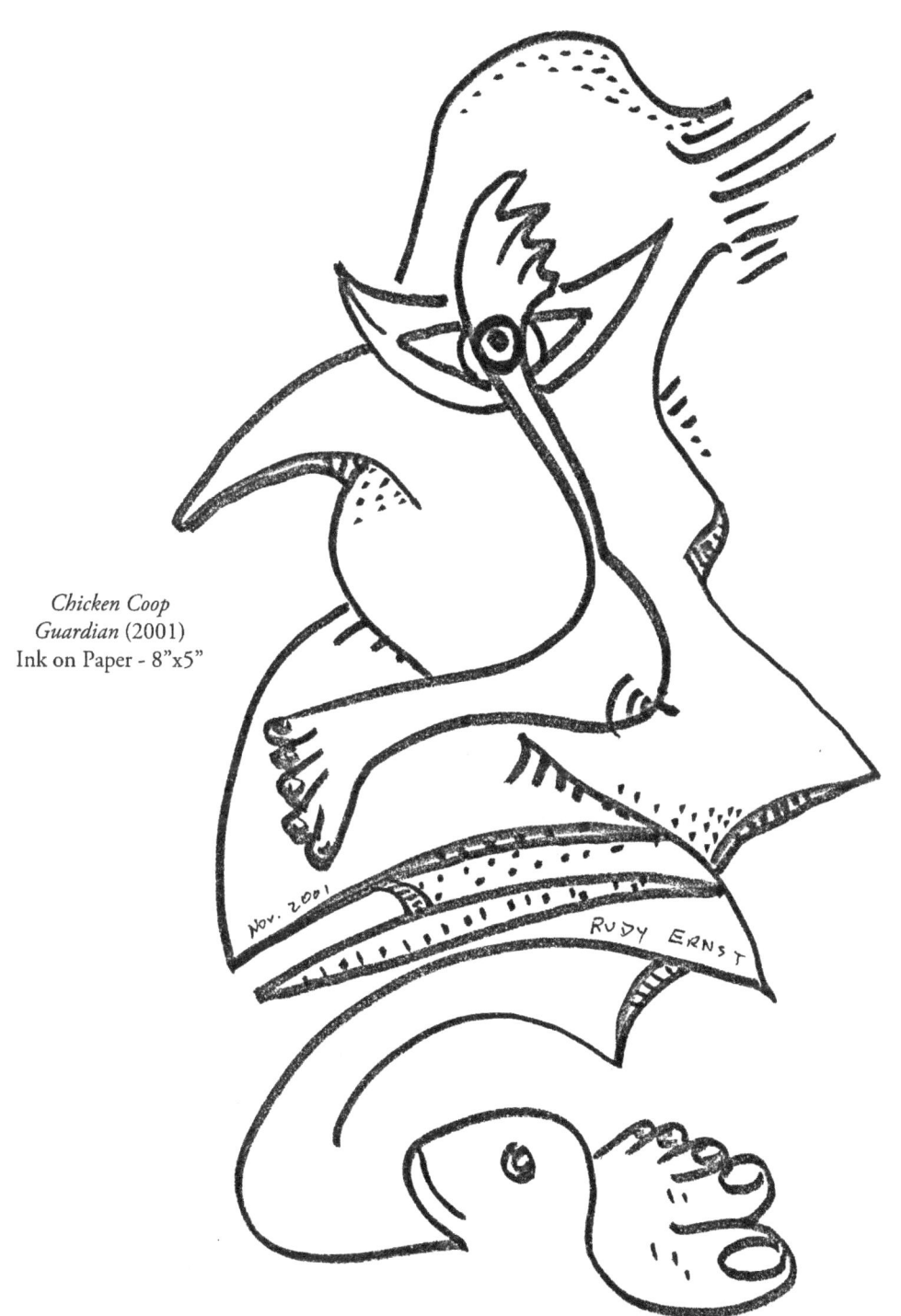

Chicken Coop
Guardian (2001)
Ink on Paper - 8"x5"

Nov. 2001

RUDY ERNST

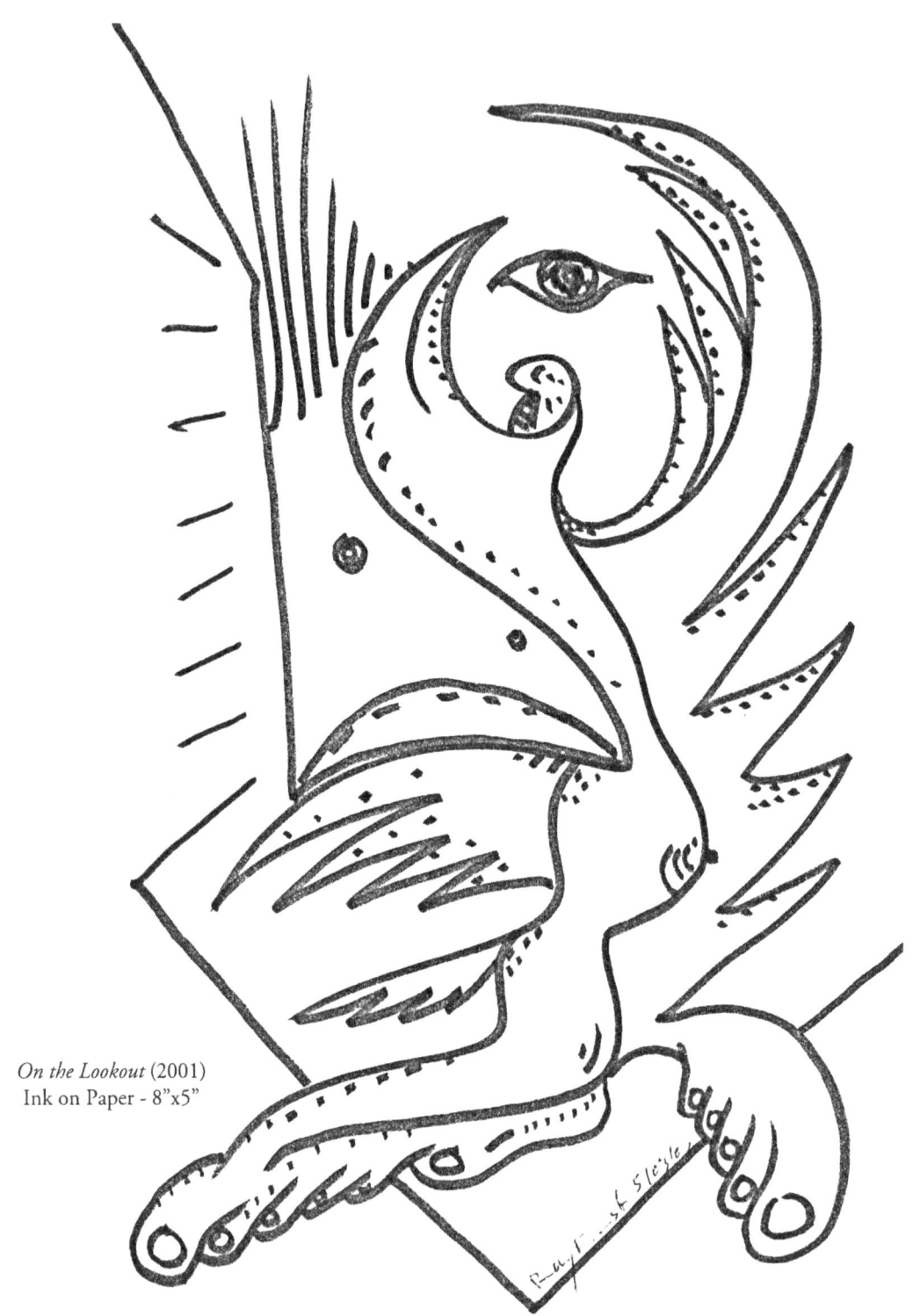

On the Lookout (2001)
Ink on Paper - 8"x5"

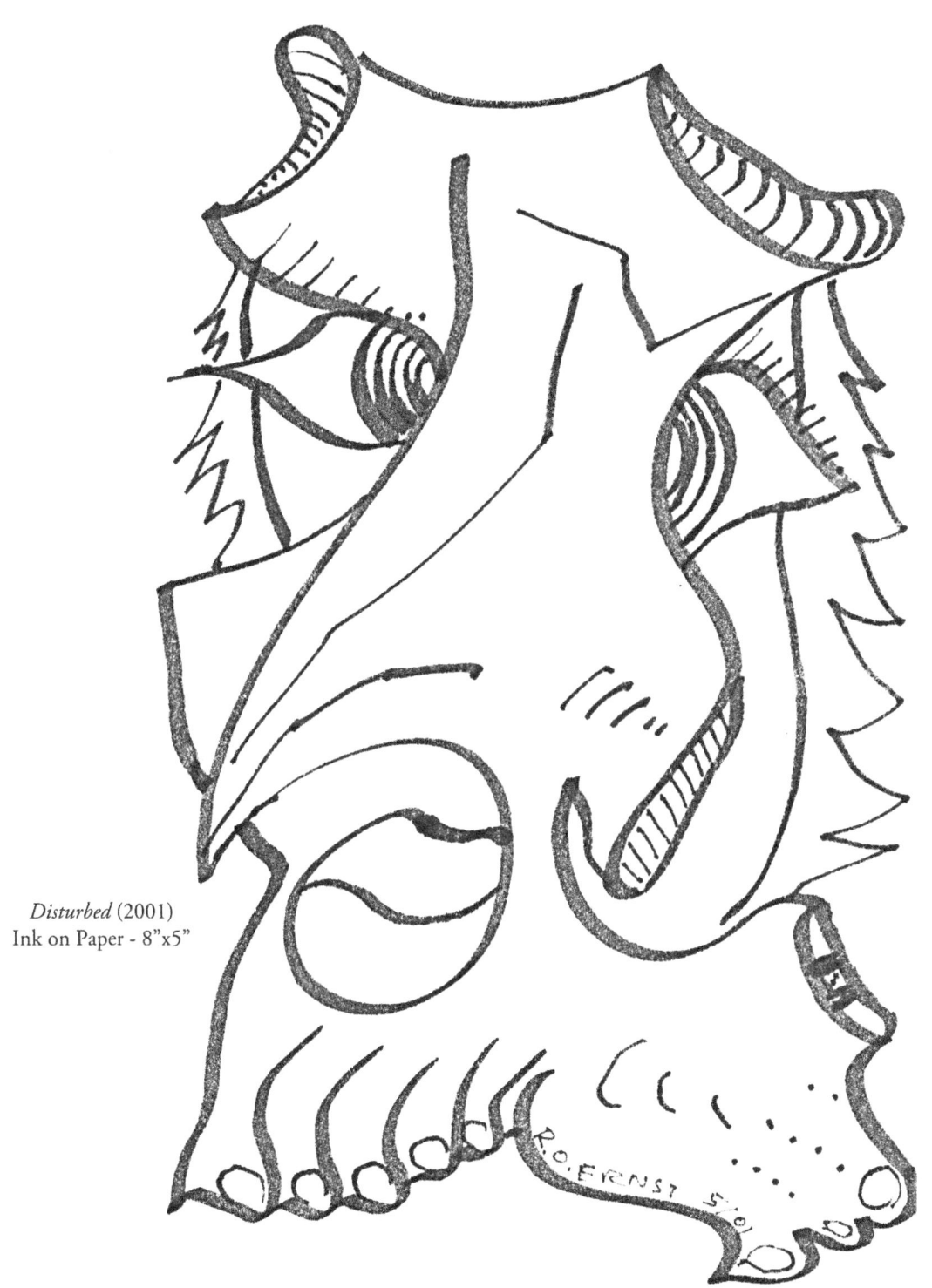

Disturbed (2001)
Ink on Paper - 8"x5"

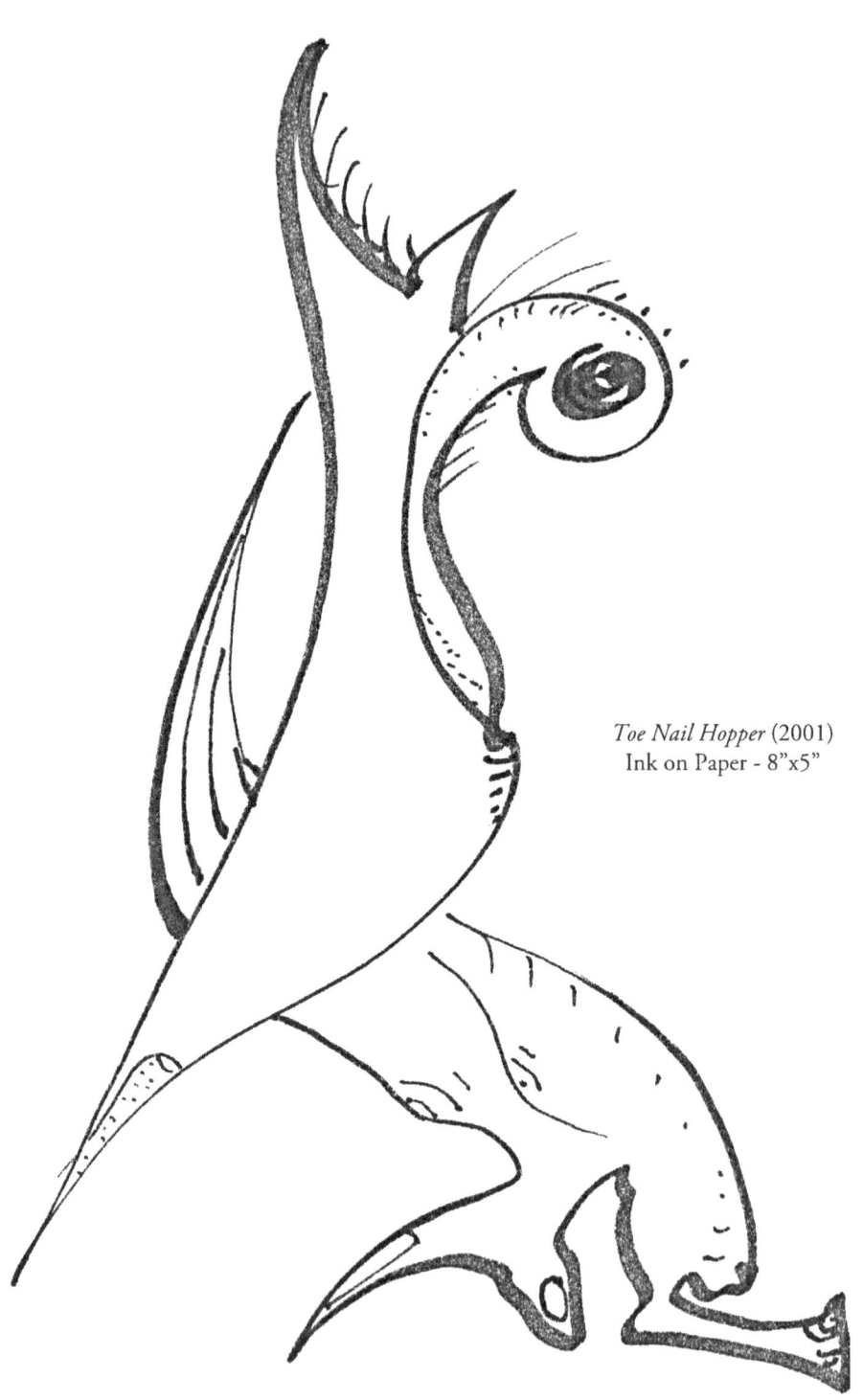

Toe Nail Hopper (2001)
Ink on Paper - 8"x5"

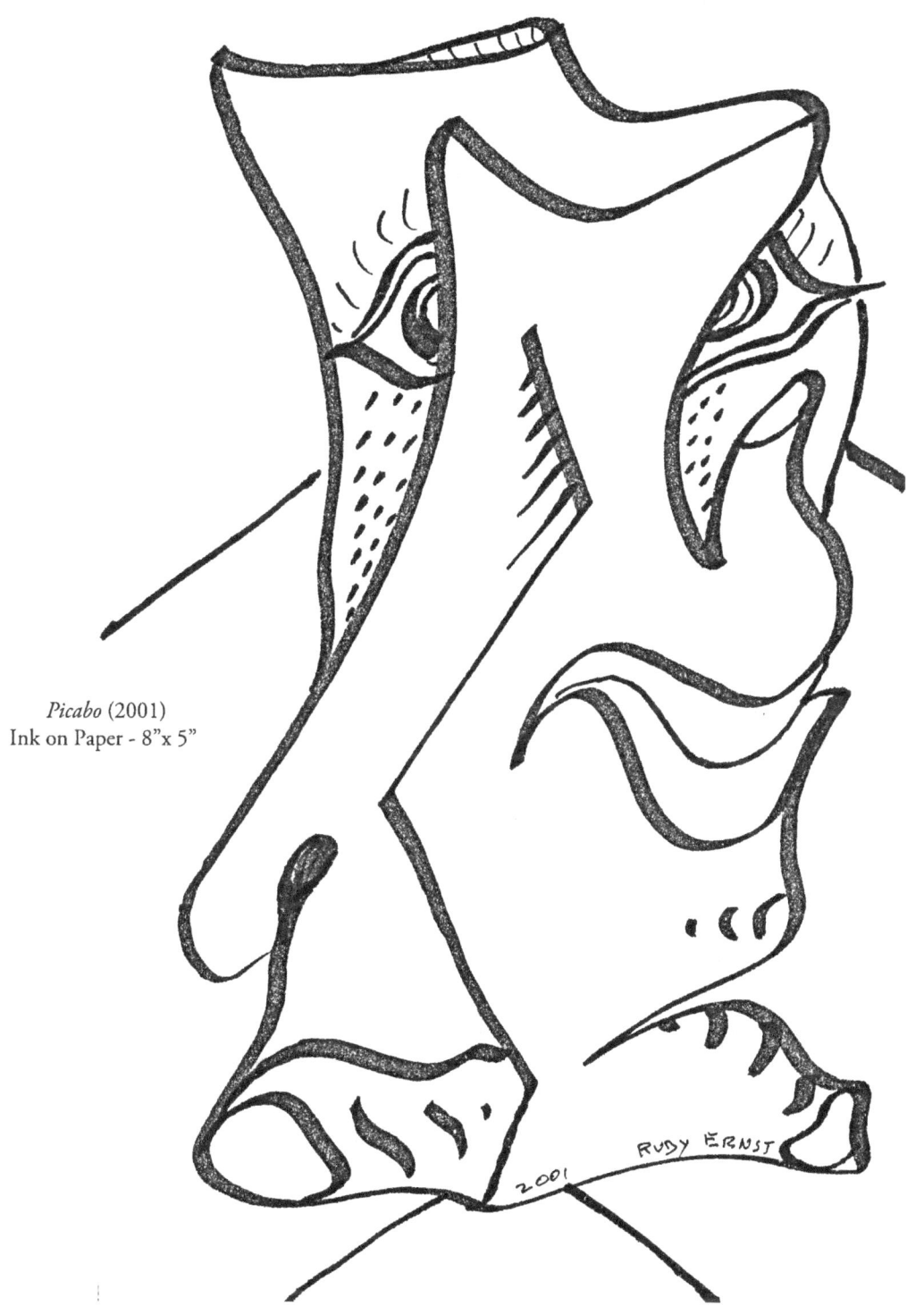

Picabo (2001)
Ink on Paper - 8"x 5"

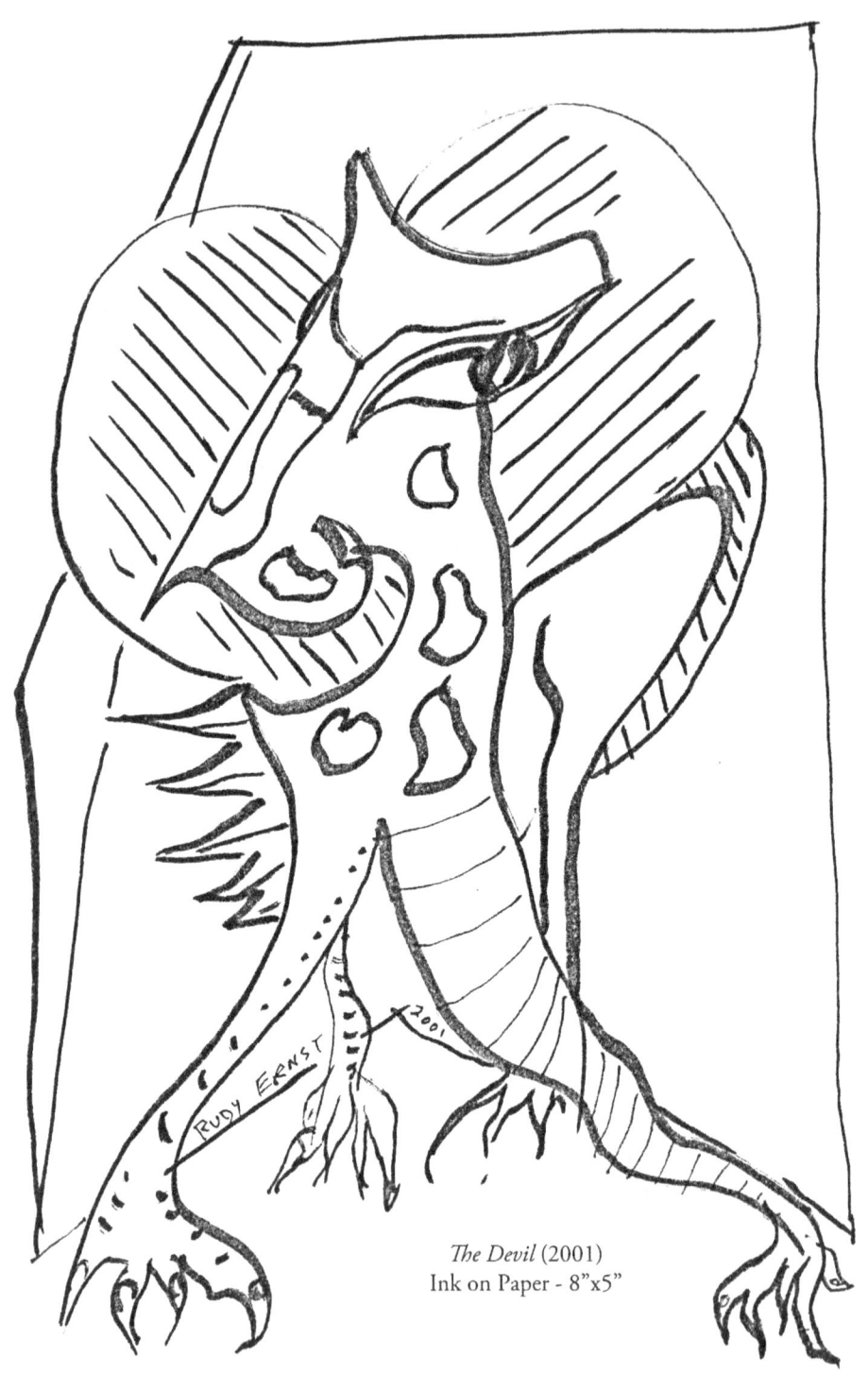

The Devil (2001)
Ink on Paper - 8"x5"

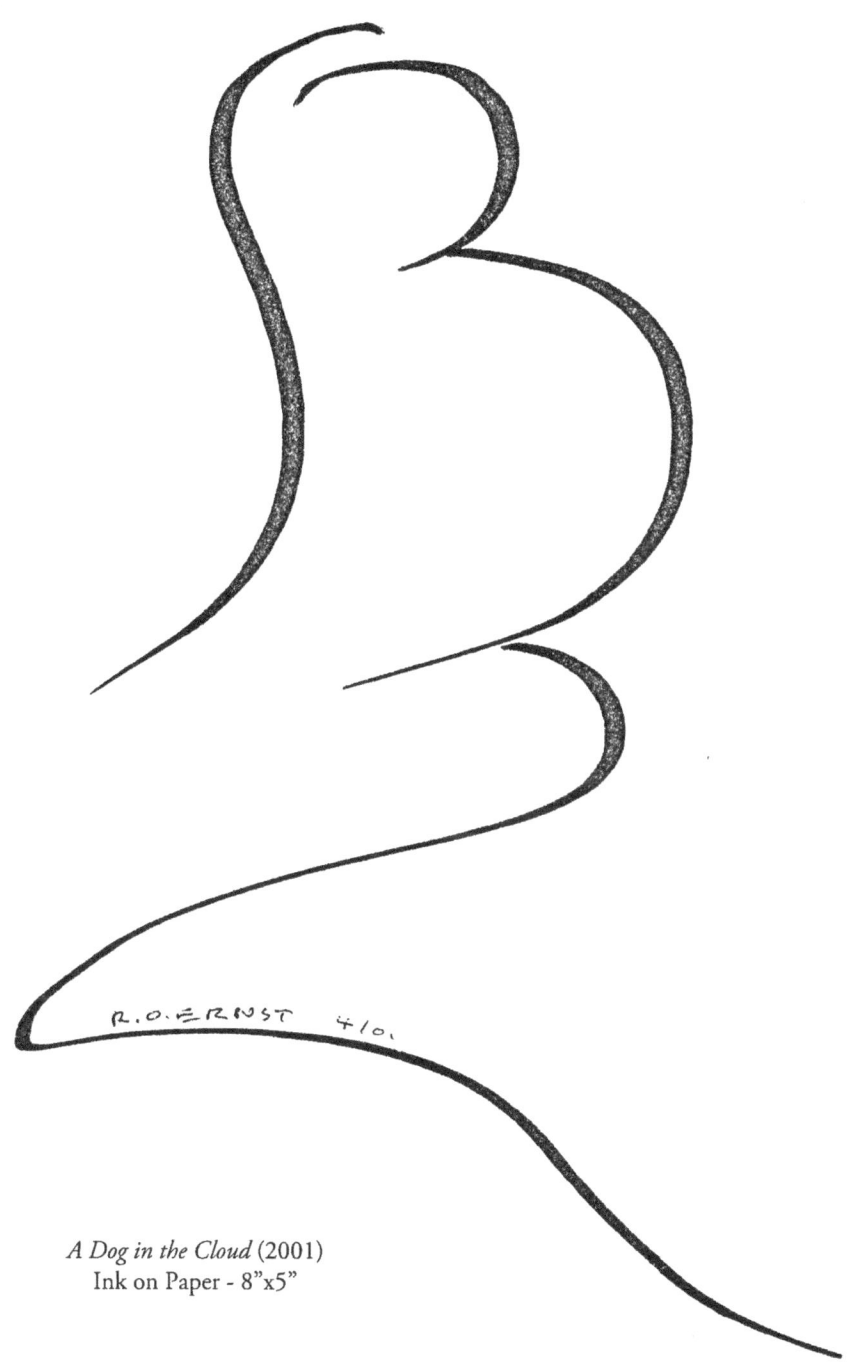

A Dog in the Cloud (2001)
Ink on Paper - 8"x5"

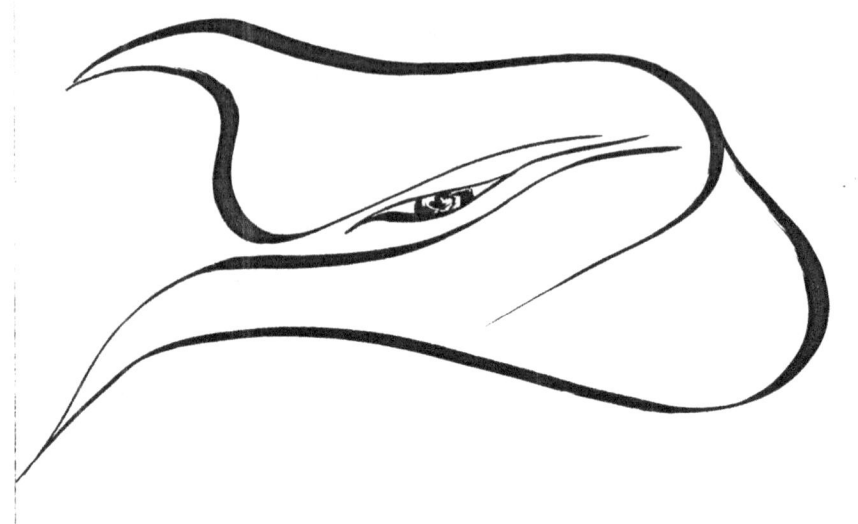

Wind Currents (1987) - Ink on Paper - 5"x 8"
(Reduced Size)

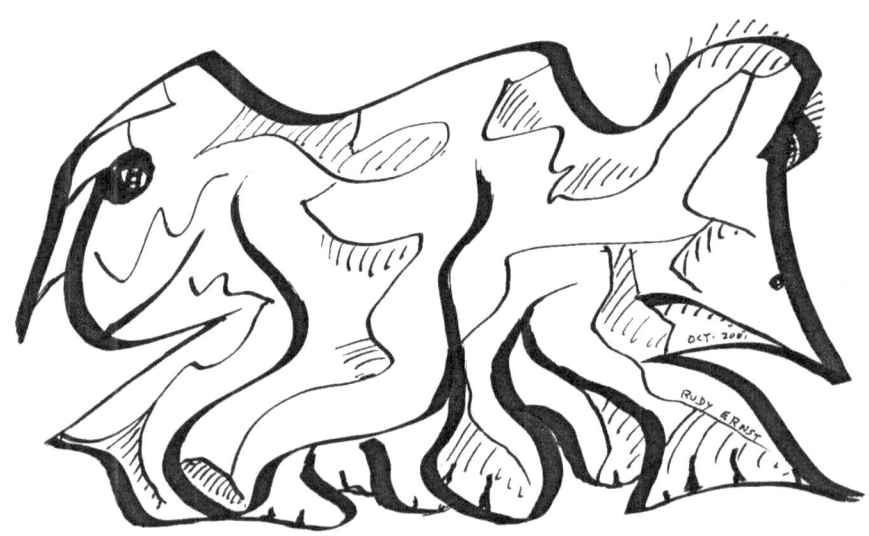

Two Way Puzzle (2001) - Ink on Paper - 5"x8"
(Reduced Size)

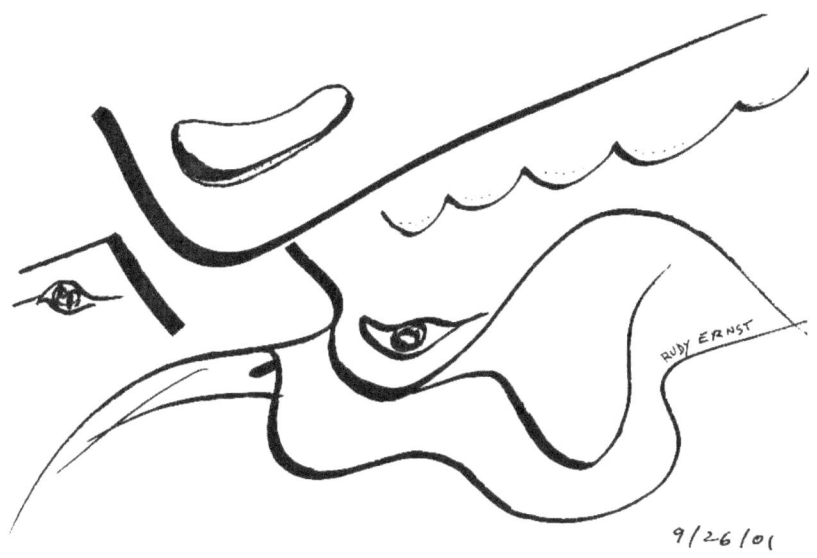

An Eagle in the Sky (2001) - Ink on Paper - 5"x8"
(Reduced Size)

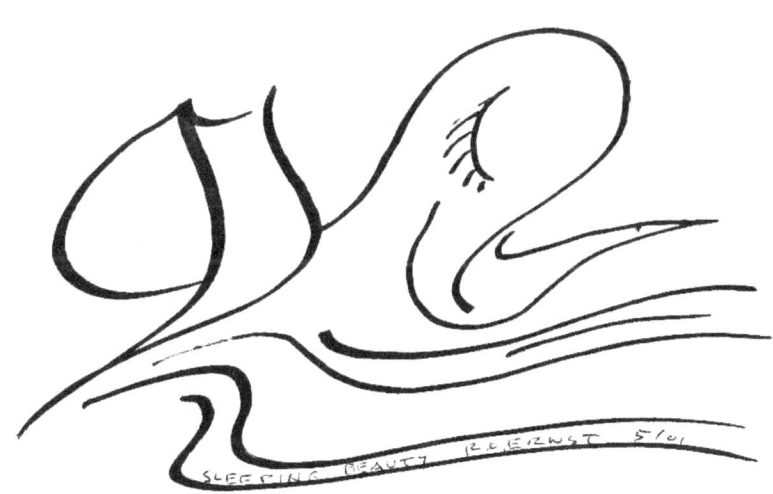

Somebody Watches over You! (2001) - Ink on Paper - 5"x8"
(Reduced Size)

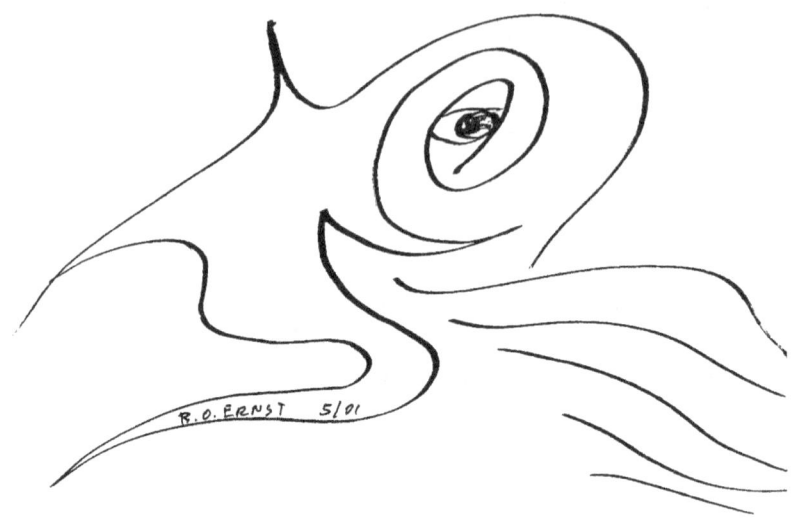

Keep Smiling! (2001) - Ink on Paper - 4"x 6"
(Reduced Size)

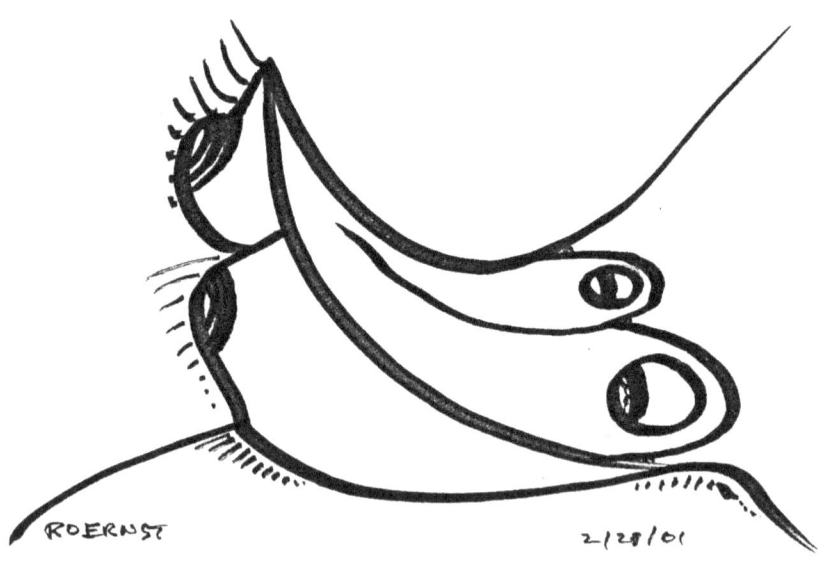

Eye-Toe Symphony (2001) - Ink on Paper - 5"x 8"
(Reduced Size)

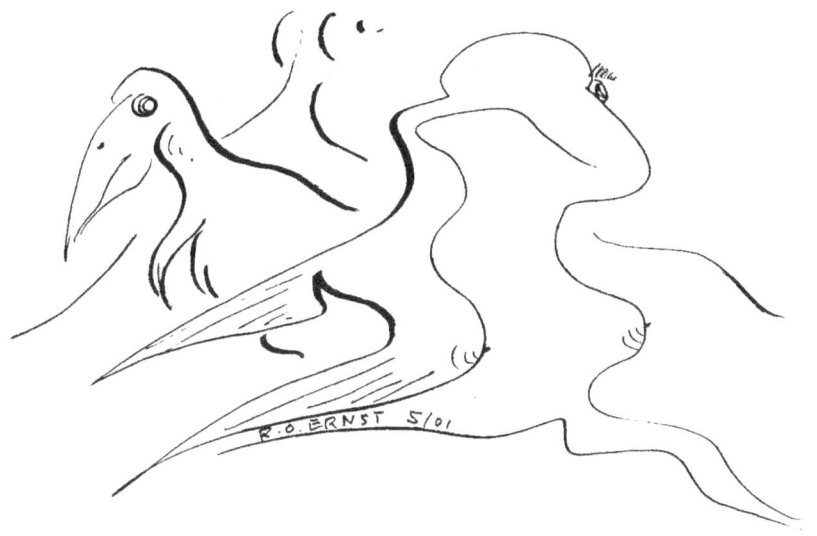

Paleontological (2001) - Ink on Paper - 5"x 8"

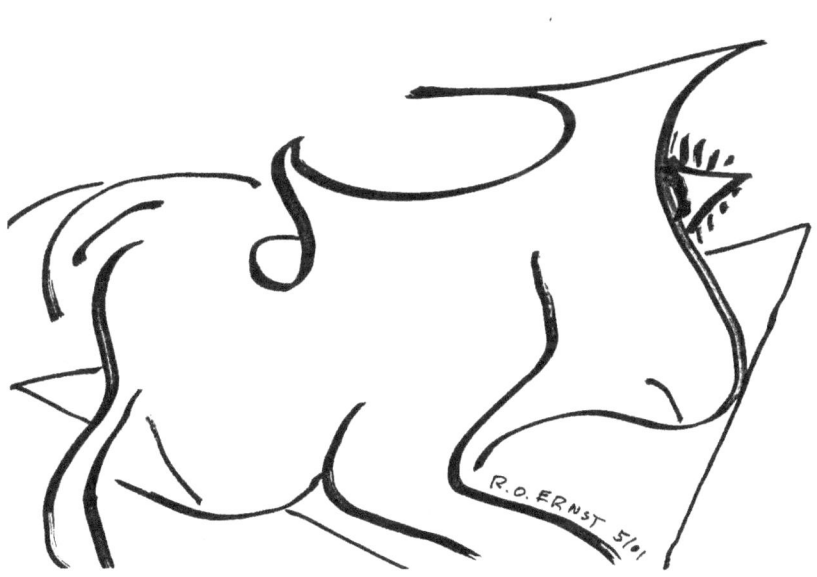

Teen Age Bull (2001) - Ink on Paper - 5"x 8"

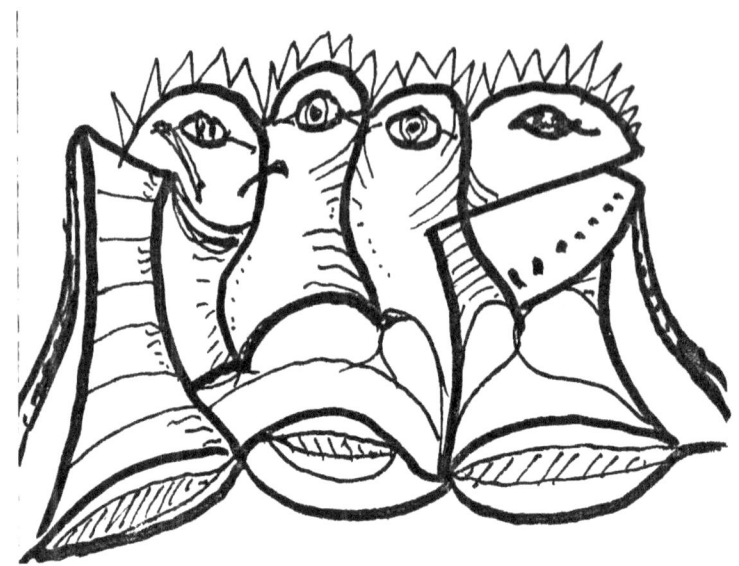

Double Talk (2008)
Ink on Paper - 2.25"x 4"

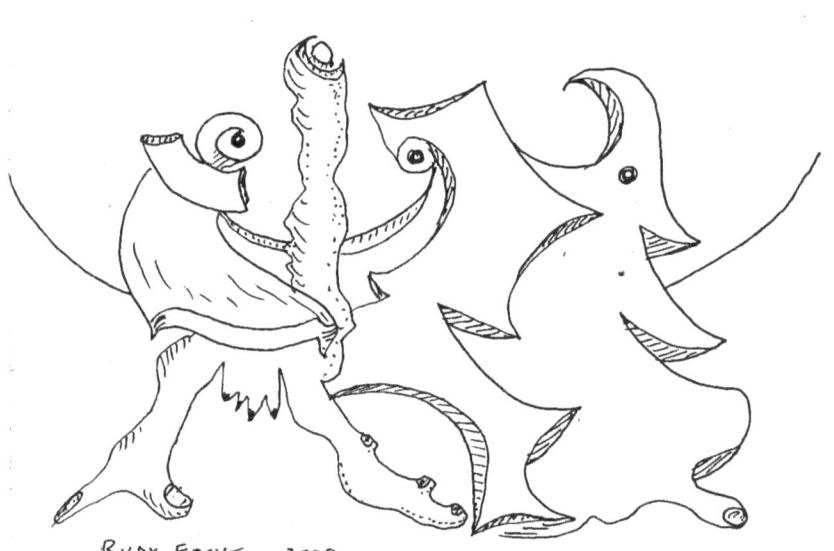

Milking the Goat (2008)
Ink on Paper - 4"x 6"

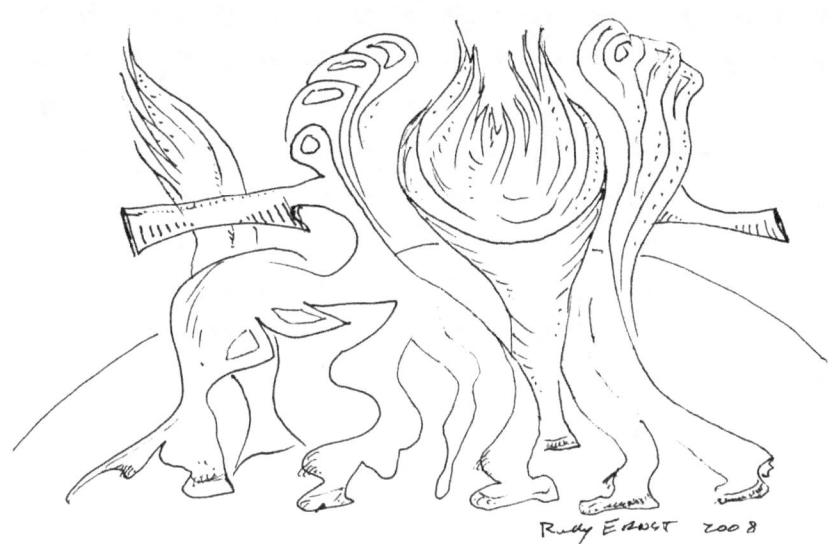

Ancient Sacrifice (2008)
Ink on Paper 4"x 6"

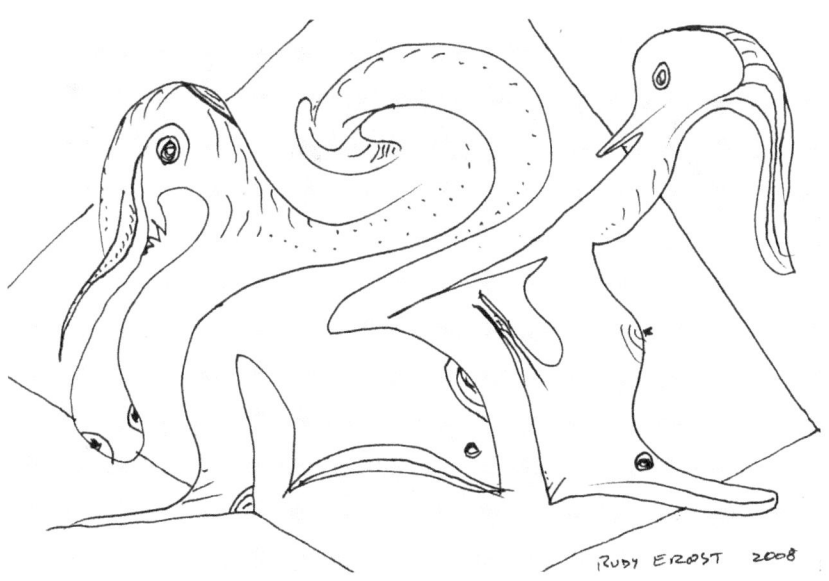

Teen Age Girl Entering the Cold Water (2008)
Ink on Paper 4"x 6"

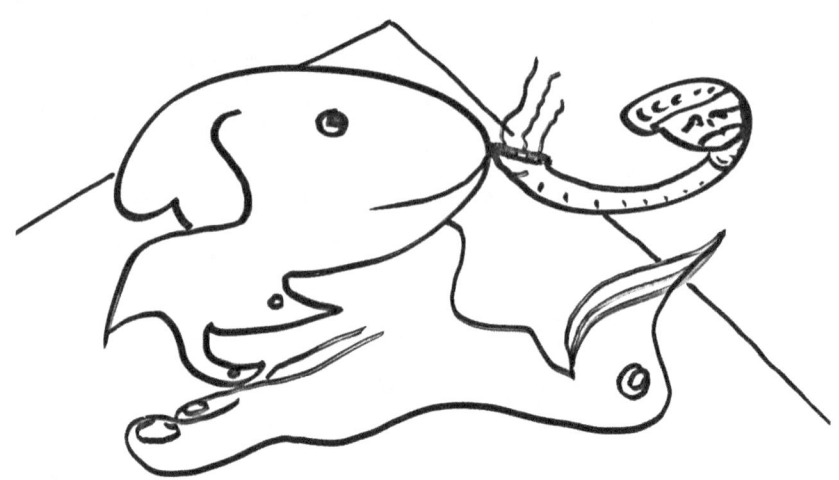

The First Cigar (2008)
Ink on Paper - 5"x8"

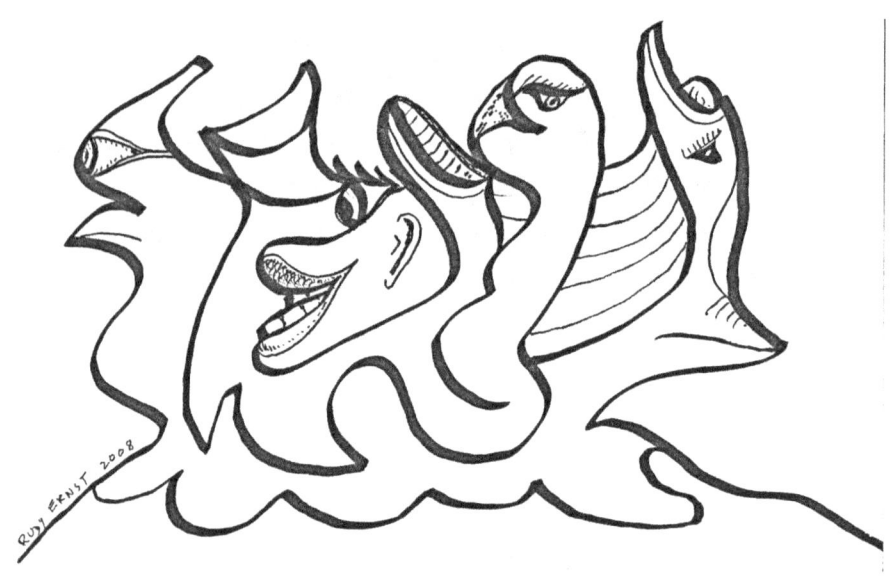

A Peaceful Crowd (2008)
Ink on Paper - 5"x 8"

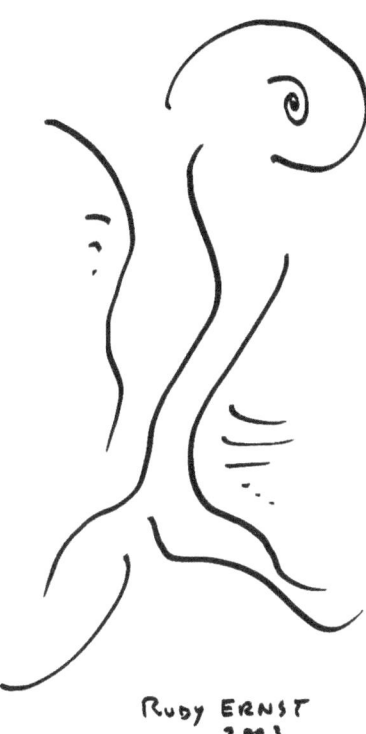

Bypasser (2003)
Ink on Paper - 8"x 5"

Happy Man
With Angry Woman (2003)
Ink on Paper - 8"x 5"

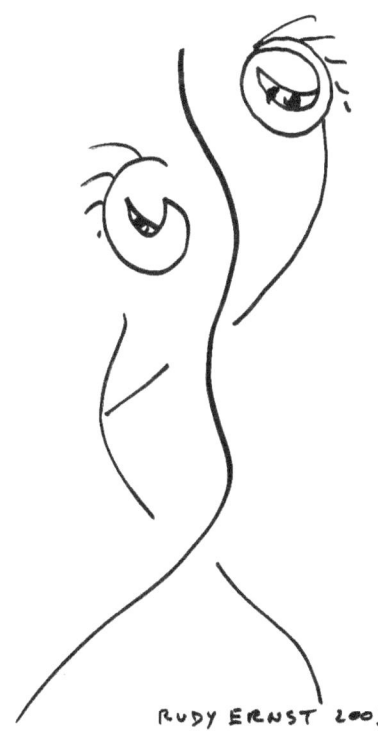

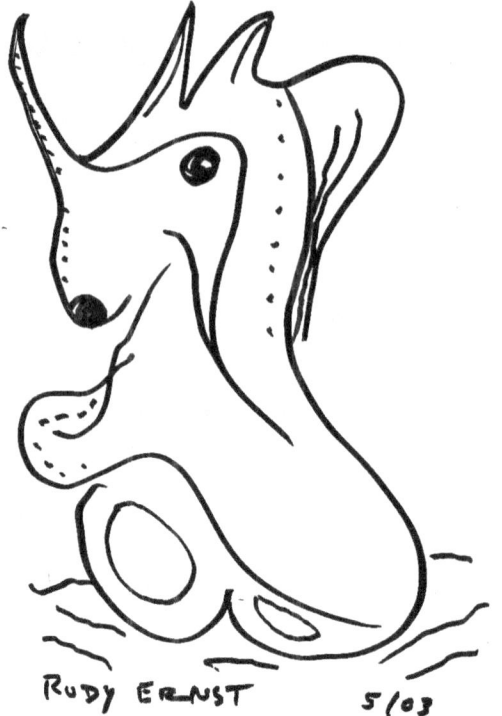

Unicorn Kangaroo (2003)
Ink on Paper - 6"x 4.25"

Rabits Emerging From a Hat (2004)
Ink on Paper - 6"x 4"

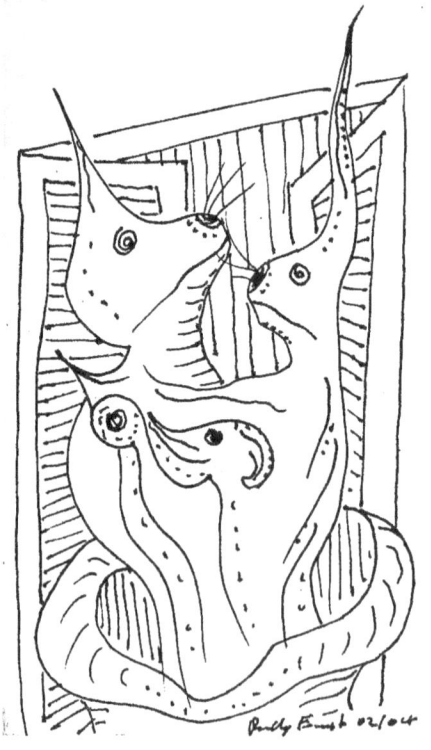

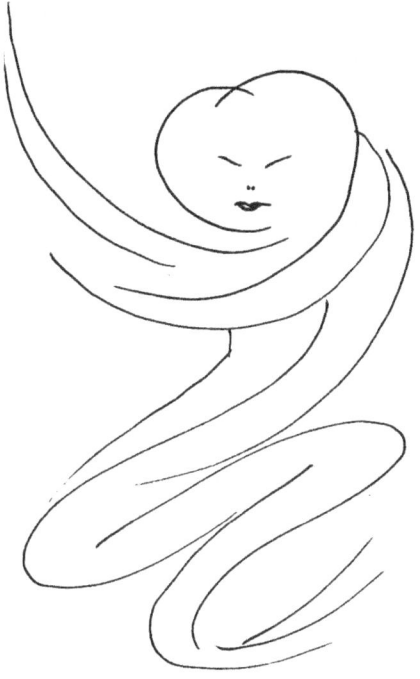

Buddha on the Move (2008)
Ink on Paper - 5.75"x 4"

A Touch of Spring in the Air (2008)
Ink on Paper - 5.75"x 4"

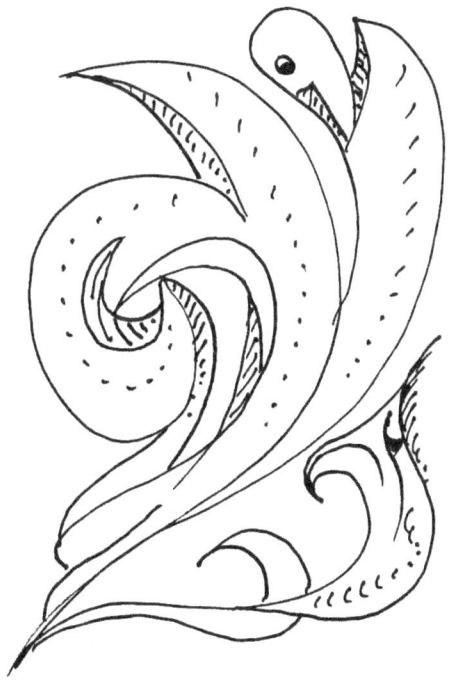

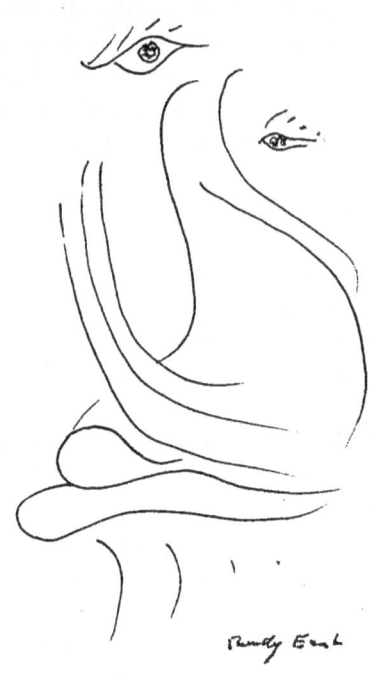

Tight Lipped (2004)
Ink on Paper - 6"x 4"

Donald Duck Flower (2006)
Ink on Paper - 6"x 4"

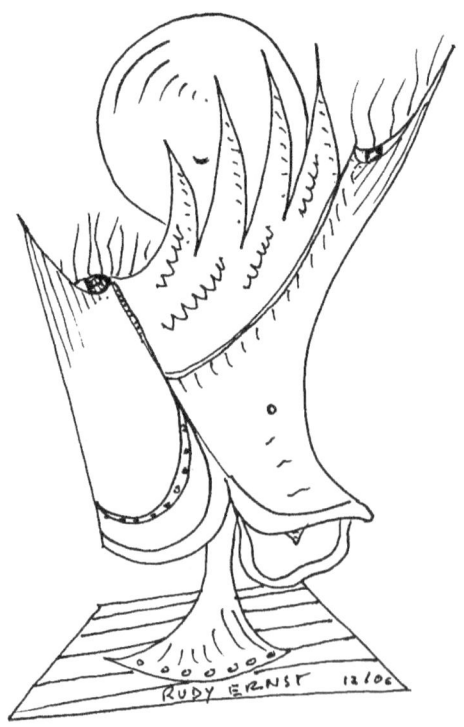

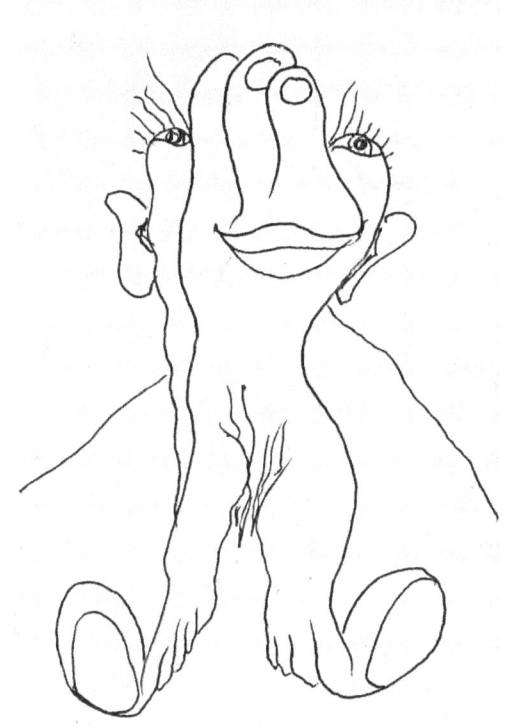

Finger Nose (2004)
Ink on Paper - 6"x 4"

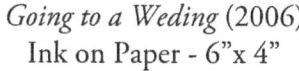

Going to a Weding (2006)
Ink on Paper - 6"x 4"

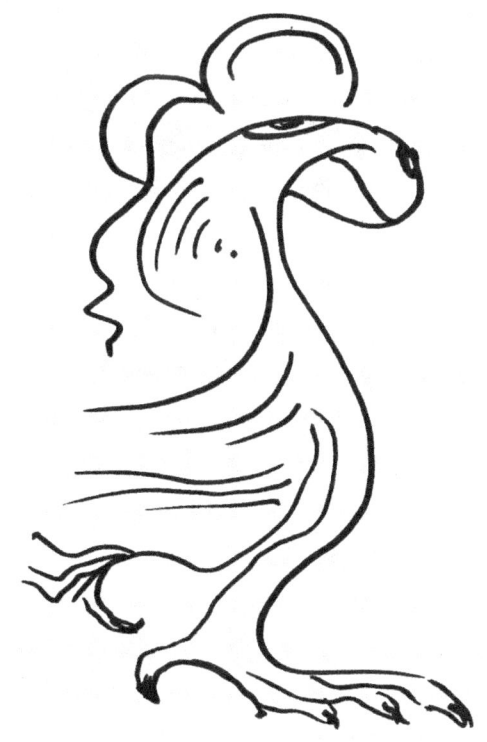

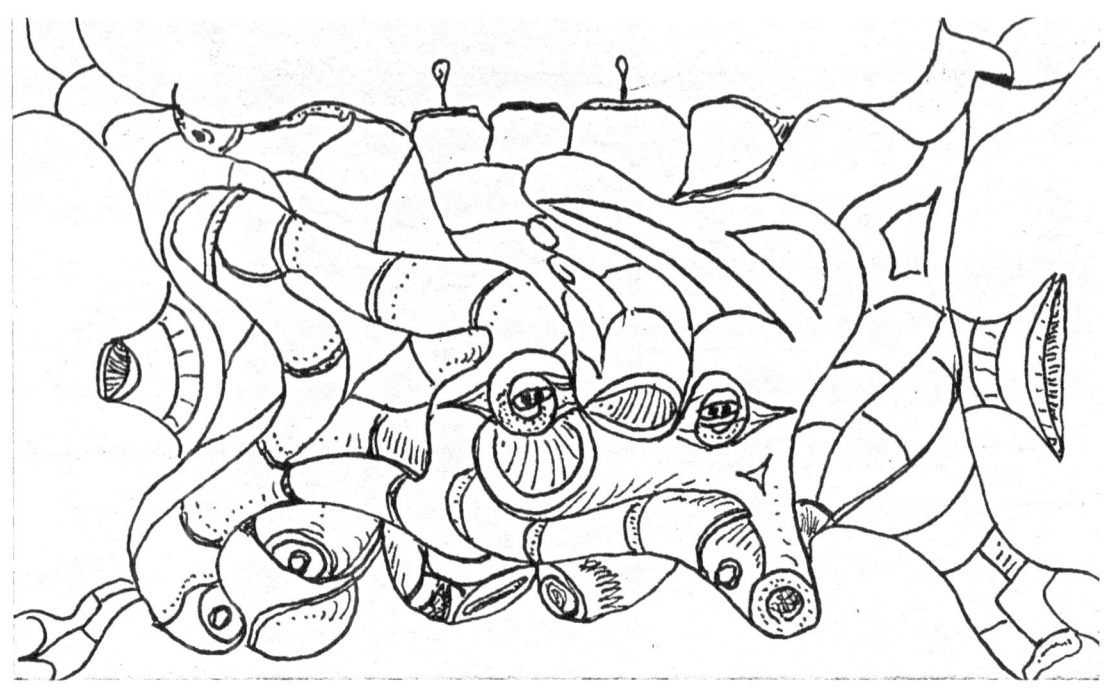

Opossum Hideaway (2007)
Ink on Paper - 3"x 5"

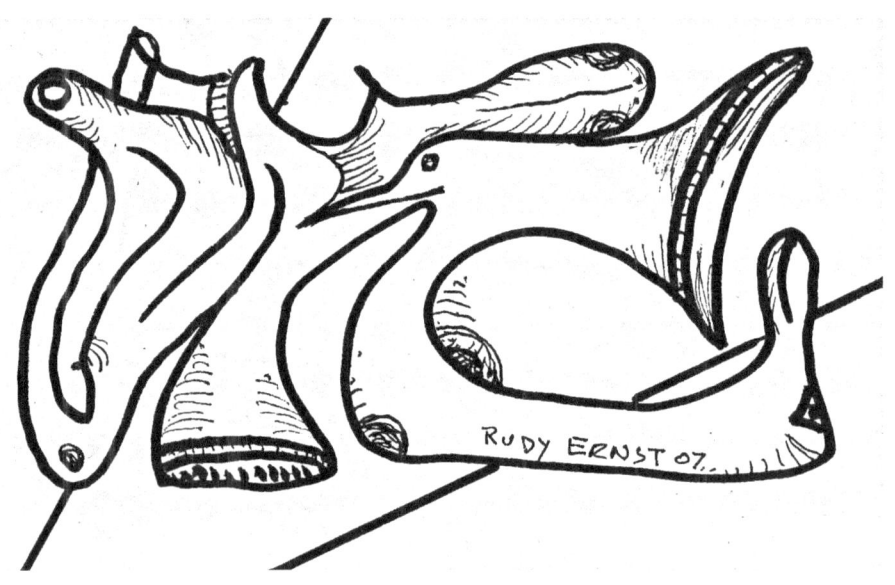

Fish Pond (2007)
Ink on Paper - 3"x 5"

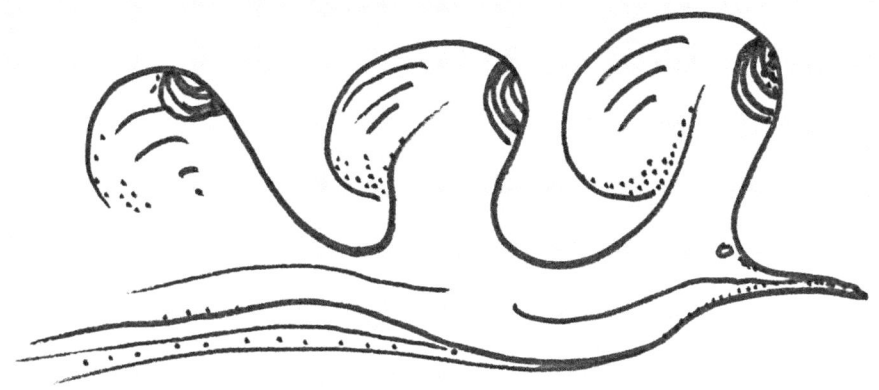

Flying Octopussies (2007)
Ink on Paper - 3"x 5"

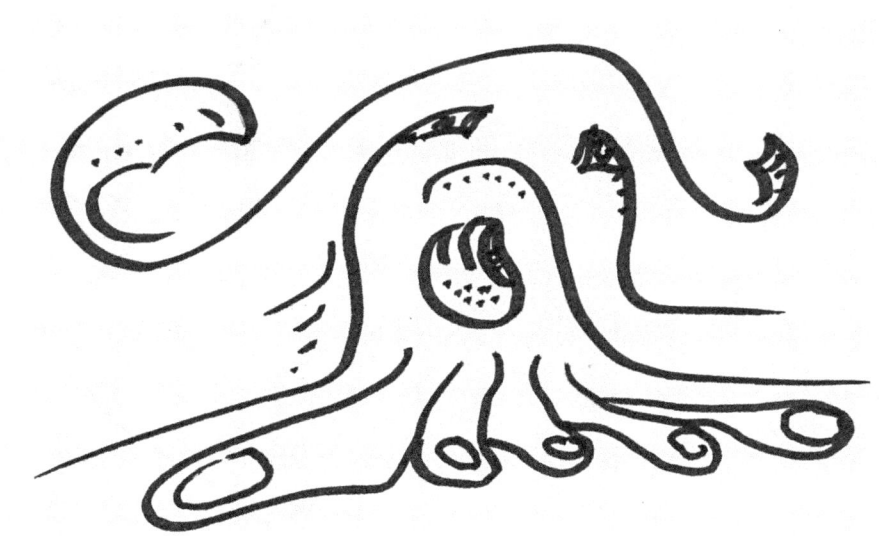

Finger Ghost(2007)
Ink on Paper - 3"x 5"

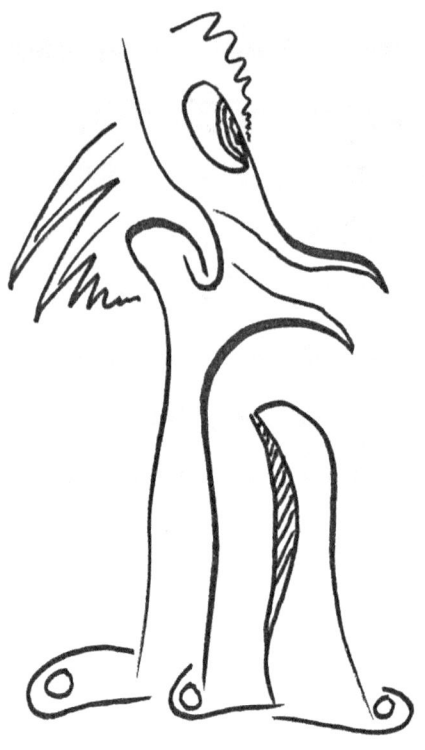

Talk to the Micro! (2007)
Ink on Paper - 5"x 3"

Elephant Tears (2007)
Ink on Paper - 5"x 3"

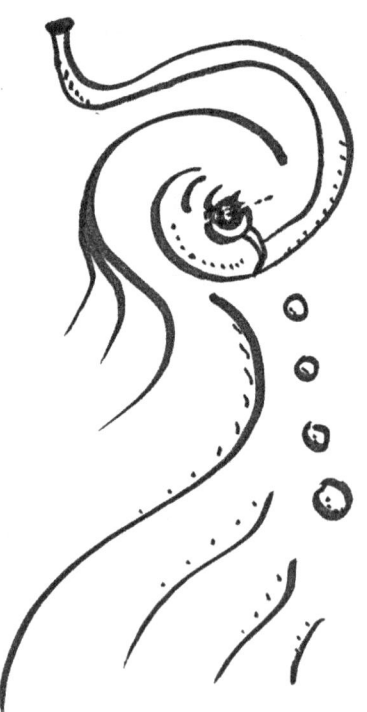

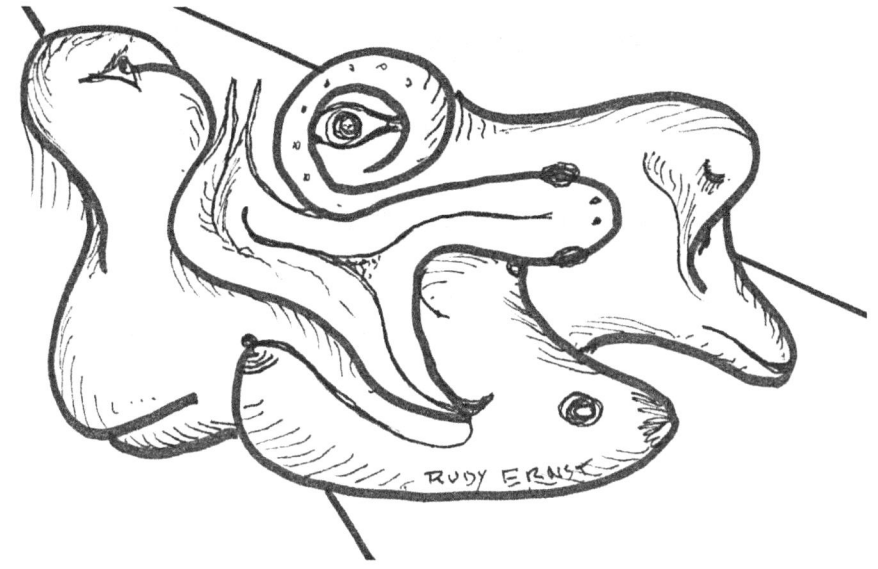

Sleeping Beauty (2007)
Ink on Paper 3"x 5"

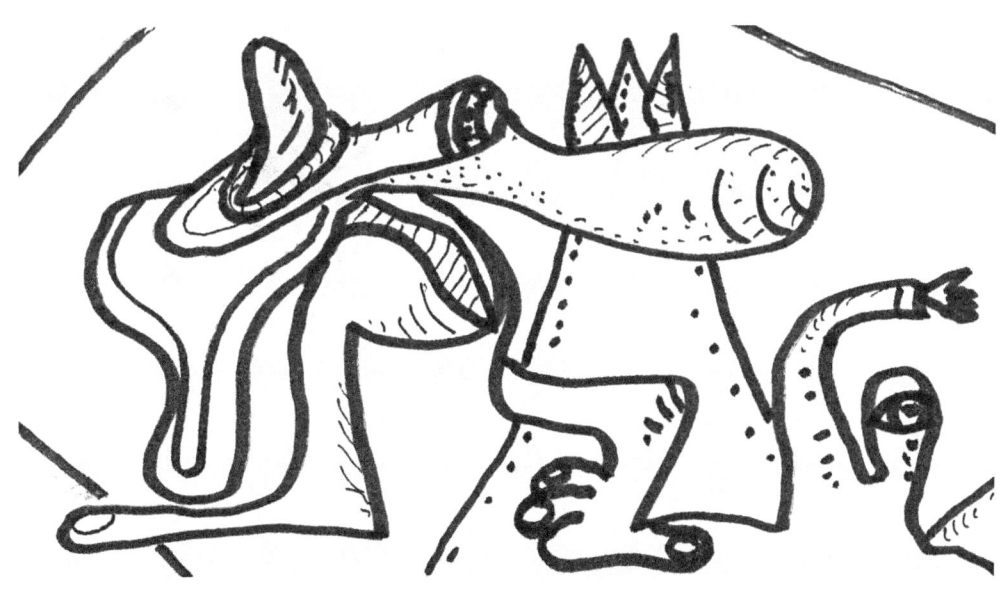

Sniff Sniff (2007)
Ink on Paper 2.5"x 4.5"

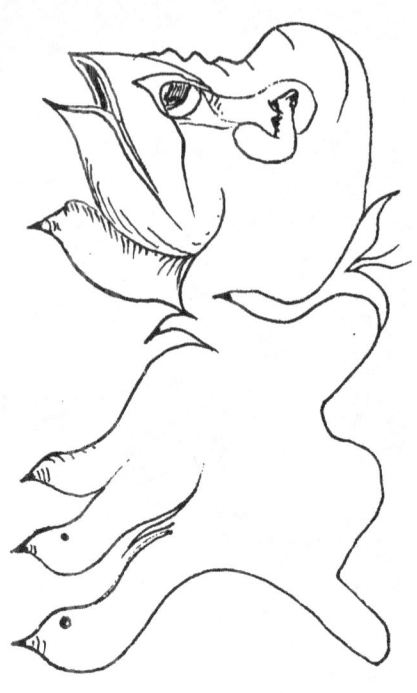

Prehistoric (2007)
Ink on Paper - 5"x 3"

A Foot in Disguise (2007)
Ink on Paper - 5"x 3"

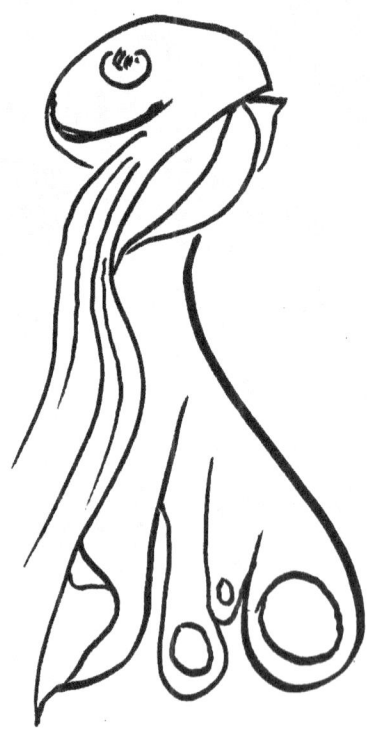

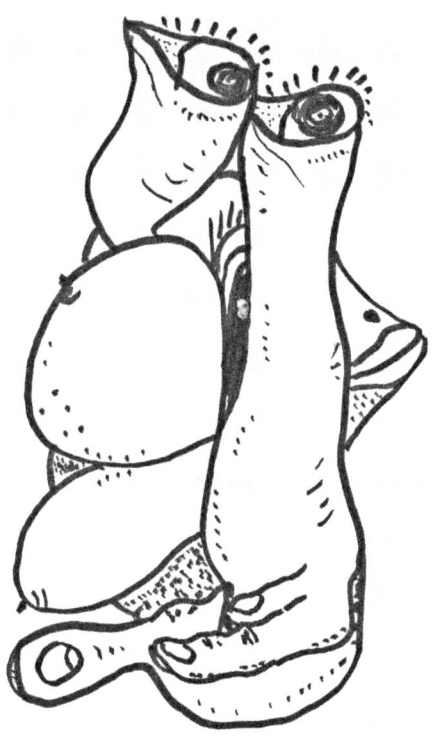

Bra Not Fitting (2004)
Ink on Paper - 5"x 3"

Greek Philosopher (2007)
Ink on Paper - 5"x 3"

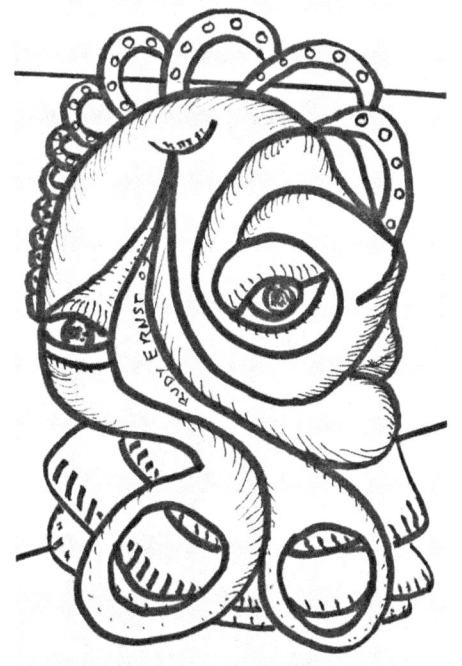

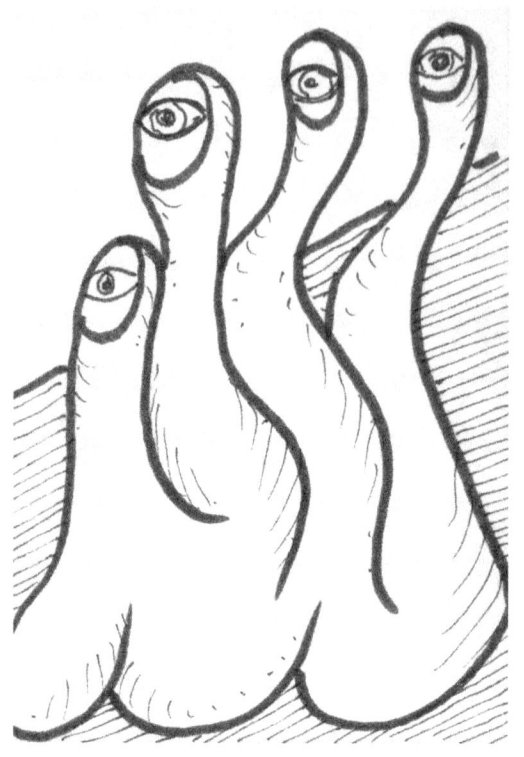

Geese (2007)
Ink on Paper - 4"x2.75")

A New Level of Complexity (2007)
Ink on Paper - 5"x 3"

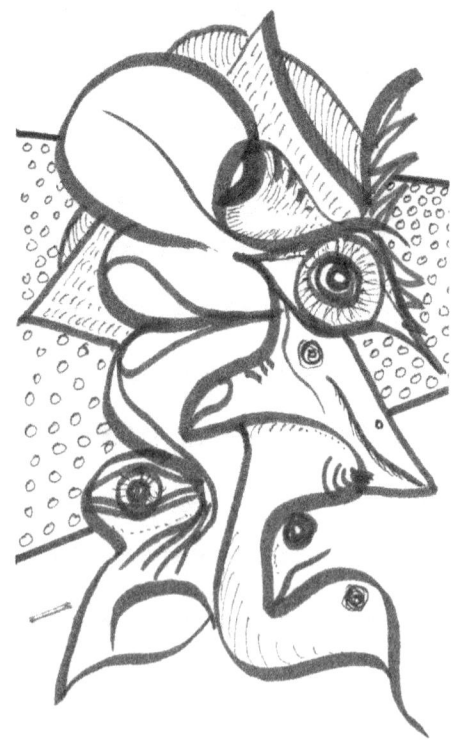

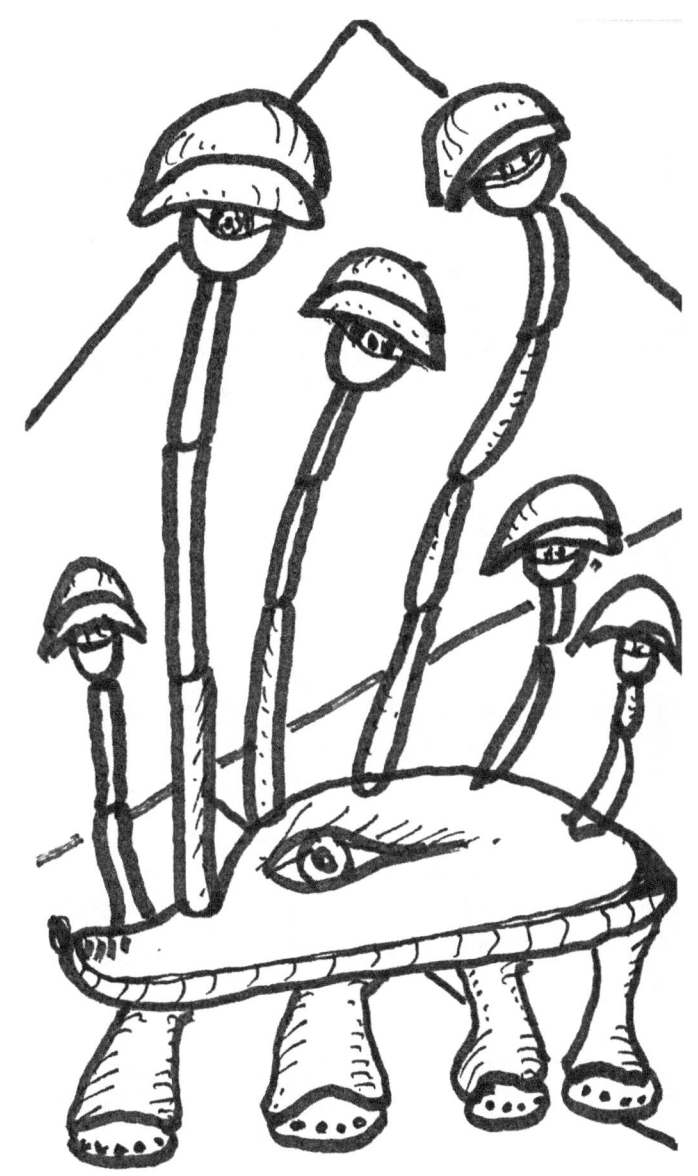

Colonial Army (2007)

Ink on Paper – 4.75" x 2.75"

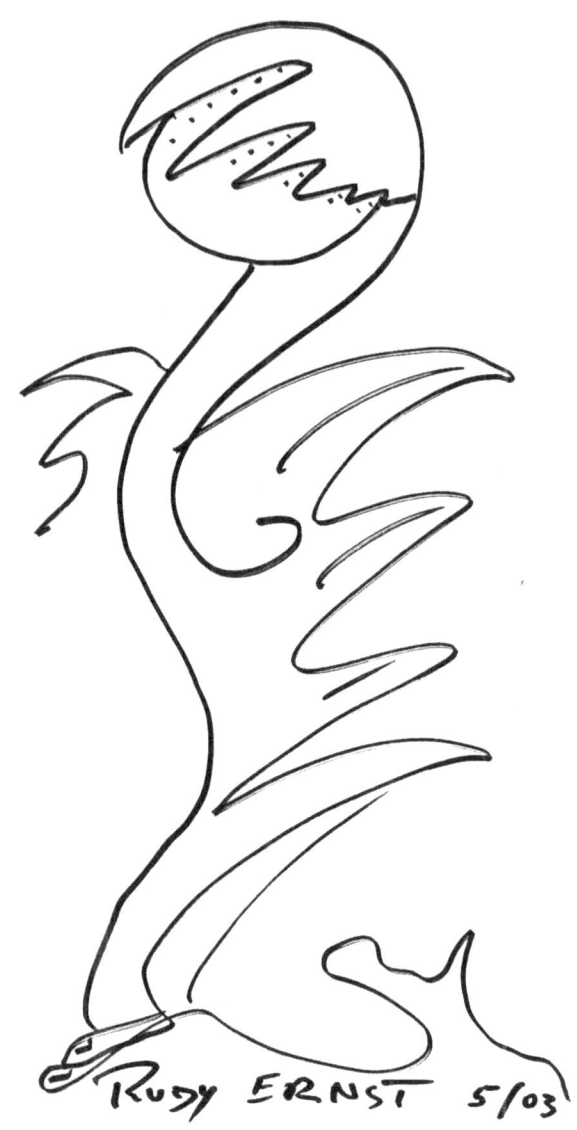

First Attempt to Fly (2003)
Ink on Paper – 8.75" x 4.75"

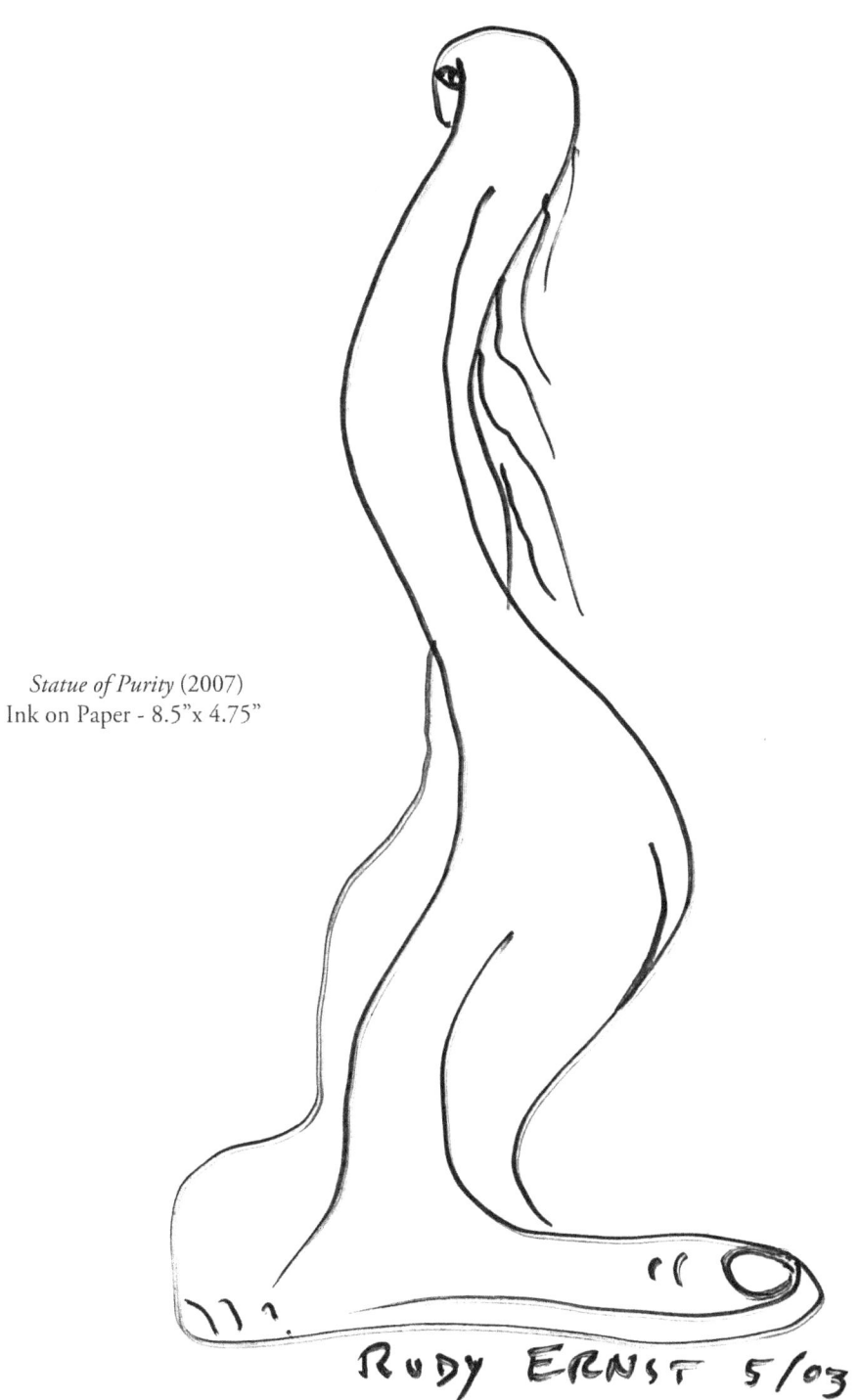

Statue of Purity (2007)
Ink on Paper - 8.5"x 4.75"

RUDY ERNST 5/03

PART V:

THE DADA-POMS

PART V:

THE DADA-POMS

About the Dada-Poms

The most fascinating aspect of the Dada-Poms is that they make no sense. Yet, like so many other things in life that make no sense, once you are able to project your own sense into something that didn't have any in the first place, you will suddenly enjoy that liberating sensation of accomplishment inside you that only a few of us ever had the privilege of experiencing.

I used to write poetry that did not only make sense, but was embedded in rhyming and rhythmic qualities, which elevated them to a level of boredom that was often criticized as being outdated.

My Dada-Poms changed that. They may come across as a bit confused, but that is exactly their inherent charm (at least I wish that were the case). Why does everything in life have to make sense, since not much in life ever seems to make sense anyhow?

To illustrate my theory I have written a number of Dada-Poms, both in English and in other languages, of which a few are hereafter reproduced.

English Dada-Poms

The Dada-Gene

The Dada-Gene
Is mostly green
And like your money
Tastes like honey.

And yet, I'd rather
Be a father
Than a gene
That's never seen;

Thank God my stand
In Dada-Land
Relieves my guts
From going nuts!

February 20, 2009

Your Dada-Gene…

…wakes you up in the morning.

What a great day it is going to be!

You may have to go to work,

But that still leaves you

With eight hours

Of your own!

Be creative!

They are

Yours!

A Wedding Tragedy

A Shadow and a piece of Bread
Went on a trip as newlywed;
Their honeymoon was rather short,
Because they had it to abort
When Mrs. Shadow's sunny side
Dried out the bread and cut their ride;
All that was published of their fate
Was that they vanished as of late.

A prosecutor known as "Mike"
Drove to the crime scene, on his bike,
And introduced the case in court,
Which cut this Dada-Story short.

Blurry

The Dada drank her Guinness Beer
And thought: How it is cold in here!
She drank some more to warm her soul
And thought and thought about her role
In general, and in the art,
And then her thoughts went off the chart,
Which is to show you what occurs
When Guinness Beer your Dada blurs

March 13, 2009

Dada Come as Dada Go

Now Dada come,
Then Dada go,
Like also coming moon,
But never is like other some
Who always coming soon.

September 16, 2009

Was the Easter Bunny

funny
my dear,
this year?
Did he bring
anything?

Or was he mad
that things are bad,
took the eggs off the shelf
ate them all by himself
and left you alone,
without a bone?

It isn't funny
as Easter Bunny
in such trying times
when nothing rhymes
down to the core
any more.

So if you got nada
don't blame it on Dada,
instead fault the moon,
or blame a tycoon,
and remain sappy
and happy!

Unequivocally Ambivalent

When roses blossom in the sky
And rusty bridges wonder why
They don't collapse from all that noise
That children cause with Chinese toys
In spite of Dada's happy face,
Just as he won the greyhound race:
That's when your soul is really blessed
And murmurs while it is caressed
By so much love that hates your world
And in it all the hair that's curled.

11_02_15

The Multi Language Dada-Poms

In good old Dada tradition, where the sound of words is more important than their content, I wrote a nonsensical *sonnet* written in my own *Dada-Language*, as well as some multi-language Dada-Poms.

The English version of my sonnet is inspired by Johann Wolfgang von Goethe's famous poem *The Fisherman*

The Story of Quig

There was a quampa in the gosh'
It had a bolo mang,
Yet while its baba was a mosh'
It never lala bang.

A quig came by and saw the gosh
"Polala manga tune?"
The quampa quizzled notabosh
"Ya mama cola pune!"

Su whereupon the quig begued
"Po quara nuna lee
Sopanagur quelesta gued
Ne bama never Bee!"

Two Language Dada-Pom

Da war auch the Man in the Moon,
But he didn't know was zu tun.
Er kaufte some Wine,
And now he is fine,
Doch schon bald he'll be back by balloon.

Nophretete International

(4-Language Dada-Pom)

The Lullaby is

Eins-zwei-drei

a nenuphar

ganz wunderbar,

but Nophretete

(diese Flöte)

hat per se

in volupté

sich (falsch belichtet)

selbst gerichtet!

In Vino Veritas

(6-Language Dada-Pom)

Nel mezzo del camin von meinem Leben
I drank the wine, qui est si bon, von meinen Reben;
ya no me souviens what time I went to bed,
pero ich weiss genau: the wine was red,
because das Weisse de mes yeux was rather rot
y en mi cama, from that wine, I felt halb tot.
Ein Glück nur que mon Dada kept me sane,
sinon le sense von dem Gedicht would be in vain.

Auf alle Fälle lautet die Conclusion:
De temps à autre Dada breeds confusion!

PART VI:

DADA-MICROMANIA

PART VI:

DADA-MICROMANIA

Micromania

Since the world is playing crazy with *Micromania* at an age when the new computer technologies are reaching molecular levels, why should I not engage on a similar path with my Dada-Micromania drawings? This idea was probably my subliminal guideline for many years, before I began doing my *tiny Dada-Drawings*, which look quite interesting under magnification.

But since my really small Dada-Drawings measure barely an inch square and are therefore too small to be reproduced in this book, I chose the next larger level of which a few samples are shown here below.

Micromania Pieces

These are a few Dada-Micromania drawings, first in bulk, then individually as magnified pieces in order to show how they hold their own in a magnified environment.

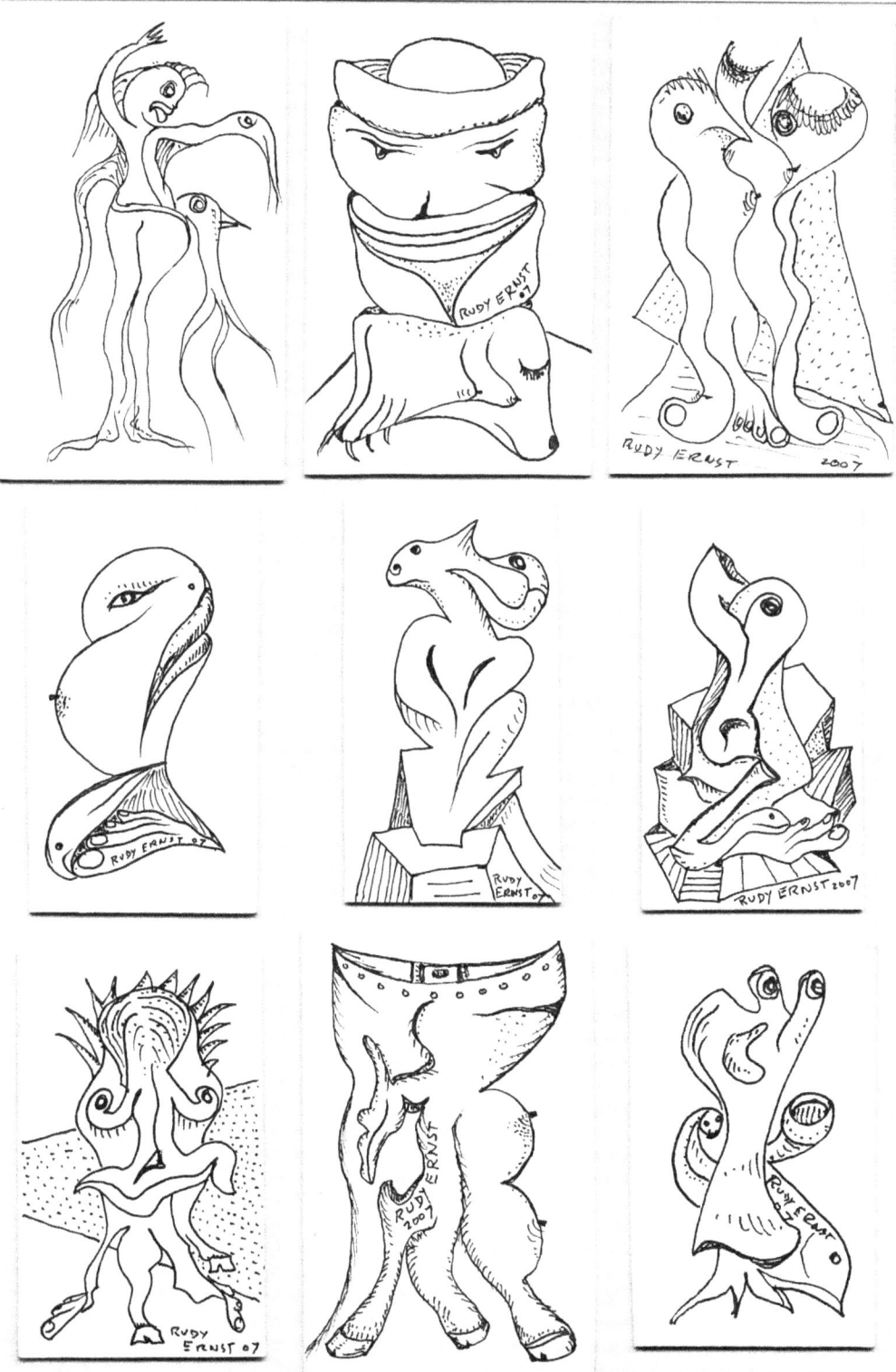

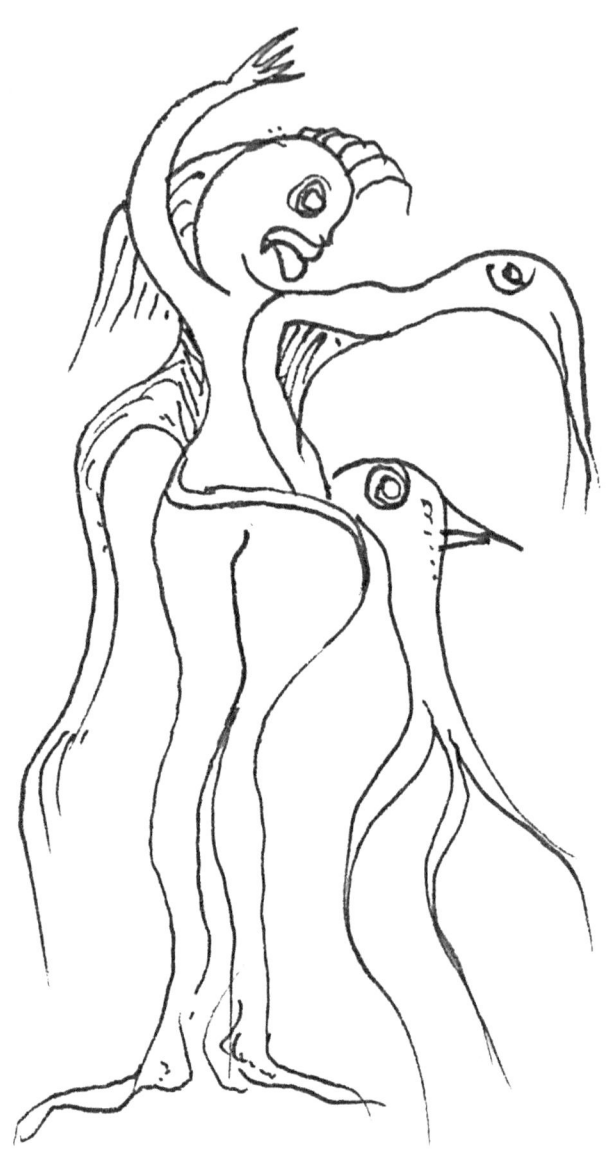

A Circus Act (2007)

Ink on Paper – 3.25" x 2"

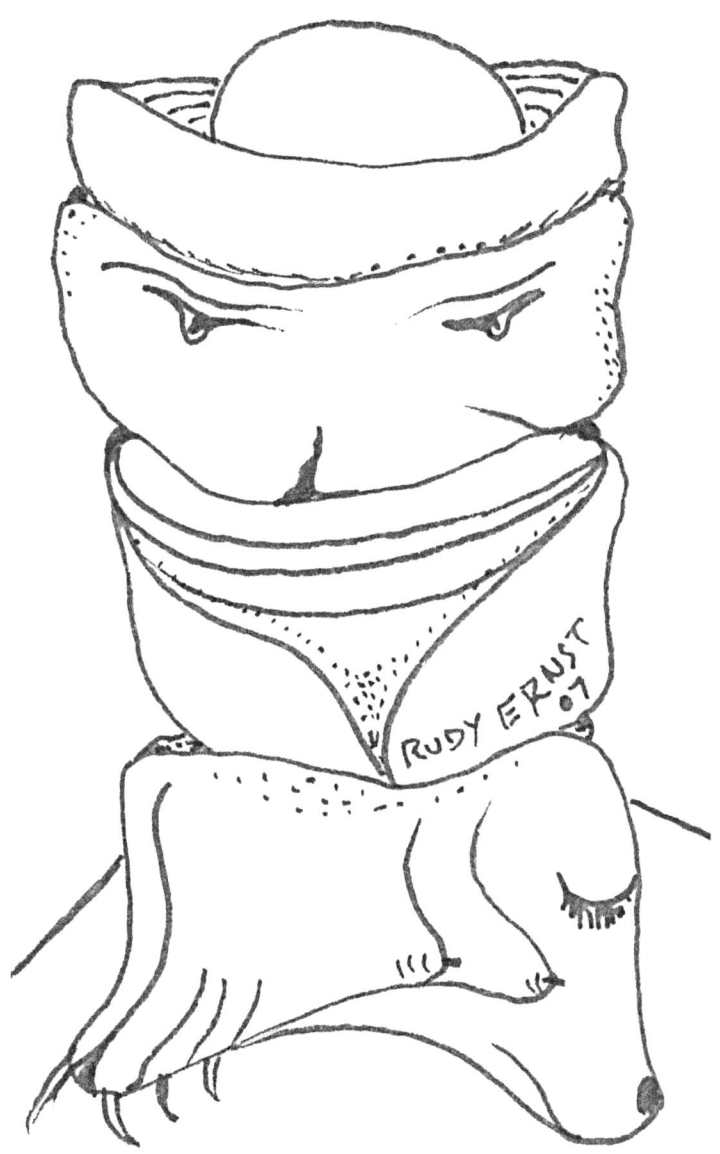

All is in Divine Order (2007)

Ink on Paper – 3.25" x 2"

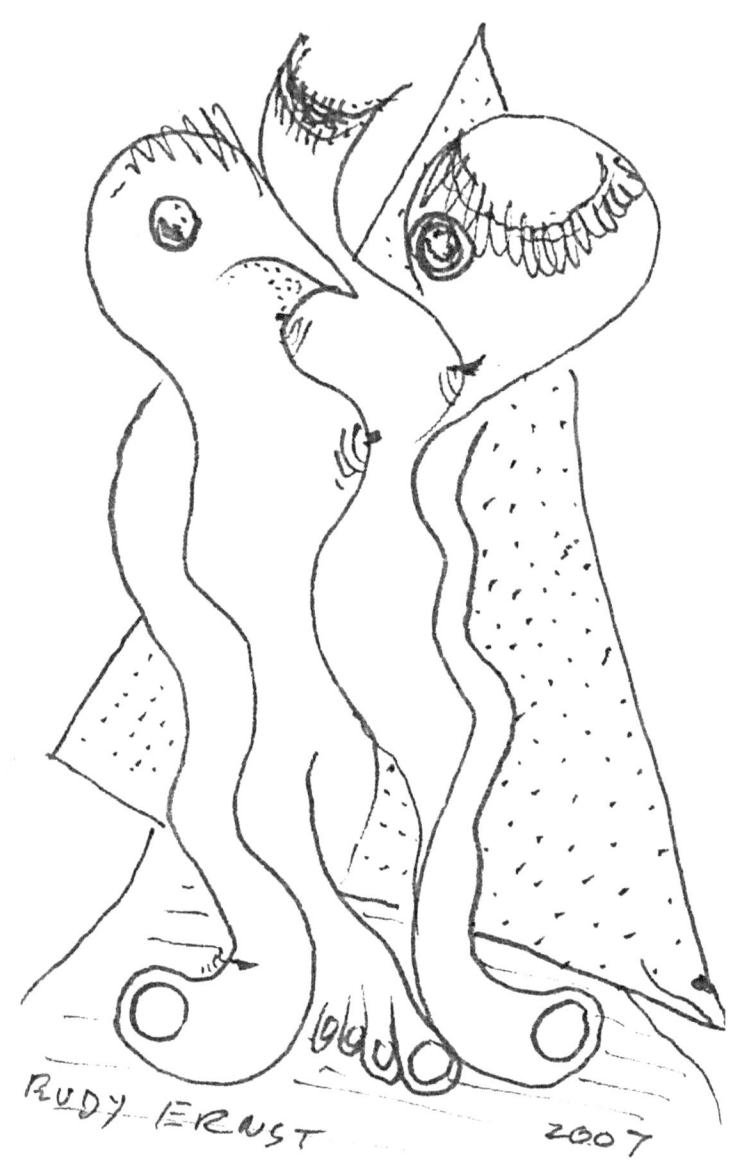

Are You Sure? (2007)

Ink on Paper – 3.25" x 2"

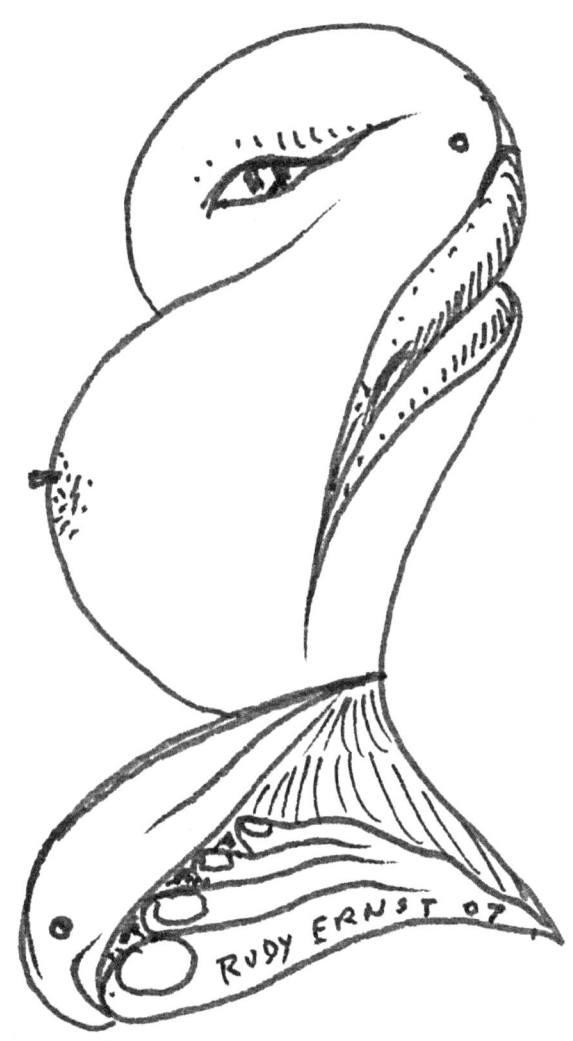

Excessive Pride (2007)

Ink on Paper – 3" x 1.75"

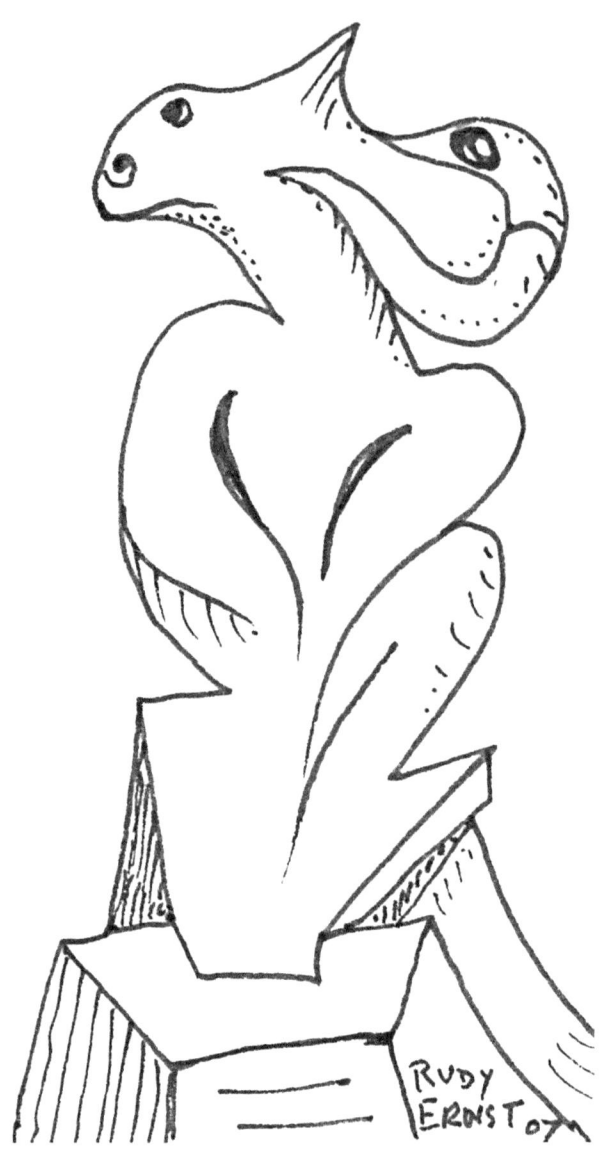

Statue of Isis (2007)

Ink on Paper – 3" x 1.5"

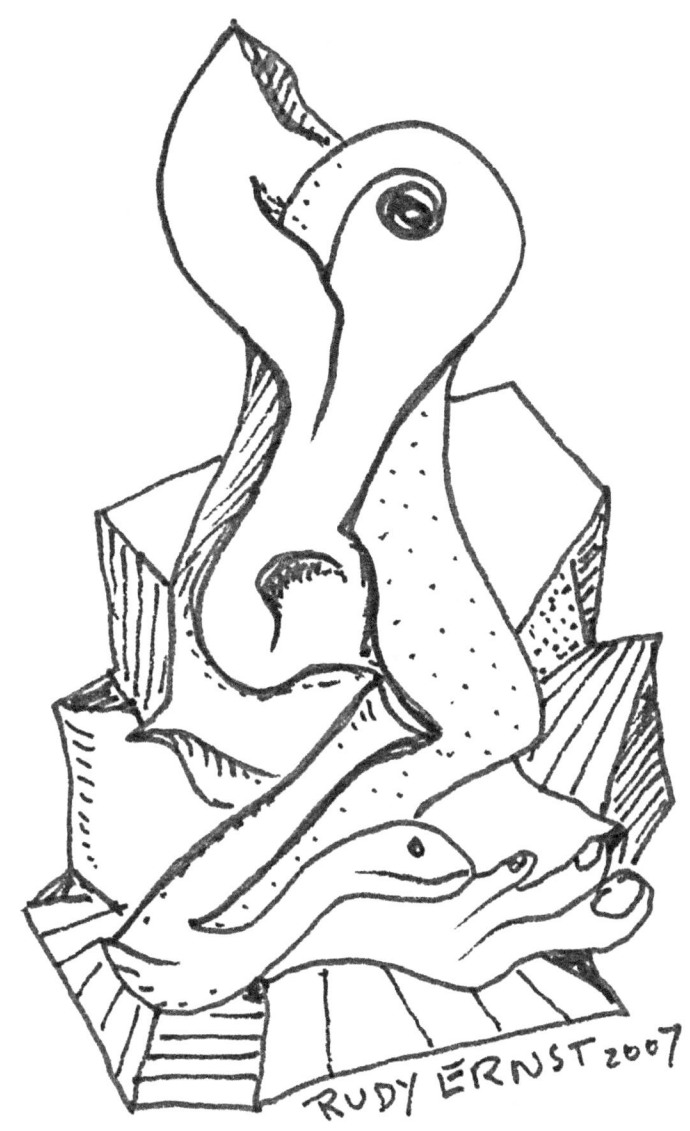

A Proud Marble Piece (2007)

Ink on Paper – 3" x 1.5"

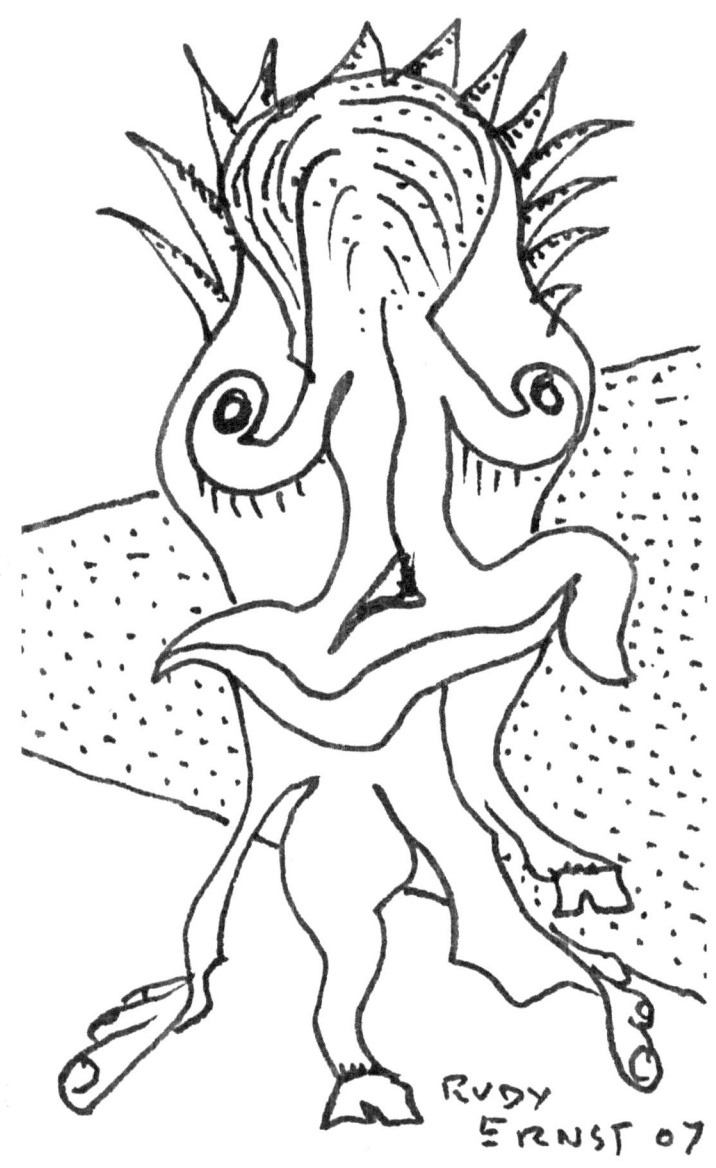

Mondo Cane (2007)

Ink on Paper – 3" x 2"

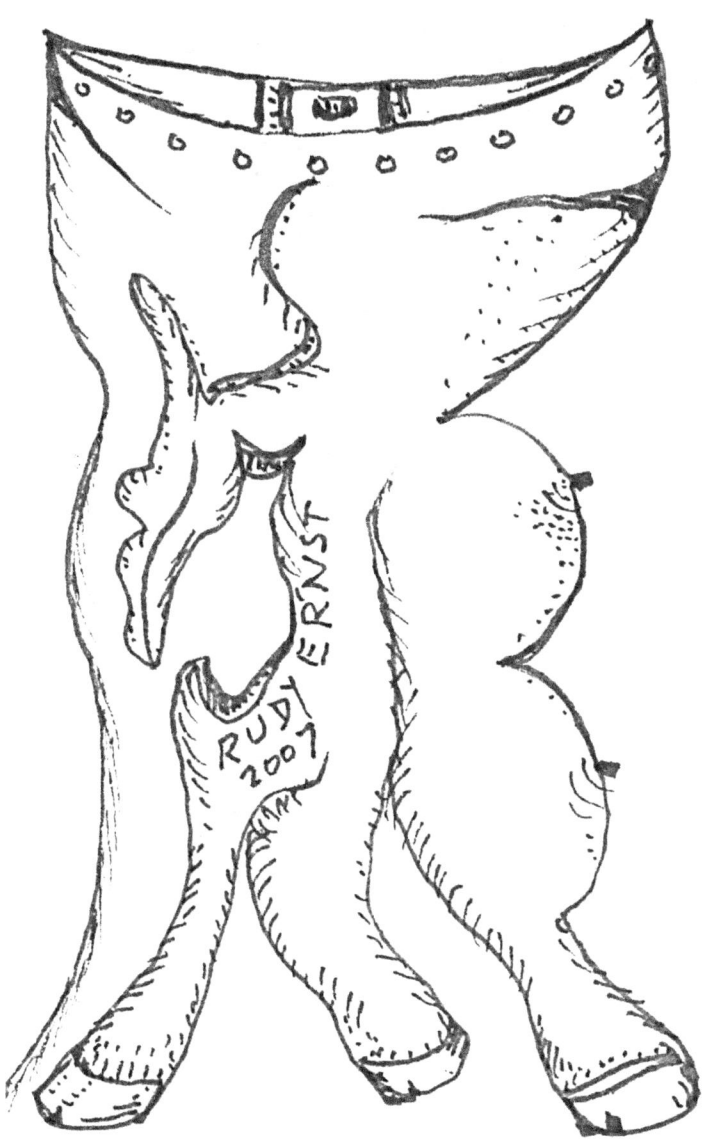

Nude (Lower Part) (2007)

Ink on Paper – 3.25" x 2"

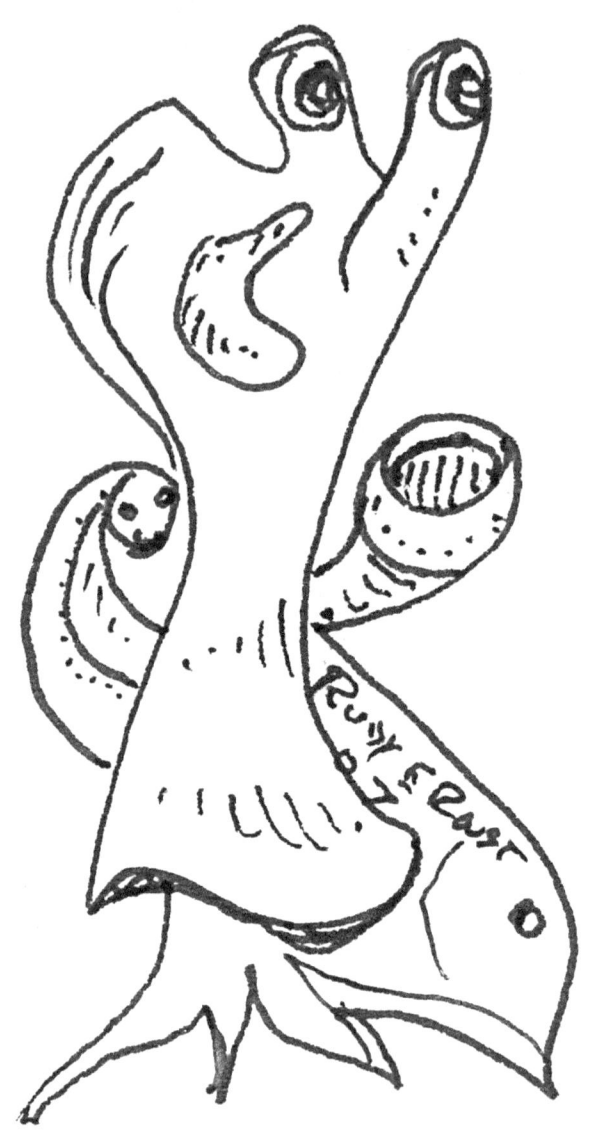

Confusius (2007)

Ink on Paper – 3" x 2"

PART VII:

THE DADA-SCULPTURES

PART VII:

THE DADA-
SCULPTURES

My Own Bauhaus

In my book *Sculptomania* (pp. 70-71) I explain how fortunate I was to grow up with what I have since called *my own Bauhaus*. Recently, I came across an old picture of that workshop in my hometown in northern Switzerland where I first learned to weld metal and do woodwork when I was still in my early teens.

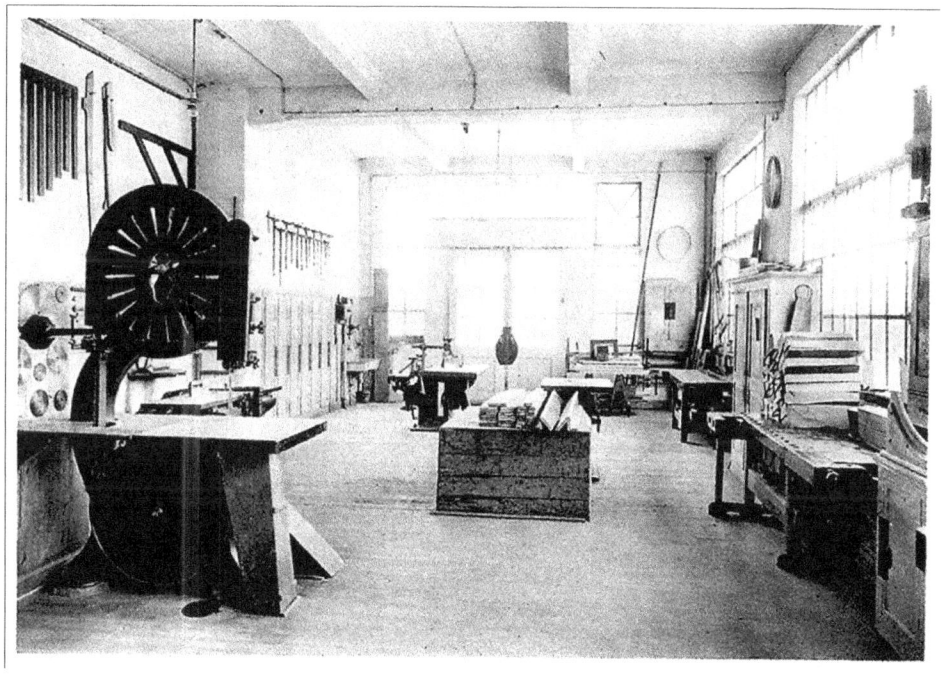

North View of *My Own Bauhaus* Workshop

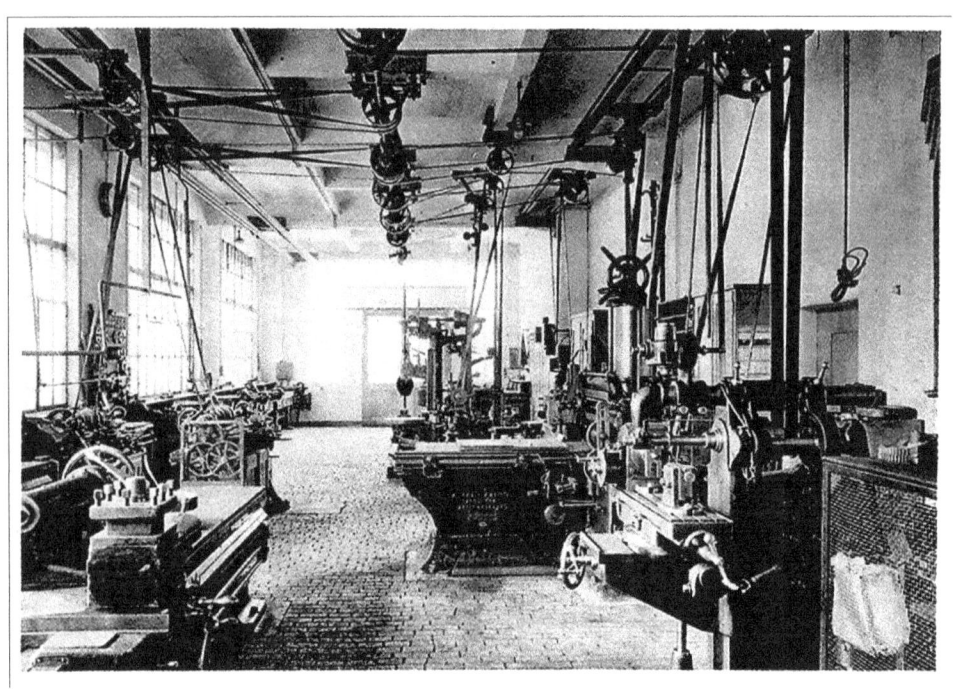

South View of *My Own Bauhaus* Workshop

Becoming a Sculptor

While, at the time, I was sure I would never become an artist, the knowledge that I had accumulated during the early days of my life came in handy when the creation of my own sculptures became the main focus of my life and had grown to be nothing short of an obsession.

*

Few things stimulate my Dada-Mind like walking around a scrap metal place and having my imagination assemble a bunch of weird objects in my mind into what I came to call my *Reverse Engineered Dada-Sculptures*, just before actually welding them together into my *dadaesque* art pieces.

Over the next few pages the reader will find some recent pieces of my *Dada - Sculptures*.

The Dada Angel -- Year: 2010

Height: 14 ½ "

Scrap Metal Pieces Welded Together

(Photo: Arpi Pap 2011)

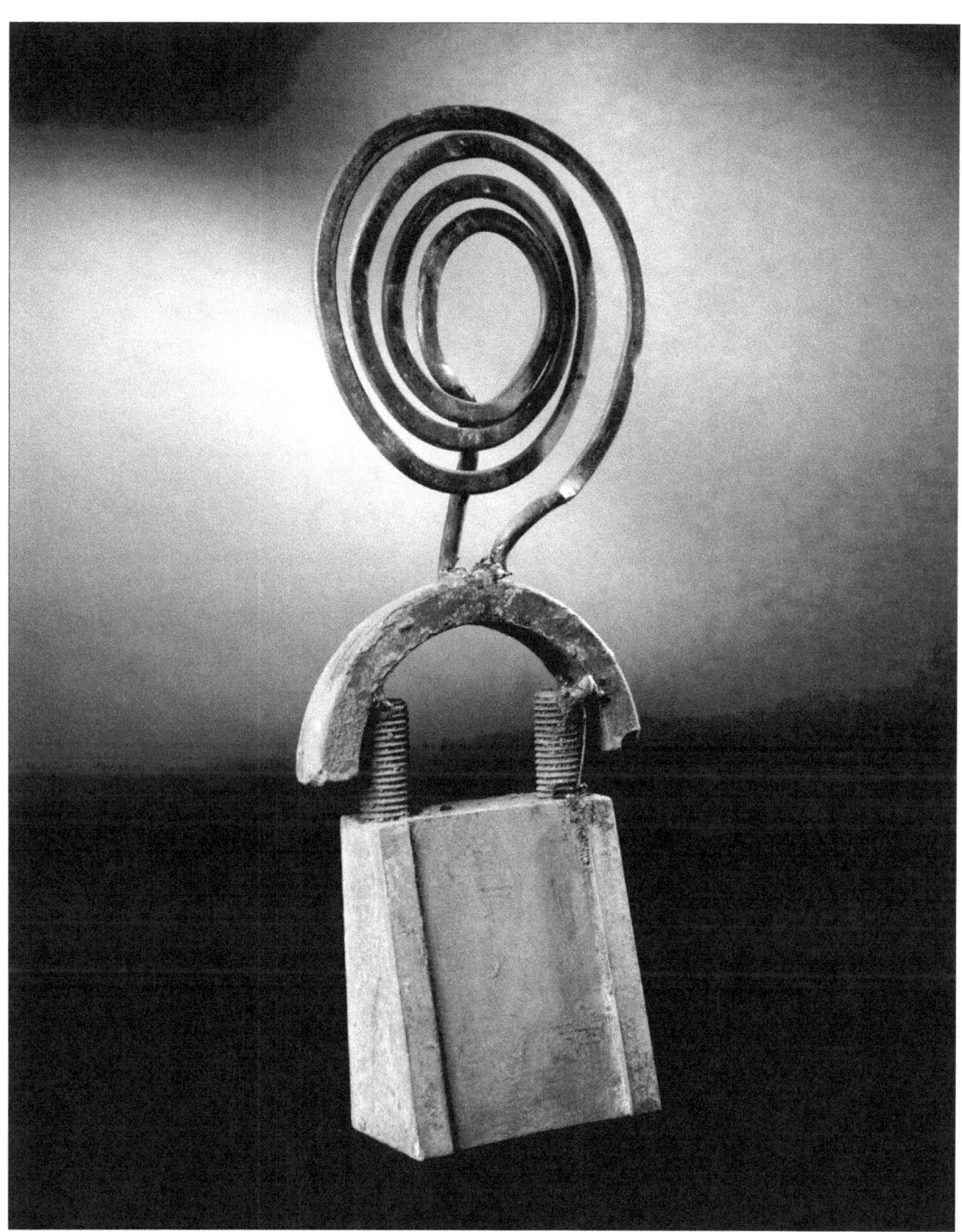

Dada Brain Monitor -- Year: 2010

Height: 9"

Scrap Metal Pieces Welded Together

(Photo: Arpi Pap 2011)

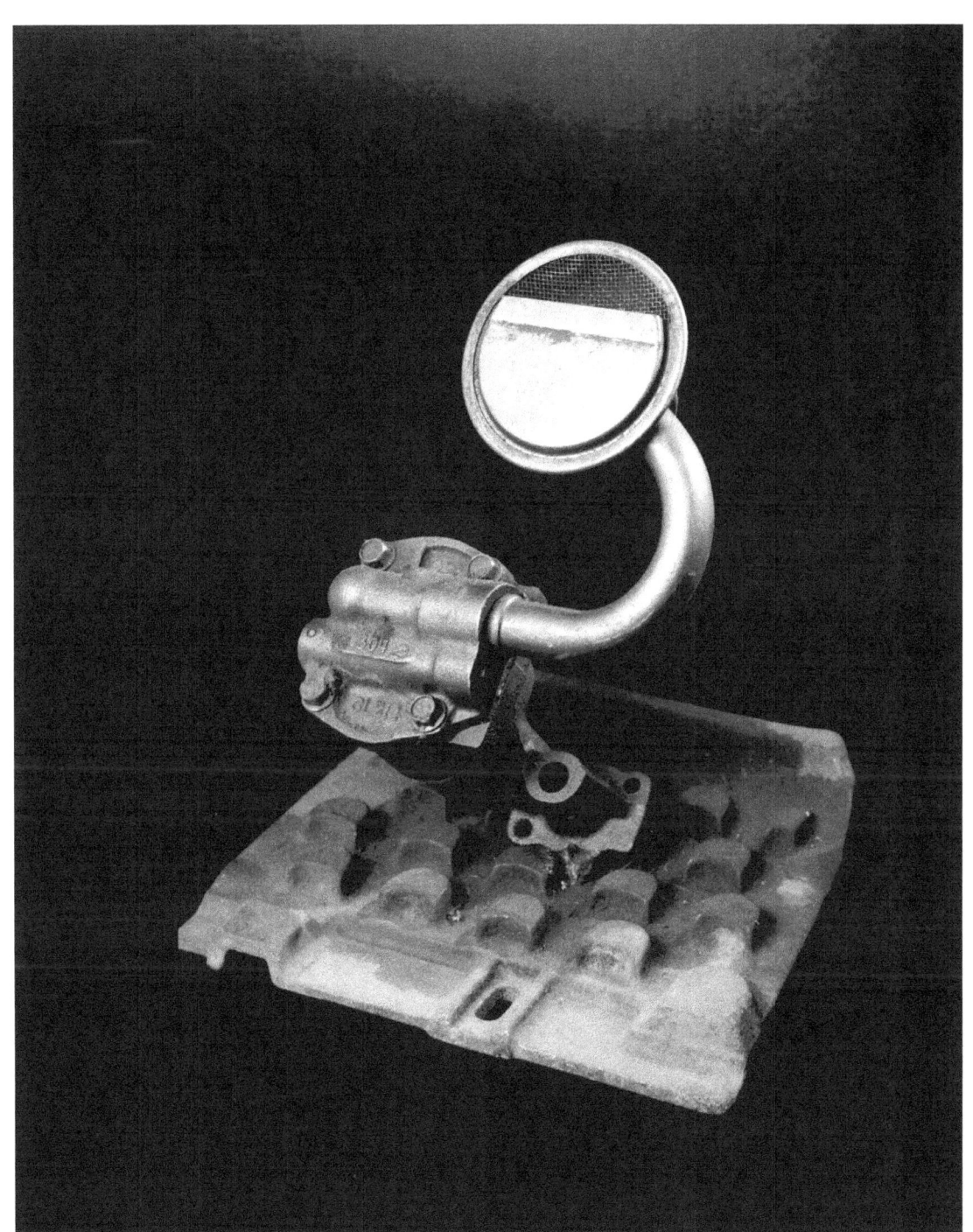

Dada Moon Rocket -- Year: 2010

Height: 14"

Scrap Metal Pieces Welded Together

(Photo: Arpi Pap 2011)

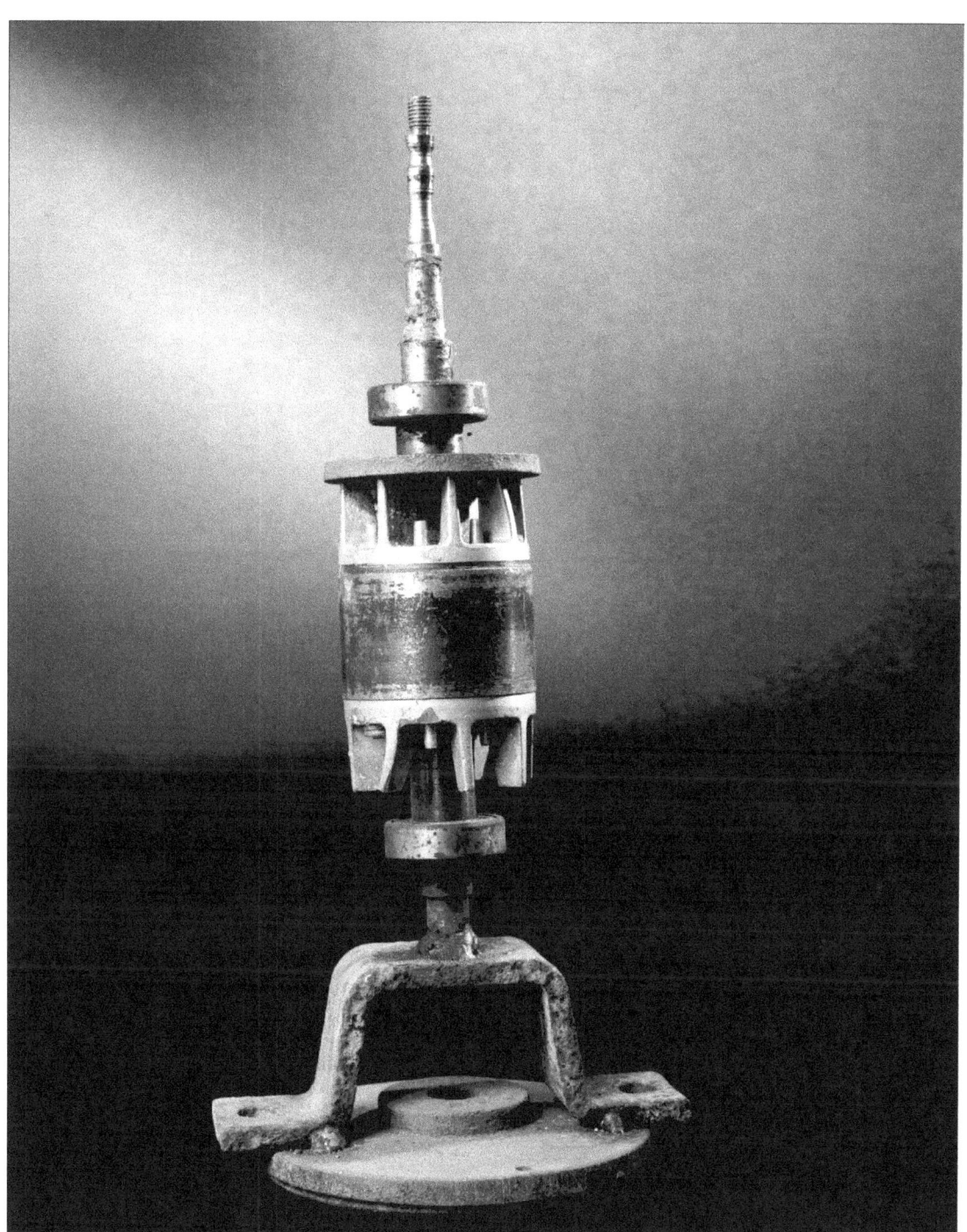

Listen To Me! -- Year: 2010

Height: 9"

Scrap Metal Pieces Welded Together

(Photo: Arpi Pap 2011)

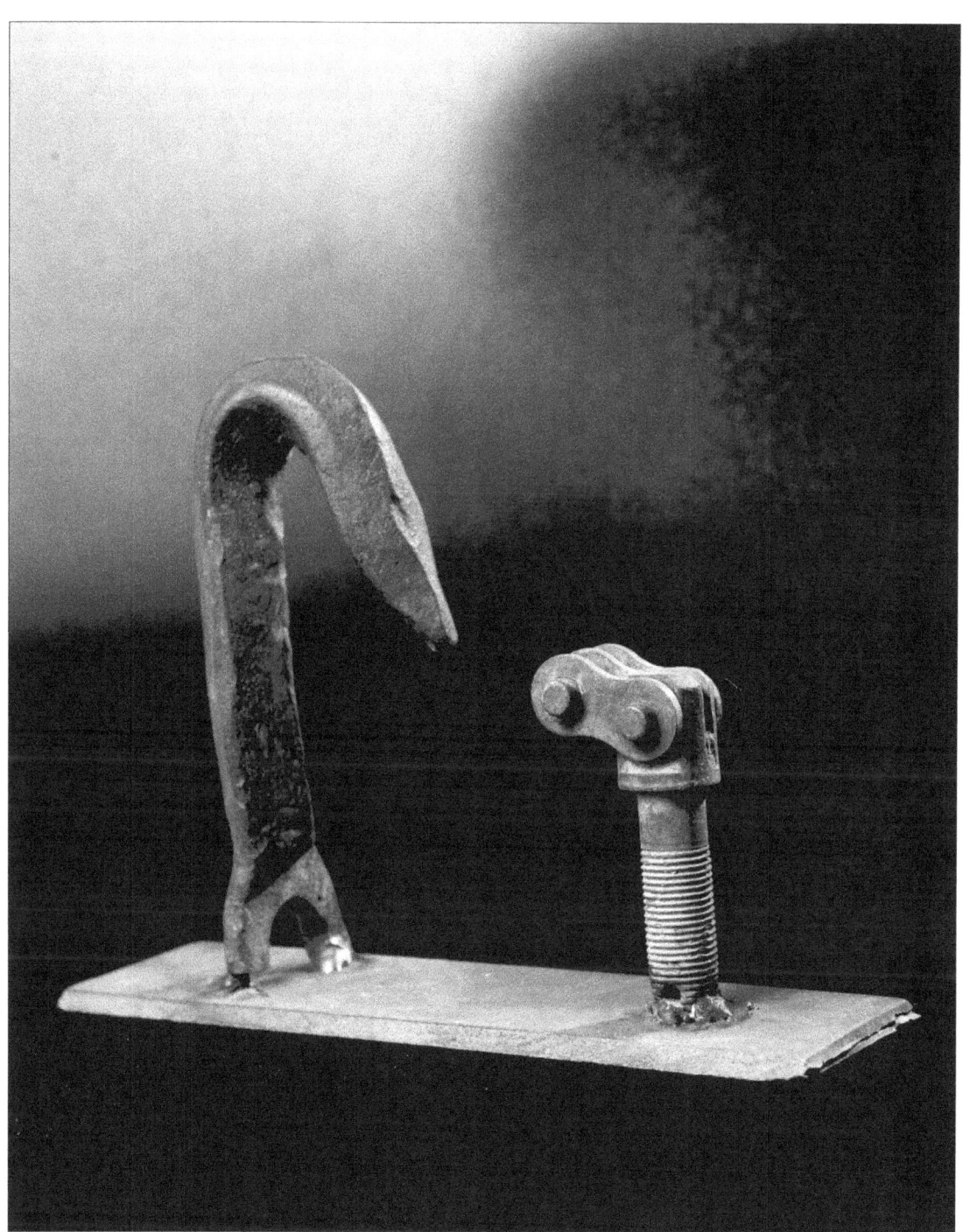

Dada Hobby Horse -- Year: 2010

Height: 9"

Scrap Metal Pieces Welded Together

(Photo: Arpi Pap 2011)

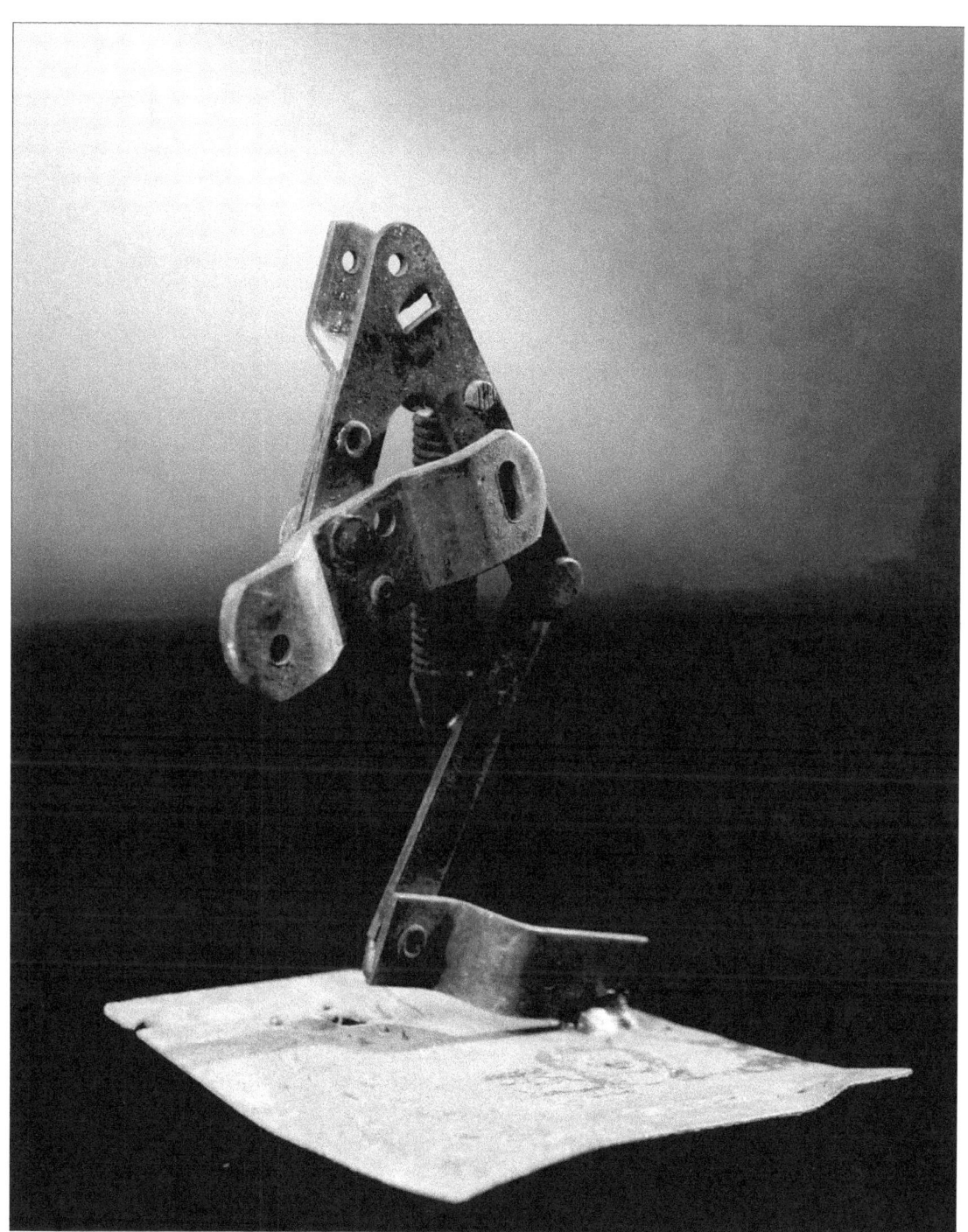

Dada Bird Ready to Fly -- Year: 2010

Height: 8"

Scrap Metal Pieces Welded Together

(Photo: Arpi Pap 2011)

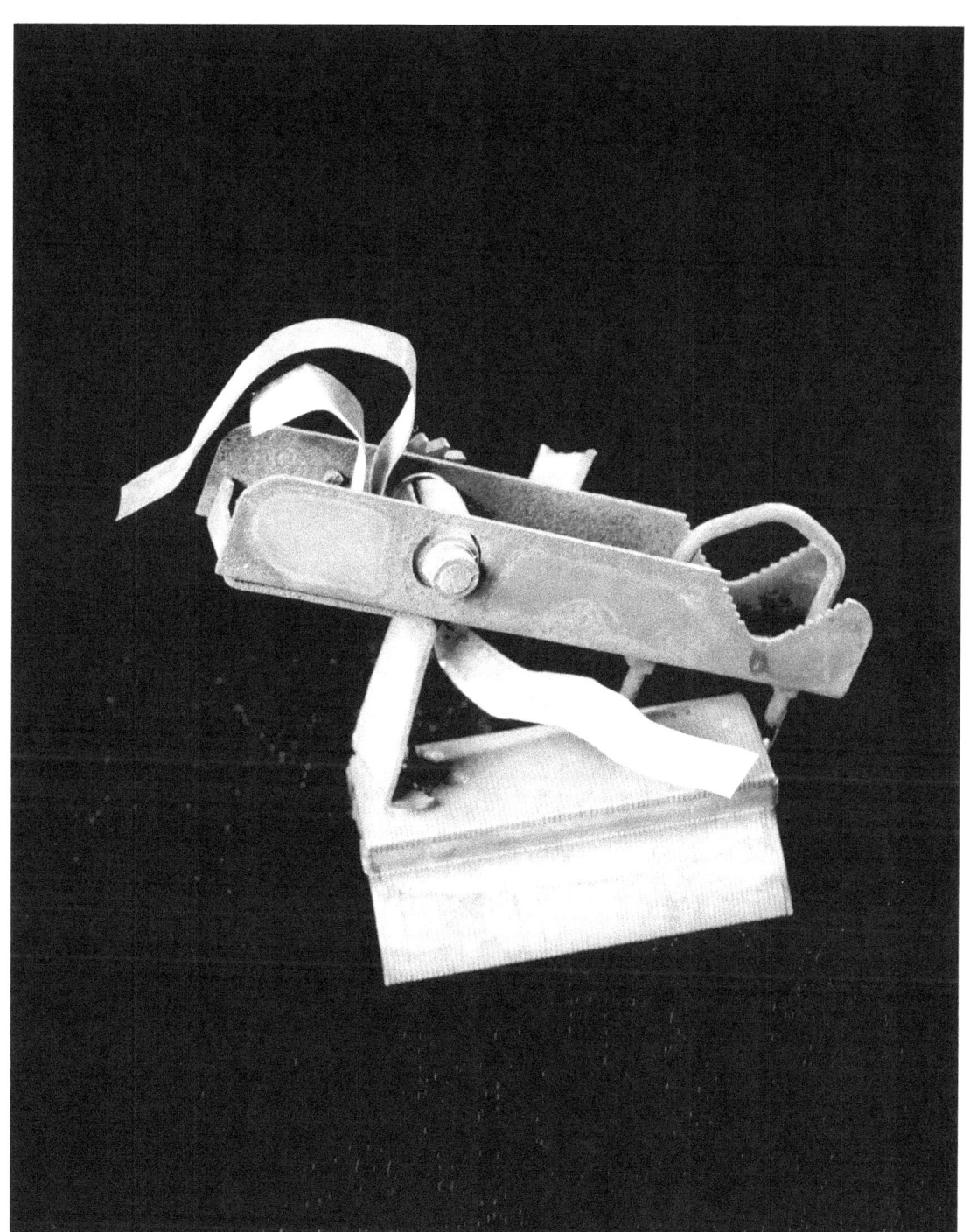

The Dada Tower of Babel -- Year: 2010

Height: 26"

Scrap Metal Pieces Welded Together

(Photo: Arpi Pap 2011)

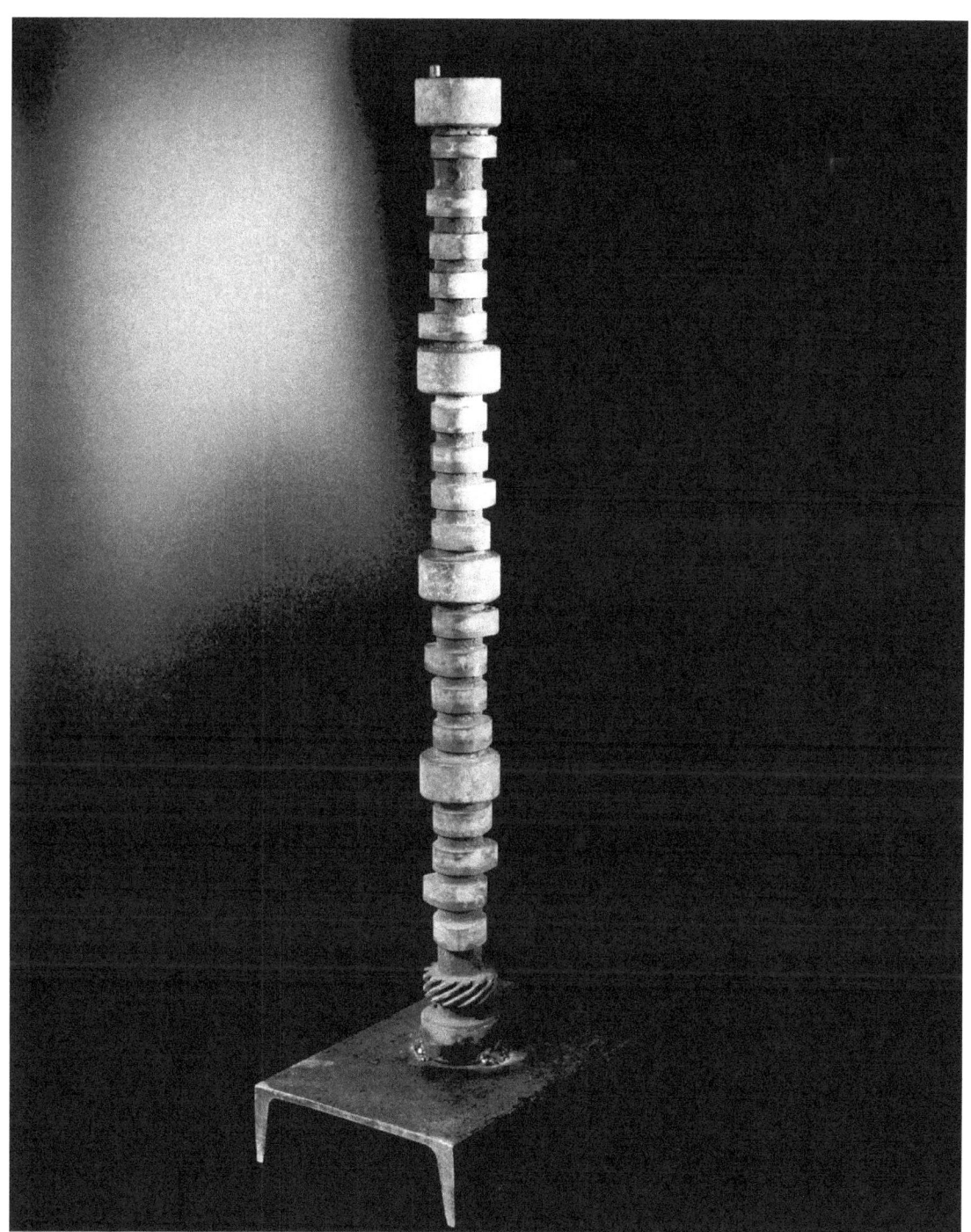

www.ingramcontent.com/pod-product-compliance
Lightning Source LLC
Chambersburg PA
CBHW081110170526
45165CB00008B/2401